RACING POST
ANNUAL 2015

Racing Post One Canada Square, London E14 5AP.
020 7293 2001
Irish Racing Post The Capel Building, Mary's Abbey,
Dublin 7. 01 828 7450

Editor Nick Pulford
Art editor David Dew
Cover design Samantha Creedon and Jay Vincent
Chief photographers Edward Whitaker, Patrick
McCann
Other photography Caroline Norris, Martin Lynch,
Getty, Mark Cranham, Alain Barr, John Grossick
Picture editor David Cramphorn
Graphics David Cramphorn, David Penzer, Jenny
Robertshaw
Picture artworking David Cramphorn, Nigel Jones,
Stefan Searle
Feature writers Tom Bull, Scott Burton, Steve Dennis,
Alastair Down, Nicholas Godfrey, David Jennings, Lee
Mottershead, Jonathan Mullin, Julian Muscat, Nick Pulford,
Brough Scott, Peter Thomas
Contributors Paul Curtis, Steve Mason, John Randall,
Martin Smethurst, Craig Thake

Advertisement Sales
Racing Post: One Canada Square, London E14 5AP.
0208 2630226 Cheryl Gunn, cheryl.gunn@racingpost.com

Archant Dialogue Prospect House, Rouen Road,
Norwich NR1 1RE. 01603 772554
Gary Stone, gary.stone@archantdialogue.co.uk
Kay Brown, kay.brown@archantdialogue.co.uk
Dean Brown, dean.brown@archantdialogue.co.uk

Distribution/availability 01933 304858
help@racingpost.com

Published by Racing Post Books
27 Kingfisher Court, Hambridge Road, Newbury,
Berkshire RG14 5SJ

Copyright © Racing Post 2014

ISBN 978-1-909471-43-6 [UK]
ISBN 978-1-909471-44-3 [Ireland]

Printed in Great Britain by Buxton Press
Every effort has been made to fulfil requirements with
regard to copyright material. The author and publisher will
be glad to rectify any omissions at the earliest opportunity.

www.racingpost.com/shop

Timeless them
year of magic r

The Racing Post Annual is living proof of the eternal vibrancy and charm of this great sport. At the start of every year we have a blank page — in fact, 208 of them — and the wonderful world of racing never disappoints in providing the stories and colour to bring them to life.

This year is no exception, even if we have missed the presence of an undisputed great such as Frankel and Sprinter Sacre — the cover stars on previous editions of the Annual. But we cannot expect superstars of their ilk every year — after all, it is their rarity value that tells us they are so special — and there was no shortage of memorable moments in 2014 with Kingman, Treve, Australia, Sire De Grugy, Jezki, Quevega, Taghrooda and many others.

Their stories — encompassing timeless themes of destiny, triumph, disappointment, revival and fairytale — are told here by the Racing Post's best writers and accompanied by the outstanding photography of Edward Whitaker and Patrick McCann.

The human tales of the racing year are no less engrossing. Tony McCoy, who at the age of 40 has had another record-breaking year, talks to Alastair Down, and we also look at the fabulous seasons enjoyed by John Gosden, Willie Mullins, Paul Nicholls, Ruby Walsh, Jonjo O'Neill, Richard Hannon, James Doyle and Paul Hanagan.

But racing is not all about the big names and one of the most captivating aspects of 2014 has been the major successes enjoyed by some of the smaller stables. Encapsulated in the triumphs of Champion Chase hero Sire De Grugy, Grand National winner Pineau De Re and the globetrotting Gordon Lord Byron are dreams turned to reality in the most unexpected and unlikely ways.

In these pages, too, are lesser-told personal triumphs against the odds — not only the people who overcame age-old battles with the scales, loss of form and thoughts of packing it all in, but also the survivors of heart attacks and broken backs who enjoyed golden moments in 2014.

Of course, racing is always looking forward to the next race, the next season, the next dream — and this book is no exception. The Annual 20 is our pick of the horses and people to watch in 2015, while several trainers — not least Mullins, with his awesome firepower — discuss their big hopes for the coming months.

Racing moves on quickly but the Annual is an opportunity to pause and reflect on a memorable year packed with great moments.

Nick Pulford
Editor

INSIDE Great feats, great writing and great photography

Treve the wonder filly Page 20

Popular hero Sire De Grugy Page 80

Record-breaking Quevega Page 98

BIG STORIES

Tony McCoy
Page 38

Treve
Page 20

FINAL FURLONG

STATISTICS

James Doyle
Page 10

David O'Meara
Page 68

Richard Hannon
Page 110

Grand National
Page 122

'I appreciate things all the more because I know there's a lot more behind me than there is still in front. But enjoying it is all about being successful and going on riding winners'

Tony McCoy Page 38

'By training I feel close to Henry. Winning the Champion Stakes really accentuated that feeling. It made me think of Henry a lot'

Lady Cecil Page 14

'There was a big story about Leighton Aspell and his comeback, quite a story about a small trainer winning the National, but the bit that was missed out is how good Pineau De Re is'

Richard Newland Page 122

'I've thoroughly enjoyed it. Yes, it's been stressful at times but I'm a very lucky boy'

Richard Hannon Page 110

'Handicappers? They're the worst judges in the world. I'd like to see Sprinter Sacre try and give mine 18lb in a handicap, but I bet Nicky Henderson wouldn't'

Gary Moore Page 80

'I thought we were certain to lose it given my luck. They were the worst few minutes of my life'

Jim Culloty Page 72

'I'd never done a flying dismount before – I'm 6ft 3in. I was afraid in case my foot got stuck in the irons and I ended up making a fool of myself'

Robbie McNamara Page 185

STAR QUALITY

Kingman and Taghrooda, Britain's top three-year-old colt and filly, gave John Gosden a season to remember with a string of major triumphs

By Nicholas Godfrey

MAIN event or mere sideshow? Definitely the latter according to John Gosden, who insisted the outcome of his race with Richard Hannon the younger for the British Flat trainers' title was a frivolity. "I enjoy joking with Richard and we have a lot of banter about it," he said. "I regard it as a bit of fun and no more than that."

Rather more serious than personal accolades is the performance of his Clarehaven team and fortunately the man who must now surely be regarded as Britain's pre-eminent trainer can reflect on a superlative season for his Newmarket stable. With major victories in Ireland and France, this most international of trainers by no means concentrated his efforts on chasing domestic prize-money, yet still he easily surpassed his previous-best earnings total in Britain. For the first time, two trainers topped the £4m mark; Hannon saddled many more winners, but he also had more than twice as many runners as Gosden.

Doubtless more significant for Gosden, whose raison d'etre is quality rather than quantity, was a multitude of major successes. When he was champion trainer in 2012, Gosden won seven Group 1s; before the start of October this year, he had already won eight across Europe, among them Classics in Britain and Ireland plus a second King George victory via the Oaks winner Taghrooda.

Gosden narrowly missed out in a photo-finish for Royal Ascot top trainer, where Sir Michael Stoute showed there is plenty of life in the old dog. Gosden's four winners included dazzling displays by Kingman in the St James's Palace Stakes and The Fugue, who banished the demons of a succession of luckless efforts when defeating Treve in the Prince of Wales's Stakes. Eagle Top (King Edward VII) and Richard Pankhurst (Chesham) completed the Gosden haul.

Throw in lesser-light Group horses like Nassau Stakes winner Sultanina, Pomology and Western Hymn and it is clear Gosden enjoyed a wonderful season. "I'm very clear on this," he reflects. "It's great if you're involved for the title because it means the horses are running well and you're having a good year. And if you have the top three-year-old colt and the top three-year-old filly then it has to be an exceptional year in any person's life."

Gosden is a rarity these days in that he is supported by several leading owner-breeders and his two outstanding

▶▶ Continues page 6

performers of 2014 arrived from such sources. Kingman, the latest homebred star from Khalid Abdullah's Juddmonte production line, was a son of the sprinter Invincible Spirit out of high-class mare Zenda, who was trained by Gosden to win the French Guineas. Taghrooda, homebred by Hamdan Al Maktoum's Shadwell outfit, came with much more a middle-distance pedigree: by Sea The Stars, she was the second foal of the Sadler's Wells filly Ezima, who won three Listed races for Jim Bolger from a mile to a mile and three-quarters. Little wonder that this massively talented pair played in diverse spheres, their career trajectories advancing at somewhat different speeds.

Kingman was the miler with such a deadly turn of foot that his trainer readily and repeatedly asserted he had enough speed to win the July Cup; Taghrooda was the more stoutly bred filly who had already won at a mile as a juvenile and would never again race at such a distance. After just a single winning outing (as supposed second string, sent off 20-1) at Newmarket in September of her two-year-old campaign, Taghrooda was something of a dark horse at the start of 2014, though she had been nibbled at in the ante-post betting for the Oaks.

Kingman, on the other hand, was anything but a dark horse. His entire juvenile career – all two races – had been conducted amid a blizzard of hype, prompting his trainer to suggest Guineas quotes after his initial Newmarket maiden win came from the "theatre of the absurd". Kingman followed up in the Solario Stakes under James Doyle, freshly appointed Abdullah's retained rider, before minor surgery to remove a chip in an ankle joint kept him off the track until his spring reappearance in the Greenham Stakes, where he thrashed the Hannon-trained Night Of Thunder in a manner that drew comparisons with a recent predecessor in the Abdullah silks.

The Racing Post analysis comment on the Greenham read: "One could not help but think of Frankel, who won the 2011 running, when watching Kingman, in the same colours and also sporting the cross-noseband, absolutely demolish his rivals to maintain an unbeaten record in this 2,000 Guineas trial." Gosden was well aware of what he

A DIFFERENT VIEW

The Racing Post's James Milton watches at the start on Kingman's big day at Glorious Goodwood

On the Wednesday of the Glorious Goodwood meeting around 20 racegoers board a minibus at the East Gate to enjoy a trip to the starting stalls and a privileged view of the Sussex Stakes.

For all the hype surrounding the duel between Kingman and Toronado, there's a palpable sense of calm down at the start. A vast expanse of downland turf and Sussex sky separates us from the grandstands. Over there, thousands of spectators, giddy with sunshine and Pimm's, are preparing to savour the race of the week. Over here, the four runners mill around patiently as the jockeys await their instructions.

Toronado's jockey Richard Hughes, whose Goodwood record entitles him to regard the place as his own private fiefdom, chats contentedly with the stalls handlers. On Kingman, James Doyle – far less experienced than Hughes, and with the additional pressure of favouritism – sits quietly, radiating a kind of controlled tension.

The starter, like a bored schoolmaster, calls out the draws – "Buick, one. O'Brien, two. Doyle, four. Hughes, five" – and it wouldn't be a great surprise to hear him bark: "Are you chewing, boy? Spit it out. It's your own time you're wasting."

Languidly, the runners enter the stalls and then, in ludicrously low-key fashion, they're off. Not quite off and running, though – they amble through the early stages while we scramble back to the minibus to catch the radio commentary: "Kingman is taking some time to get himself organised . . . now he comes at Toronado . . ."

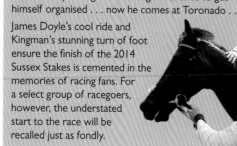

James Doyle's cool ride and Kingman's stunning turn of foot ensure the finish of the 2014 Sussex Stakes is cemented in the memories of racing fans. For a select group of racegoers, however, the understated start to the race will be recalled just as fondly.

had on his hands. "Without doubt he has the highest cruising speed of any I've trained over this trip," he said after the race.

Kingman was starting to look unbeatable, yet he was beaten on his very next start in one of the messiest Classics for some time. Sent off 6-4 favourite, Kingman led with a furlong to go but was edged out by none other than his Newbury victim Night Of Thunder, a virtually unconsidered 40-1 chance, with subsequent dual Derby winner Australia in third. With the field splitting into two groups, the Guineas was a wholly unsatisfactory affair, but it had nevertheless cost Kingman his unbeaten record. He was never to be defeated again, appearing to consider it a matter of personal pride not to let a Hannon-trained rival get the better of him in four subsequent outings.

Hannon was to throw everything bar the stable cat at Kingman, all to no further avail. Shifting Power, fourth at Newmarket, was dismissed with contemptuous ease by five lengths in testing ground in the Irish 2,000 Guineas and then Kingman exacted revenge on Night Of Thunder in the St James's Palace Stakes at Royal Ascot, where he produced a devastating turn of foot after being held up.

Hannon's older milers were next in the firing line, starting with the top-class Toronado, who got first run

in what amounted to a two-furlong dash off a dawdling pace in a fast-ground Sussex Stakes. Just like his younger stablemates, however, the Queen Anne winner was brushed aside as Kingman scored with plenty in hand. Olympic Glory, Hannon's representative at Deauville in the Prix Jacques le Marois, could finish only third as Kingman confirmed his status as Europe's top miler. He quickened well out of the soft ground for yet another comfortable triumph, this time from the French-trained Anodin.

Without question, Kingman was now on the verge of greatness, his near-flawless record not a million miles away from that of the exalted Frankel at the same stage of his career, albeit with that one unfortunate reverse on his CV. But he had already run his last race; in September came the announcement that the four-time Group 1 winner had been retired before his intended engagement in the Queen Elizabeth II Stakes owing to treatment for what was colloquially described as a sore throat.

Frustratingly, handicappers felt unable to offer a rating commensurate with the impression given by his string of victories. "We will never know how good Kingman was," suggests Paul Curtis of the Racing Post Ratings team. "He achieved a peak RPR of 128 but that was surely not his limit. His rating

CLASSIC PAIR
KINGMAN IN NUMBERS

7 Wins in eight starts

£970,834 Career earnings

4 Group 1 victories

1 Classic win (Irish 2,000 Guineas)

128 Highest Racing Post Rating, recorded in the St James's Palace Stakes

TAGHROODA IN NUMBERS

4 Wins in six starts

£1,476,101 Career earnings

2 Group 1 victories

1 Classic win (Oaks)

126 Highest Racing Post Rating, recorded in the King George

was restricted by his patient style of racing, which, although exhilarating to watch, meant his performances were always limited by his opponents and the shape of the race."

Gosden, who, lest we forget, has also trained a Derby winner (Benny The Dip) and a Breeders' Cup Classic winner (Raven's Pass), did not hold back in his assessment. "He was a long way the most exciting colt I have ever trained. Royal Heroine won the Breeders' Cup Mile and broke American records but this horse was just in another league, a horse with quite the most

extraordinary acceleration and a horse who captured the imagination.

"He just missed the last dance but he had six runs this year and five wins. Ascot, the Sussex Stakes, the Jacques le Marois were performances out of the top drawer. He could change from cruising along in second gear to the afterburners and eighth gear. He had some turn of foot. What he did in the Sussex no horse was meant to do. To pick up Toronado like that was an example of his extraordinary speed. He was an exciting horse to have trained."

KINGMAN will stand alongside Frankel at Abdullah's Banstead Manor base in 2014, while his former stable companion Taghrooda is destined for life as part of Shadwell's broodmare band after a season in which she rose quickly to the status of Europe's champion three-year-old filly. Despite having raced only once as a two-year-old, she was no longer an unknown when she reappeared in the Pretty Polly the day after Kingman's Guineas defeat, having been steadily backed for the Investec Oaks from 33-1 over the winter to single figures.

She lived up to expectations with a wide-margin victory – as in her maiden win, looking strongest at the finish – and was promoted to favouritism for the Epsom Classic. Even so, it would have taken a leap of faith to foresee what was

▸▸ Summer of fun: (from left) Kingman beats Toronado (centre) and Darwin (left) in the Sussex Stakes; John Gosden with Kingman in the Goodwood winner's enclosure; Paul Hanagan salutes the Epsom crowd after winning the Oaks on Taghrooda; (previous page) Gosden with Kingman after the Irish 2,000 Guineas

to come in the next couple of months as Taghrooda went from an emphatic Oaks success to a no less clear-cut victory in the clash of the generations (and sexes) that is the King George.

Run in memory of Sir Henry Cecil, the Oaks looked pretty competitive with Marvellous, the Irish 1,000 Guineas winner, 4-1 favourite on the day and no fewer than four supplementary entries in the 17-runner field. Taghrooda, though, proved in a different league to her rivals as she extended her unbeaten sequence to three. After travelling strongly in midfield she powered away from Tarfasha, who completed a one-two for a resurgent Sheikh Hamdan; it was also a first Classic success for the owner's retained jockey Paul Hanagan, who had never before even ridden in the fillies' Classic.

Gosden said he was keen to follow
▸▸ *Continues page 8*

the softly-softly approach by keeping Taghrooda against the fillies, which made his next move something of a contradiction of himself. The Oaks winner took her chance in a compelling renewal of the King George as one of a trio of Clarehaven representatives alongside Eagle Top and the Derby third Romsdal.

The bold move to reroute Taghrooda from a penalty kick in the Irish Oaks was amply rewarded with a fantastic display as she stayed on strongly after a patient ride from Hanagan to draw three lengths clear of Telescope, thereby becoming the seventh individual of her sex to win Ascot's midsummer championship. Although Taghrooda received 15lb from the older males, this was clearly a superb performance from an outstanding filly, worthy of a career-best RPR of 126.

Asked if the filly had always shown such brilliance at home, Gosden reveals a little of his modus operandi. "We don't ask them those questions at home," he explains. "She'll work nicely on the bridle and you hope when you ask them to go that she's not a bridle horse. When she won her maiden she picked up well first time out; it's only in races that you ask them to do that, you tend not to do it at home. You definitely don't want to find out how fast they are before they run. But she's a filly that when you want her to put it in, she can. She travels at any pace and has a great turn of foot."

Taghrooda would start favourite on her final two outings and run creditably but without reaching the level of her King George triumph. A shock defeat at odds of 1-5 in the Yorkshire Oaks did little to dim her lustre as she was worn down close home by a persuasive Ryan Moore on Tapestry to join a surprisingly

long list of Epsom winners to have come to grief on the Knavesmire.

At the time Gosden felt she had simply been outstayed after being in front for plenty long enough but a more valid explanation was soon to come to light. "She showed no signs going to York that she was coming into season but she was certainly in discomfort the next day," Gosden says. "We made no excuses on the day but she was very tender and in season the next day. She obviously wasn't quite feeling herself but that's life. On the day she was beaten."

The merit of Taghrooda's performance in finishing third on her final start in the Prix de l'Arc de Triomphe may have been overshadowed by Treve's tearful triumph but it was noteworthy nonetheless as she (and fourth-placed Kingston Hill, for that matter) made the best of a bad job from unpromising wide draws.

"She ran a great race in the Arc," Gosden says. "We were forced wide all the way, we never had any cover, but that's the effect of the draw. On ground as quick as that it's impossible for a horse stuck out there. We just didn't get the rub of the green. I don't say we would have beaten Treve but we might have been able to give her a real race."

Retirement was beckoning for Taghrooda, leaving Gosden to reflect: "She has a great mind on her, just like her father, very little bothers her, she is a wonderfully relaxed filly, a pleasure to be around. She also has a great physique and was always a very classy filly."

With The Fugue having joined Kingman and Taghrooda in departing the scene, Gosden will start 2015 without at least three of what the US legend Bob Baffert likes to refer to as his equine 'cannons'.

▶▶ In the clear: Taghrooda scores by three lengths in the King George VI and Queen Elizabeth Stakes at Ascot

"When you've been fortunate enough to train the top three-year-old colt and the top three-year-old filly in the same year it would be a little audacious to think you're going to repeat the feat in a hurry," Gosden says. "Similarly we had The Fugue, a really classy older filly, but it's something like a football manager, because the older players move on and you've got to develop the younger ones."

A period of restocking and replenishing lies ahead. "I think we'll be in the same position as at the end of 2012, when I said 2013 was time to build again," Gosden says. "I have exactly the same feeling about 2015. It's a rebuilding time. But one good thing about being a racehorse trainer is that people are kind enough to send you young horses and therefore fresh new material to work on and that's always exciting. It's a regenerative process – we're sent new material in the autumn of every year which gives you a chance of building up for a brighter future."

The likes of Richard Pankhurst, Snoano, Faydhan and Christophermarlowe mean the cupboard is not exactly bare of three-year-old prospects and, while it might be stretching things to suggest there could be another Kingman among them, who knows what may be lurking relatively undiscovered by the public? After all, Taghrooda was just a once-raced maiden winner at the start of 2014 and she turned out pretty well.

HOME RUN

Richard Pankhurst was the least important of John Gosden's four Royal Ascot winners in terms of prestige but the most personally significant

The Chesham Stakes winner was bred by Gosden himself and raced in the colours of his wife Rachel Hood, president of the Racehorse Owners Association and this year elected mayor of Newmarket. The juvenile is a son of Raven's Pass, winner of the 2008 Breeders' Cup Classic for the trainer, who received a nomination to the sire from Sheikh Mohammed and sent family mare Mainstay to him.

"It's overwhelming," Hood said in the Royal Ascot winner's enclosure. "I'm speechless and that's just as well. It's very exciting. The horse has exceeded my expectations, although the trainer usually doesn't quite fill me in on what might possibly happen."

Gosden, however, came perilously close to denying his wife her moment of Royal Ascot glory with Richard Pankhurst, who had finished fourth in a Newmarket maiden on his only previous start.

"We're very lucky," he said. "I'd been planning to come here for three months but if he'd won first time out I would have put him in the Goffs sale this week and the horse would have been sold. He would have won for someone else and I would probably be an ex-husband."

Richard Pankhurst was sold later in the summer and will now race under the Godolphin banner.

ARROWFIELD

WHERE **CHAMPION SIRES** ARE MADE
1st and 2nd Australian General Sires Premiership

SNITZEL
The Hottest Young Sire
in Australia

REDOUTE'S CHOICE
The World's Best Sire Son of Danehill

KING JAMES

James Doyle was in the spotlight every step of the way with Kingman but he handled the pressure with impressive calm in a season to savour

By Lee Mottershead

JAMES DOYLE never wanted to be just a jockey. He determinedly set himself the task of becoming one of the weighing room's elite members, not just a successful rider but one of the best around. Had he not fulfilled that ambition the 26-year-old would probably not be riding now. But he is and in 2014 he showed repeatedly what has taken him to where he wanted to be.

It now seems barely believable that in 2010, with his fortunes in the doldrums and a mortgage needing to be paid, Doyle famously signed himself on to a plumbing course. He partnered just 29 winners that year but he did not give up and, having forged a relationship with Roger Charlton, he had a life-changing day at Meydan in March 2012 when he landed the Dubai Duty Free for the trainer on Cityscape. He would have needed to unblock many a sink to earn his percentage of the £1.94m first prize.

Instant wealth was his and, most significantly, he had made a lasting impression on Cityscape's owner Khalid Abdullah and his advisers. Little more than a year later Doyle was offered a retainer to ride all of Abdullah's British-trained string.

That meant the Abdullah team wanted Doyle not Ryan Moore to ride their Sir Michael Stoute-trained horses, Doyle not William Buick to ride their John Gosden-trained horses and Doyle not Tom Queally to ride their Lady Cecil-trained horses. To have been preferred to just one of those jockeys would have been something. To be preferred to all three was something else.

Waiting for him in Gosden's stable was Kingman. Two days after the announcement of the retainer in August 2013, Kingman was Doyle's first ride in the job when he contested the Solario Stakes at Sandown. Great horses bring with them great opportunities but also immense pressure and potential pitfalls. More than any other, Kingman was the horse Doyle would be judged on.

Sandown went smoothly and so did Newbury on Kingman's reappearance as a three-year-old in the Greenham Stakes. Then came Newmarket and the 2,000 Guineas, which was anything but smooth. Doyle was defeated and perhaps should not have been. The whys and wherefores barely mattered. All that counted was that in the most important race of their lives to that point, Kingman and Doyle had lost. Even if Doyle considered himself to be under no pressure, he surely felt a point had to be proved. As Kingman's campaign continued, he proved it.

What was evident most was the clarity of Doyle's thinking. Classic consolation in the Irish 2,000 Guineas was achieved simply and without fuss, as it should have been, but on Kingman's next two starts Doyle had to react to contests unfolding in ways that would have been hard to predict. In the Sussex Stakes, Richard Hughes set a funereal pace on Toronado, reckoning the only way he could beat Kingman was by momentarily catching him napping. Doyle was not caught out. Nor had he been one start earlier in the St James's Palace Stakes, in which Hughes had unexpectedly set out to dictate on Night Of Thunder. The way Doyle dealt with the situation left Gosden deeply impressed.

"A lot of jockeys," said Gosden, "would have thought 'Ah, this is not good, I will get a bit closer, I will go three wide, I'll move early.' He did the right thing, cruised into the straight, checked the Ascot crowd numbers were right and burst forward."

Gosden could not have told Doyle what to do in those circumstances because no-one anticipated them materialising. The jockey, however, was adept at taking wise counsel. He showed as much at Deauville, where Kingman was drawn nearest the stands rail in the Prix Jacques le Marois. To his immediate right was Olivier Peslier on Anodin; one

> *'He did the right thing, cruised into the straight, checked the Ascot crowd numbers were right and burst forward'*

place wider was Frankie Dettori on Olympic Glory. Gosden warned his rider not to end up on the fence as Dettori and Peslier would conspire to get him boxed in. Doyle ensured that did not happen and instead reined back his mount in the early stages before delivering the winning challenge to the right of his main rivals. Once again keen to praise Abdullah's chosen one, Gosden noted: "James has a cool head on young shoulders."

So cool, in fact, that at no point has Doyle's presence on a horse ever been deemed to be anything other than a positive influence on his mount's chances. There has been no lamenting the absence of Moore or Buick – superb though both are – on Abdullah's finest performers.

Doyle has shown himself to be worthy of his station, highlighting his ability more than once on the previously frustrating Noble Mission, who became a serial winner after his new jockey adopted front-running tactics that released in Frankel's brother a level of commitment to the cause that had been hitherto unseen.

Their partnership reached its glorious zenith in the Qipco Champion Stakes when Doyle drove the willing Noble Mission to a neck victory over Al Kazeem. "James gave him an incredible ride. I can't thank him enough," said winning trainer Lady Cecil.

For Doyle, it was a third Group 1 victory of the year aboard Noble Mission to go with his four on Kingman. "This has put the icing on the cake in a fantastic year," he said after the Champion.

It was the year that proved Doyle was the right choice to wear the fabled Abdullah colours.

CLASSIC ANSWER

Paul Hanagan proved himself as Sheikh Hamdan's jockey with a string of big-race winners led by Taghrooda

By Peter Thomas

THERE can be very few sporting arenas in which the winning of more contests than anybody else over a two-year period can end up being a stick with which to be beaten by the critics. Winning back-to-back championships is generally viewed as a badge of honour and pre-eminence, but for Paul Hanagan the questions persisted. Where were the winners in Group 1s, the Classics, that proved he belonged in the same league as Richard Hughes, Ryan Moore and the other big names?

In his first two years as number one rider to Sheikh Hamdan Al Maktoum, the mild-mannered man from Warrington had not given the doubters a satisfactory answer. He had broken his Group 1 duck in 2012, on Mayson in the July Cup, but that was for his old boss Richard Fahey, the mainstay of his title-winning seasons in 2010 and 2011.

Success at the top level in his new colours remained stubbornly elusive. Never mind that Sheikh Hamdan had been short of top-grade ammunition before Hanagan arrived; for some it was easy to see the new jockey as part of the problem.

Patience and faith – both from Hanagan and Shekih Hamdan – were finally rewarded in 2014, and everyone had their answer about the former dual champion's abilities on the big stage. In winning the Oaks and King George on Taghrooda and the Eclipse with Mukhadram, as well as bringing along the next generation led by Estidhkaar, Hanagan displayed all the craft learned during his hard graft on the northern circuit.

Sheikh Hamdan's racing manager, Angus Gold, found the ideal opportunity to praise the 34-year-old in the wake of Taghrooda's Oaks triumph – a first Classic for the jockey and the first British Group 1 for the sheikh in almost five years. "He works incredibly hard," said Gold, "and he's adapted to a very different role. We've thrown him to the wolves with all these different trainers and we've had a few quiet years, so it's nice to get back into the big time."

If that recognition for his adaptability and professionalism sounded like faint praise, Hanagan also won the admiration of Taghrooda's trainer John Gosden for his ability to act coolly in the white heat of Classic competition, persuading the winning filly to change her lead leg coming down Tattenham Hill after she had been buffeted and become unbalanced.

Little moments like that can mean the difference between a Group 1 and a damp squib, and Hanagan's formative years in gritty northern handicaps stood him in good stead at Epsom, even if they had received scant respect in some quarters.

Gosden was fully aware of the unassuming rider's contribution to a major day for the organisation. "He's very modest and a good team man," he said. "He gets to know his horses and he's a pleasure to work with. Full marks to him for getting her back on an even keel after that bump, he was very quick to get her on the near fore, and that takes some doing."

Hampered by his natural inability to make a big fuss out of doing his job well, Hanagan only slowly gained full credit in what was turning out to be a return to the golden years for Sheikh Hamdan's Shadwell empire. Taghrooda, after all, was a 'steering job' that your granny could supposedly have won on. Mukhadram, however, was a different kettle of fish.

The five-year-old had shown himself to be a little shy of Group 1 class on several occasions and was sent off a 14-1 shot when he lined up for the Eclipse. But, with Hanagan alive to the possibilities presented by a tactical pace, he was sent on early in the straight and stayed on too stoutly for the trailing pack.

It may well have been a race won by jockey genius rather than horse superiority, but Hanagan would never be caught blowing that particular trumpet. Luckily, Mukhadram's trainer William Haggas did it for him. "Paul gave the horse a marvellous ride," he said. "He was in the right place throughout the race."

By now, the diminutive 'numbers man' was beginning to emerge as a big man for all occasions and he showed his full range of attributes when suffering patiently through the discomfort and frustration of a fractured left arm, sustained at Glorious Goodwood, to be ready for the moment when Taghrooda, redirected from a penalty kick in the Irish Oaks, was ambitiously sent to Ascot for the King George.

No tactical magic or quicksilver thinking was required this time. The perfect execution of a simple plan on a brilliant filly was enough to deliver another win at the top level. Gosden declared himself "delighted with the ride, which was lovely and patient".

Hanagan went on to land the Gimcrack for Charlie Hills on Muharaar and the Champagne Stakes for Richard Hannon on Estidkhaar, in a season that finally delivered the goods he had left Yorkshire to find. He still found time to ride a sackful of winners for old guv'nor Fahey, but emerged as a well-respected work rider in the eyes of many of the land's major trainers and an undemonstrative, efficient Group-race pilot to boot.

He also seems to have mastered the art of conserving his energies for the big days, where once he felt the need to quest for quantity on a draining day-to-day basis. "This job is all about the big races," Hanagan said a few days before the Oaks, when expectation and pressure still weighed heavy on him.

In lifting that burden, he made sure he would be recognised for quality as well as quantity.

ACCOMPLISHED MISSION

Noble Mission came of age in 2014 and evoked memories of his brother Frankel and the late Sir Henry Cecil with an emotional victory in the Champion Stakes

By Lee Mottershead

HIS was the most wonderful transformation of the year. What he did and how he did it came as an unexpected but welcome surprise. We thought we knew him but we were made to think differently and on what turned into an unforgettable Qipco British Champions Day, the new, improved, reformed Noble Mission provided what, for many, was the highlight of the Flat season.

You had to wonder where it had come from. Then you remembered from exactly where Noble Mission had come, namely the same mother as Frankel and thereafter Warren Place, and you realised it made more sense. Yet those two ingredients had always been part of Noble Mission's racing life and it was only as a five-year-old that the thoroughbred with the most illustrious sibling in the sport finally lived up to his early billing. Given the pleasure he brought us on that glorious day at Ascot, it was worth the wait.

As he returned for the spring of 2014 the story so far was hardly desperate, but there was certainly a sense of frustration about what the white-faced son of Galileo and Kind had achieved. Nobody could deny he had been anything other than consistent, never finishing worse than fourth, but he had not reached

the heights he might have been capable of reaching. Moreover, there was a feeling the reason for this was he probably had not wanted to.

Raced only once at two, he was considered Derby class by Sir Henry Cecil but was an Epsom absentee. Cecil, famed for his patience, considered him not ready for the challenge. He had, however, felt him ready for a hood from the very first run of his three-year-old season. It became increasingly clear why.

That year he was beaten into second by no more than half a length on three occasions. Nobody could say for sure he had thrown in the towel, and he did win the Gordon Stakes on the nod from Encke, but it was hard not to think of Noble Mission with a question mark next to his name. To an extent the same was true at four when he managed just a single success, once again at Goodwood, in a small-field Listed event. At best Noble Mission seemed like a solid Group 3 performer, far removed from the mighty Frankel. He would remain far removed from Frankel but his efforts in 2014 went a long way to narrowing the gap.

BEFORE things got different there was more of the same. By now Noble Mission was racing for Lady Cecil. Her husband had died only 17 days after the horse's second Goodwood win. In her name he finished a

distant fourth in the Prix Dollar in the autumn of 2013 when James Doyle, appointed two months earlier as Khalid Abdullah's retained rider, was on board for the first time. Doyle stayed on board but in the season-opening John Porter Stakes at Newbury he found what Tom Queally had found in the same contest 12 months earlier. Noble Mission raced in the rear, made eye-catching headway down the straight and looked sure to win; only to lose, this time beaten a neck.

The process of change began at home. Lady Cecil, aided by assistant George Scott and groom Martyn Peake, began working Noble Mission from the front. He seemed to like it but there is little benefit to be had from merely liking it at home, so 13 days after Newbury he was sent to Sandown for the Gordon Richards Stakes.

The ground was appalling, the rain pelted down and Noble Mission was in front. After no more than a furlong Doyle made a conscious effort to urge his mount, blessed with a long, powerful stride, into the lead. After turning for home Doyle started applying pressure and, to his rear, the returning Telescope began to struggle. The horse in front was relentless and up Sandown's hill, galloping into a barrage of driving rain, he strode increasingly further clear. At the line it was nine lengths and a revelation.

"This is as impressive a performance resolution-wise as we've seen from this horse," said Richard Hoiles in commentary. He was right, but in the winner's enclosure Lady Cecil noted her team had always felt there was a big race in Noble Mission – and she was not talking about this one.

Nor was she talking about the Huxley Stakes, which Noble Mission won, in the same way and with the same opponent, Telescope, in second. That was another Group 3 but the Noble Mission camp had long since believed the big one in him was bigger even than a Group 2. The Warren Place team felt their stable star could claim a Group 1. He could and he did, on his very next outing producing an admirable display of relentless galloping to defeat Magician in the Tattersalls Gold Cup. In the space of a month Noble Mission had won three times, culminating in a Group 1 win at the first attempt.

The Curragh victory also gave Cecil her maiden win at the highest level and enabled her to fly the fabled Warren Place flag once more.

▶▶ Continues page 16

▶▶ Lady and the champ: Lady Cecil and Noble Mission at Warren Place the day after the Champion Stakes

She had done so with a horse who, crucially, now believed in himself.

"He has got his confidence and that's what Henry was so great at doing," she explained. "He was able to get horses to do their work without even realising they were doing it." But this horse was doing an enormous amount of work and doing it the hard way. That is what made his final-stride defeat in the Grand Prix de Saint-Cloud so heartbreaking. He had not deserved to lose and, eventually, he did not, with first-past-the-post Spiritjim later disqualified for failing a medication test. Noble Mission was a dual Group 1 winner. But for an unhappy trip to Germany in late July there might have been a hat-trick.

THROUGH August and September we did not see him again but he continued to blossom. It had long since been evident testing ground was his clear preference and, with underfoot conditions on the quick side for the Irish Champion Stakes, he stayed in Newmarket.

On Qipco Champion Stakes day the conditions were as far removed from quick as you could get. The Grey Gatsby, who had shocked Australia at Leopardstown, was ruled out because of the ground, while Australia was ruled out because of retirement. Noble Mission had not been retired and loved heavy ground. He went to Ascot.

Frankel had gone to Ascot two years earlier. He ended his unblemished, unbeaten career in the Champion with a 14th straight success. The ground had been only a little less gruelling than that which faced Noble Mission and eight others in the highlight of a British Champions Day that had yet to fully ignite. At around 4.10pm it exploded.

From start to finish the first two places were occupied by Noble Mission and Al Kazeem, a rival who was once a friend to Doyle. It was in part due to impressing aboard Al Kazeem, winning three Group 1 events in the summer of 2013, that Doyle had caught the eye of Abdullah.

But while Doyle spent the spring of 2014 looking forward to his first full season as a retained rider, Al Kazeem spent the spring proving to be a flop at stud. The Queen, who had bought the horse as a stallion prospect, kindly gave him back to owner-breeder John Deer, who in turn returned him to trainer Roger Charlton.

To bring a horse back to the track after a period spent indulging in frisky fun, however briefly, is no mean feat. Al Kazeem took a while to find his form of

old but he went to Ascot having arguably run better in the Arc than he had in 2013. Even so, just a few months earlier who would have believed he would be competing in the Champion Stakes? Probably around as many people as believed Noble Mission would be doing the same.

Yet they not only competed, they dominated. Down Ascot's home straight they fought a furious battle. Noble Mission responded to every one of Doyle's urgings but George Baker was similarly well served by Al Kazeem. Back in third the far less exposed Free Eagle closed in but without ever looking like winning. That honour was always going to fall to Noble Mission or Al Kazeem. It went where the packed grandstands wanted it to go, to a horse whose hood still bore the initials 'HRAC'.

Those who adore racing adored Henry Cecil. The joyful reaction to Noble Mission's triumph showed the goodwill had been transferred to his widow, who had watched the closing stages in a state of tearful shock.

▶▶ Grand finale: (clockwise from top) Noble Mission and James Doyle set the seal on a fantastic season with victory over Al Kazeem in the Champion Stakes; Doyle salutes the crowd in the winner's enclosure; Noble Mission at home the next day; (below) the Racing Post front page on October 19

"There is a lot of sentimentality about this, but it has actually happened," she said. "I know a lot of the reception was for Henry. It's so wonderful to feel all the love everyone has for him."

Ascot was indeed a wonderful place that afternoon. Memories of the greatest trainer and his greatest horse had been reawakened. It was the same for Lady Cecil.

"On the way home I was getting texts and emails from everywhere and everyone," she said. "It was lovely. It reminded me of the Frankel and Twice Over days and it brought back memories of coming back in the car with Henry after their races. By training I feel close to Henry. Winning the Champion Stakes really accentuates that feeling. It made me think of Henry a lot. It made me feel close to him."

And it made an awful lot of people leave Ascot with a warm glow inside them. The legacy of the greatest trainer and his greatest horse lives on. Those who picked up the batons have done them proud.

THE ULTIMATE RACEHORSE TRAINING EXPERIENCE

With a 10 year career as a professional jump jockey, David and the experienced team at Tyre Hill Stables have one aim:
to develop the very best in equine talent.

Over 140 acres of privately-owned farmland, which facilities include:

- Three purpose-built all-weather gallops
- Equine pool
- Solarium
- Indoor school
- Horse walker

- Turn-out paddocks
- Treadmill
- All-weather schooling ground
- EasyFix hurdles and fences

Contact David today to discuss your training needs.

Tyre Hill Racing Stables, Hanley Swan, Worcestershire WR8 0EQ
07867 974880 | info@ddracing.co.uk | www.ddracing.co.uk

DAVID DENNIS
RACING

ROYAL ASCOT
in pictures

1 Racegoers wait for the royal procession on Ladies' Day

2 All dressed up in the fashion bar

3 The runners pass the stands in the Ascot Stakes. The race was won by Domination, a first runner at the meeting for Irish trainer Charles Byrnes

4 Relaxing on the tea lawn

5 The runners in the Buckingham Palace Stakes split into two groups as they set sail down the home straight. Louis The Pious, one of the closest to the stands rail throughout, scored at 33-1 to give trainer David O'Meara his first Royal Ascot winner

6 Trainer Aidan O'Brien and his jockey son Joseph had a fruitless meeting for the first two and a half days and the relief is palpable on Joseph's face after finally breaking the duck with Bracelet in the Ribblesdale Stakes

7 Ryan Moore touches the Duke of Edinburgh Stakes trophy after his victory on Arab Spring, the first leg of a final-day treble that sealed top jockey honours. Sir Michael Stoute, who had a double with Arab Spring and Telescope (Hardwicke Stakes) on the final day, was the meeting's top trainer

8 William Buick celebrates the Chesham Stakes victory of Richard Pankhurst, bred as well as trained by John Gosden and owned by Rachel Hood, Gosden's wife. Hood later sold the colt to Sheikh Hamdan Bin Mohammad Al Maktoum

9 An artistic touch to the headwear on Ladies' Day

10 William Buick coasts home on the John Gosden-trained Eagle Top as they score an emphatic victory in the King Edward VII Stakes

11 The Richard Fahey-trained Baccarat (pink cap, leading nearside) gives 3lb claimer George Chaloner a first Royal Ascot winner with a 9-1 success in the Wokingham

TREMENDOUS

Another Arc triumph
for Treve and trainer
Criquette Head-Maarek
was one of racing's
greatest comebacks

By Scott Burton

"We choose to go to the Moon and do the other things in this decade, not because they are easy, but because they are hard"

STANDING in the centre of her yard on Avenue du General Leclerc in Chantilly, Criquette Head-Maarek may not quite be able to summon the majesty of John F Kennedy's famous words that inspired the space race of the 1960s. But her message, five days before Treve bids to become double Arc champion, is cut from the same stone.

"She deserves to be there at the finish and I think she has a chance on Sunday. When you get an unbeaten horse like her, there is only one way to guarantee they stay that way and that's to send them off to stud. We decided to keep going in the full knowledge that she could get beaten."

The hard path had been chosen for Treve, not the easy way out. It has been harder than anyone could have imagined but she has just crossed from the dark into the light – literally in the case of her final piece of work in fog-shrouded Chantilly. In a very real sense the four-year-old is emerging from a season cloaked in doubt and disappointment. Her trainer is convinced she can finally see improvement. For the rest of us, faith is not yet quite enough and the proof will have to wait for Longchamp.

SIX months earlier, everyone is a believer. Just three days after the Grand National, a watery spring sunshine greets the first semi-public glimpse of the previous year's Arc heroine and her reunion with Frankie Dettori, who later enthuses about her double acceleration. The smiles are broad and are by no means confined to jockey and trainer. There is no hiding the quiet satisfaction of head lad Pascal Galoche, who has become as reliable an indicator of Treve's position in the first-lot line-up as the filly's white star and four bandages.

Yet the sunny optimism is soon to be washed away by a series of high-profile defeats and injury-enforced absence. This becomes the story of a plan gone badly awry, of a horse in pain, and of Head-Maarek's

▶ *Continues page 22*

determination to leave no stone unturned in the search-and-rescue mission for the real Treve.

The first setback comes in late April when Treve is beaten a short neck by Cirrus Des Aigles in the Prix Ganay, but the very soft ground at Longchamp and the enduring quality of her battle-hardened conqueror offer ready excuses. Cirrus Des Aigles is already having his third run of the season and for Head-Maarek it is "normal" to be beaten in such circumstances. There is, she maintains, "nothing else" to it.

Optimism still abounds when Treve goes to Royal Ascot for the Prince of Wales's Stakes and is sent off at odds of 8-13. But the alarm bells are ringing even before the start of the race and she produces a laboured performance in third behind The Fugue. Now Head-Maarek is worried. "Frankie said Treve didn't have a good action and going down to the start she didn't look good," she admits. "Her action was not right today, I don't know why. Maybe we will discover something when we go back. Something must have been wrong with her."

Head-Maarek's fears are justified. Owner Sheikh Joaan Al Thani's vet diagnoses a back injury to go alongside the problems the filly has been suffering with her feet. Lumbar arthritis is not a promising condition to deal with but, having spoken with the vet, Head-Maarek remains certain Treve will be trainable again in the autumn. "She has a sore back, it's a muscle problem and a little arthritis. It's nothing serious and with rest and a little care she will be fine for September or October," Head-Maarek tells the Racing Post the week after Ascot.

In the first week of August a chance encounter in the Deauville parade ring resets the clocks as Head-Maarek mentions that Treve is back cantering after having stopped for a full six weeks. "It's early days but all the lights are green so far," she says with a smile.

By the time the racing circus returns to Paris at the beginning of September, news of Treve's recovery and her build-up to Longchamp's all-important trials meeting has begun to reverberate more widely. Head-Maarek has already begun to make changes to Treve's routine and the personnel around her, the most public of which is her request to put Thierry Jarnet back on board in place of Dettori, for what she expects to be Treve's final two races.

Everything is geared to managing the physical problems that have prevented the filly from displaying the full range of

▶▶ Start and finish: Treve (nearside) is beaten by Cirrus Des Aigles in the Prix Ganay on her first outing of 2014; (previous page) a troubled season has a glorious conclusion as Treve (left) roars back to form to win the Arc for the second year in a row, with Flintshire (fourth left) two lengths behind in second

her abilities. "The only thing I changed [when she came back into work in August] was to put a lightweight girl on her and also the type of saddle," she recalls in October. "I put a very big saddle on her – a cowboy saddle – which didn't touch her spine. It was heavy but it rested on both sides rather than on her spine. And the girl weighs less than 50kg.

"My head lad, Pascal, who used to ride her, wasn't pleased at first. But the girl rides dressage and she is so good and she puts no weight on her back. It worked. Look at the result."

Head-Maarek's promotion of Maurine Beusnel is not the only change among the backstage crew, as the trainer seeks to soothe Treve's troublesome feet, an issue she believes is the root of the back problem.

"She had a problem as far back as the beginning of her three-year-old career when she wasn't right in front," she explains. "We x-rayed but we couldn't find anything. This year I did a scan and we discovered a cyst inside the coffin bone. We put special shoes on her. I called the smith from the stud in Normandy, who takes care of all the foals and yearlings with problems."

Head-Maarek gestures across the yard to an open stable door and what passes in rural Calvados for a hipster, working away at the hoof of a grey filly. "He's young but he's incredible," she says of David Letellier. "He did a great job and he told me straight away that her feet weren't normal. He is part of the victory, I promise you. And with that beard he looks like God!"

DUAL WINNERS

Treve became the seventh to complete a double since the Arc's inception in 1920 – the first in almost 40 years and only the second filly after Corrida in the 1930s

Ksar 1921, 1922
Motrico 1930, 1932
Corrida 1936, 1937
Tantieme 1950, 1951
Ribot 1955, 1956
Alleged 1977, 1978
Treve 2013, 2014

The call to Sheikh Joaan to ask for Jarnet is not one many trainers would relish. The sheikh very publicly backed Dettori when injury robbed him of Arc glory in 2013, while the Italian has just conjured all his experience to win the Prix Morny aboard The Wow Signal with his boss in attendance. The storm breaks while Head-Maarek is in Kentucky for the Keeneland September yearling sales but there has been no hint of ducking the issue.

"I didn't get better feedback [from Jarnet] than with Frankie. He is a fantastic boy and he is very easy to deal with. I'm sure if he had ridden Treve in the Arc he would have won the same way Thierry did. I think the mare is more comfortable with Jarnet, that's all. But it's not against Frankie, he's a

▶▶ *Continues page 24*

HH Sheikh Mansoor
Bin Zayed Al Nahyan
Global Arabian Horse
Flat Racing Festival

المؤتمر العالمي لخيول السباق العربية
WORLD ARABIAN HORSE RACING CONFERENCE

Warsaw, Poland, 2015

champion jockey and I hope I will use him again and again. Treve doesn't pull as much with Jarnet. But, saying that, when Frankie rode her this year she was not 100 per cent, so it's not his fault. It's the filly who had problems and it took me quite a long time to figure out what was really wrong with her and to deal with her."

The mind also travels back to that April morning when Head-Maarek asked the lightweight Cristian Demuro to ride work against the heavier Dettori in order to give Treve more of a workout. "Frankie needed a tiny saddle when he rode her and with her back problems . . ." She lets the phrase hang in the air.

HAVING made the brave call to replace Dettori, and with a new work rider in place and other changes at home, Head-Maarek will surely see a different Treve on her return in the Prix Vermeille. Once again she is odds-on – 4-5 in a field of nine – but once again to most eyes she looks a pale shadow of her former self and is beaten a length and a half in fourth place.

The Vermeille looks a near fatal setback for Treve's Arc challenge, as she fails to pick up behind Baltic Baroness, whom she had beaten by a combined distance of 30 lengths in their two previous meetings. Sheikh Joaan appears to sense it may be a lost cause when he says that afternoon that Treve has "nothing to prove", while Jarnet's opinion is that hard races in the Ganay and at Royal Ascot have left their mark.

But in France they're called *courses preparatoires* – not trials – for a reason. While even Jarnet feels his old partner lacks her former sparkle, Head-Maarek and her father Alec see encouragement enough to proceed.

In the heat of the moment the trainer describes Treve's run as "a good comeback" and expresses the hope that the filly will line up on Arc day. In the days that follow, she has to persuade Sheikh Joaan that the cause is worth fighting for. "He could have lost faith but I told him 'let me do it'. After the Vermeille I said: 'Please don't rule her out, let's run in the Arc, we'll see'."

By the Tuesday before the Arc, and that all-important gallop, all forecasts have been revised upwards. Head-Maarek even regards the near impenetrable bank of fog as a good omen, telling the assembled press and well-wishers: "It was like this the whole week the year that Three Troikas won the Arc."

Owing to the near zero visibility, only

Jarnet will ever really know the details of Treve's gallop that morning but a flying finish out of the mist looks impressive and leaves everyone in buoyant mood.

"Last year we were unbeaten but I was worried about Orfevre and Intello," says Head-Marek as we return through the gloom. "She just continued to improve all the way to the Arc. Even though she is older this year she has done what she did last year, which is to say that she has thrived throughout September. She might not be as good as she was on the eve of the Arc last year but she is 100 per cent better than she was at the start of this year."

Usually a trainer chooses their words carefully when it comes to the opposition but, as confidence in the form of Treve increases, Head-Maarek has started to pull at the threads of the challengers to see if they start to fray. "The Japanese horse [Just A Way] is a very good horse over 2,000 metres [1m2f] but he isn't a real 2,400-metre [1m4f] horse and in the Arc you really need to stay. The same with Ectot. The other day they didn't go hard, he came up on the outside very quickly and then he slowed near the line. It's logical because he wasn't running over his best trip. If we get a truly run race, 2,400 metres around Longchamp takes some getting. Treve has no problem staying, in fact quite the opposite. Non-stayers don't win it. They come there to win it but then what?"

Alec Head is pressed by reporter Fanny Salmon for his views on the work but French racing's elder statesman, who spends the majority of his days in the Bahamas, confines himself to a few

▸▸ Cover girl: Treve and Thierry Jarnet are led in after the Arc and (below) the Racing Post front pages on October 1, 6 and 7

general pleasantries. Fortunately his daughter is in the mood to break confidences.

"Papa was next to me during the Vermeille and he tapped me on the elbow straight afterwards and said 'she'll win the Arc'. I told him it would be difficult but he said to me: 'Listen, she has run a lot better than other people will think. Just focus on her and keep doing what you're doing and she will win the Arc.' This morning was the first time he's seen her work this year and he liked what he saw. He believes in her."

JARNET broke just about every rule in the Longchamp playbook aboard Treve in the 2013 Arc, travelling four wide before letting his partner shoot forward in the false straight. Convinced of the filly's superiority, he was prepared to give away ground around the outside rather than forfeit extra lengths tacking across to the rail from his wide draw and then trusting that a gap would appear.

In 2014 he has stall three and rides with similar confidence, albeit this time glued to the rail. Jarnet is in front before the two-furlong pole and allows himself a celebratory slap down Treve's neck before the pair cross the line between Arc winner and turf immortality.

"When I asked she accelerated straight away, she gave me exactly the same sensations as in 2013," Jarnet says. "She might have been a little bit less decisive right at the end because she has had her problems but even so the turn of foot was still there."

High up in the Longchamp grandstand, father and daughter

▸▸ *Continues page 26*

▸▸ Loving touch: Criquette Head-Maarek with Treve at her Chantilly stable the day after their astounding Arc success

embrace and at once the scene is awash with tears. Criquette and Alec are no longer alone in their certitude; now they are besieged by the reconverted.

As Head-Maarek races out on to the course amid a swarm of photographers, Alec fights his way to the winner's enclosure. His words tumble out in proud defiance. "If the mare is well, nobody can beat her. What she did last year was unbelievable, the way she won the Arc. You have to be a super champion to win that way, so she's got the class. The only thing is that she has to be sound.

"When I saw her go to post at Ascot I thought 'my God, she shouldn't be running'. She couldn't crawl at Ascot. She wasn't beaten by better horses. The other day [in the Vermeille] people didn't realise what a good race she ran because she had been stopped and she needed the race. And Jarnet didn't give her a hard race. I thought nobody could beat her and I said so to everybody."

Now everybody lines up to pay tribute to Treve and the wonderful feat executed by Head-Maarek. The trainer has the air of a proud mother whose daughter has just excelled in a school concert or sports match. "When I saw her going in the false straight I said 'we're going to win'. She's got that fantastic turn of foot. For me, she's a very special horse."

BACK in the yard in Chantilly the day after, Head-Maarek is once again entertaining media and friends. "I never thought she would win like that," she admits. "I always had the thing where I knew her spine was not perfect and, when a horse is suffering, they stop. I didn't know if she was going to stop."

Treve didn't stop and now we know she won't be stopping for a while yet. The decision to try for a third Arc comes as an about turn, after connections had gone so far as announcing Dubawi as the first stallion to whom they intended to send Treve.

But maybe the seeds of that change of mind were there on that foggy morning before the Arc. On that occasion Head-Maarek said: "There has never been a thought about retiring her during the year because there has always been

something else to try. She is wearing different shoes, for example. But if you stopped with the sort of problems she has you wouldn't run 80 per cent of the horses in training."

For the Heads and the Al Thanis, the gauntlet is there to be picked up again. As Jarnet says: "It's fabulous. I'm delighted it's turned out like this and it's a huge challenge. It's a great thing even to be trying."

Following Treve from the high of her first Arc victory to the low of Royal Ascot and her remarkable autumn revival has been the ultimate racing rollercoaster. It is the story of a trainer with unmatched skill who got Treve right for the day that mattered in the most trying of circumstances. And having discovered the key to keeping the filly happy and healthy, Head-Maarek and Sheikh Joaan now believe they have a roadmap with which to head for a historic third Arc triumph.

TRAINER PAR EXCELLENCE

WHAT THEY SAID ABOUT CRIQUETTE HEAD-MAAREK'S ACHIEVEMENT WITH TREVE

This is genuinely extraordinary. This is a training performance you can only wonder at. Many trainers would have given up. But she would not give up *Channel 4 Racing's Clare Balding*

I don't think we can quite believe what we've just seen. If we'd all listened to Criquette all the way along, yes you'd believe it, but it's incredible. She's a remarkable trainer and this is a remarkable filly *Harry Herbert, racing manager for owners Al Shaqab Racing*

Fantastic. What a triumph and what an amazing training effort. I thought Treve had completely gone *Former BBC commentator Sir Peter O'Sullevan*

Criquette was under a lot of pressure. Even though Treve hadn't performed in the prep race she had to have her right for the Arc. It is fabulous *Treve's jockey Thierry Jarnet*

An amazing training performance. Everyone had written the filly off after Ascot and to get her back to her best when it mattered was amazing *Fellow trainer Lady Cecil*

Graham Budd

AUCTIONS

THE LEADING SPECIALIST AUCTIONEER OF SPORTING MEMORABILIA IN THE UK

All sales held at Sotheby's New Bond Street saleroom, London

Dick Francis first edition, first novel, with dust jacket

Graham Budd Auctions Ltd, PO Box 47519, London, N14 6XD
Tel: 020 8366 2525 E-Mail: gb@grahambuddauctions.co.uk
web: www.grahambuddauctions.co.uk

IN THE PICTURE

Kensington Palace a fitting venue for first Frankel foal to go to public auction

The first foal by Frankel to be sold at public auction caused a stir in June when he fetched £1.15m as part of a three-for-the-price-of-one offer at the inaugural Goffs London sale staged in the magnificent surroundings of Kensington Palace.

The sale, held in the Orangery late on the Monday afternoon of Royal Ascot week, was scheduled to attract leading international owners in London for the races and the Frankel foal was the centre of attention. He was sold along with his dam, Crystal Gaze, who had been scanned in foal to Frankel again after a covering in April. Crystal Gaze is the dam of Group 2-winning sprinter Spirit Quartz and the opportunity to buy her, as well as two offspring of Frankel (the foal and his unborn sibling), was snapped up by MV Magnier, son of Coolmore supremo John Magnier.

"He could be fast by the look of him," said Magnier. "He's a good, strong colt. The lads [the ownership group of his father, Derrick Smith and Michael Tabor] liked him a lot and I have to listen to what they say. A horse like that, with that pedigree and those looks, should be making serious money. I'll tell you if it's value when he hits the track in a couple of years."

The ritzy sale had the feel of an upmarket garden party, with afternoon tea followed by cocktails and canapes, and Frankel's foal garnered plenty of media attention, with reports of his sale making the ITV News at Ten and the non-racing press.

The Frankel foal and his mother, consigned by Tweenhills Stud on behalf of Qatar Bloodstock, were the only horses sold in the flesh at Kensington Palace but 50 more, including unraced two-year-olds and horses in training, went under the hammer simultaneously at Kempton Park, via video link to those gathered in central London.

Several of the horses in training had entries at Royal Ascot, but none of them was able to win at the big meeting. Cappella Sansevero, who was knocked down to Sheikh Fahad Al Thani for the sale's top price of £1.3m, was quickly registered to run in Qatar Racing colours and was second the following day in the Group 2 Coventry Stakes behind The Wow Signal. The Ger Lyons-trained Cappella Sansevero went on to win the Group 3 Round Tower Stakes at the Curragh in August.

Sheikh Fahad also bought the most unusual lot at the London sale: a lifetime nomination to the stallion Invincible Spirit, the sire of star miler Kingman. The nomination, which will allow the sheikh to use Invincible Spirit for one of his mares every year, fetched £160,000.

Picture: ROD KIRKPATRICK/F STOP PRESS

By Jonathan Mullin

THE momentum is the striking aspect. Next spring will mark the 20th anniversary of Willie Mullins' first Cheltenham Festival winner as a trainer, the day when Tourist Attraction came in at 25-1 in the Supreme Novices' Hurdle, and since then he has taken his score to 33. But it is the momentum that catches your breath – more than half of his festival winners have come in the past five years, and in 15 of the 27 races at the 2014 meeting Mullins supplied a horse in the frame, four of them winning.

Do not expect the landscape to take on a different hue any time soon because, while stars like Hurricane Fly and the now retired Quevega will not have the same hold on the headlines they once did, Mullins'

bright bunch of youngsters are poised to become big news.

Every pocket of time gets hitched up with a name and this is quickly becoming the Willie Mullins Era. In Ireland alone last season his horses earned more than €3.8million in prize-money, a total that his four nearest challengers could barely muster between them. Not only that, but 2013-2014 was the season when Mullins' empire expanded from his base in Ireland and looked east towards Britain with more regularity. His seasonal total of 11 winners for earnings of more than £800,000 almost doubled his tally in Britain for the previous campaign and sent out the strongest signal that Mullins-trained horses will be popping up on big days in Britain from now on.

He will do so with a formidable team of young horses collected from all corners of Ireland and France.

Last season he landed both of the premier novice hurdle events at Cheltenham, with Vautour in the Supreme and Faugheen in the Neptune producing hugely impressive performances. Two of his runners finished second and fourth in the Champion Bumper, with both Shaneshill and Black Hercules joining stablemate Allez Colombieres, a three-time bumper winner in France, at the top of the novice hurdle betting for 2015.

As the wraps come off the jumps season Mullins' horses dominate the ante-post picture for next year's Cheltenham Festival and stable jockey Ruby Walsh must be licking his lips with anticipation. Annie Power looks a ready-made replacement for Quevega in the mares' hurdle division and a return to his best form for Sir Des Champs would make him a prime Gold Cup contender in a season where the field

looks as wide open as a scene from Ben Hur. Then there is the eye-popping possibility of Un De Sceaux going chasing, a tearaway tank built without brakes. It is a treasure of equine riches and, like last season, keeping them all apart for as long as possible will be a daily chore for the Irish champion trainer.

Racing people readily compare this training genius to his late father Paddy and, for those hoping that Mullins will return to the pack some day soon, the pedigree gives them little succour.

As trainer and TV pundit Ted Walsh points out. "Willie's father Paddy wasn't champion jumps trainer in Ireland until he was 63. Most people would have been thinking about packing it in if they hadn't made it at that stage – instead Paddy went on to be champion trainer ten times." The best is probably yet to come from WP.

YOUTH ON HIS SIDE

Willie Mullins has his eye on the big prizes with a new generation headed by Cheltenham Festival winners Vautour and Faugheen

For the 58-year-old trainer to continue his march, he needs the right weapons in his artillery and replacing the lost ones is perhaps the most difficult job in racing. Once-in-a-lifetime horses, by definition, do not come around a second time and the job of finding another Quevega and another Hurricane Fly, for so long the first two names on Mullins' teamsheet for the big spring festivals, will not be an easy one.

The new poster boys and girls might all be in pink – most of the big young horses mentioned above run in the colours of Susannah Ricci – but let nobody in Closutton hear you talk of Hurricane Fly's career being swatted by defeats at Cheltenham and Punchestown.

"Sure, his last two runs were disappointing but there are still lots of good races to be won with him," says Harold Kirk, the bloodstock agent who plays an integral role in the Mullins operation. "He'll stay very well and he won over two and a half miles as a four-year-old at Auteuil in heavy ground. And he is settling better in his races than he used to. There's plenty left in Hurricane Fly, you can be sure of that."

Kirk, charged with the responsibility of finding the future stars of the yard, acknowledges that, with Hurricane Fly in his veteran years and Quevega departed to the paddocks, this is a big season for the Mullins yard, and one in which they will rely heavily on the youngsters coming good.

"The last two or three years have been a period of transition for the yard, I've no doubt about that," Kirk says. That statement may appear to be contradicted by the fact that Mullins finished as top trainer at

▶ Continues page 32

Cheltenham in 2014 – for the third time in four seasons – but while the bare facts may go against Kirk, the detail supports his view. Three of the four Cheltenham victories were with novice hurdlers – Vautour, Faugheen and Don Poli – while the other, Quevega's momentous sixth, came from the opposite end of the experience range. In between is the ground where the big championship races are fought and this season will test whether Mullins has invested wisely in replenishing his stock for an assault on those contests.

THOSE exciting novices – some plucked out of Irish point-to-points, others from the fields of France that have returned such a huge dividend for the trainer – have their chance to make some noise. Faugheen and Vautour have long occupied lofty positions in the ante-post lists for Cheltenham 2015 and, while the big British yards have been scrambling to compete in the buying stakes, Mullins appears to have assembled a huge team of talented young horses.

"You need luck and the novices turned out to be very good last season," Kirk says. "I'd always be trying to work 18 months in advance to ensure there is a constant supply. But every year is scary because you hope that the batch coming through is somewhere near as good as the batch that they were bought to replace, which sometimes won't happen.

"When you have top-class racehorses that fall by the wayside or get old or aren't as good as they were, they're almost impossible to replace. Paul Nicholls went through that transition and he lost four or five of the best horses he had. We'll never find another Hurricane Fly, I'm convinced of that."

The big problem for Mullins, with Kirk at his right hand, is that their success in buying horses from France has been so overwhelmingly successful that they have illuminated the passage for others to go and do the same. That has created a feeding frenzy of demand for a relatively small pool of French horses.

"It's so hard to buy now because more and more people are there to buy the ready-made horses," Kirk says. "In France for a small pool of horses there's a huge pool of people to buy them with more and more money to spend. The horse that wins in a province now is the price of a horse that wins at Auteuil and that horse is 100 per cent more expensive now because of supply and

▶ Continues page 34

▶▶ High hopes: (from top) Faugheen, Shaneshill, Don Poli and Sure Reef

GENERATION NEXT

Ten rising stars with the potential to hit the big time

Faugheen Emphatic winner of the Neptune and followed up even more impressively at Punchestown, making it six from six in his career. A point-to-point winner with bags of speed, he looks set to stay over hurdles with the challenge of trying to become Hurricane Fly's replacement in the Champion Hurdle division.

Vautour Unbeaten in five starts last season after arriving from France, with three Grade 1 wins. Best performance was his six-length victory in the Supreme Novices' at Cheltenham and he looks set to go straight over fences.

Djakadam Fell at the fourth last in the JLT Novices' Chase when he was travelling sweetly and looked on course for a big run for a five-year-old. Two from two over fences before that and this imposing French-bred is an exciting prospect.

Black Hercules Fourth in the Champion Bumper and impressed that day with the way he travelled and battled. Ultimately chasing will be his game but that won't stop him becoming a force in the staying novice hurdle division this season.

Tell Us More One of the darker horses in this list. Won a weak Gowran bumper in impressive fashion and all of the point-to-point judges had him marked down as special after his debut win at Tattersalls last December.

Shaneshill Sent off favourite for the Champion Bumper at Cheltenham, having been unbeaten in Ireland, and found only Silver Concorde too good. Reversed the form at Punchestown and has the shape of a top novice hurdler this term.

Allez Colombieres An intriguing recruit, coming into the season on the back of three bumper wins as a three-year-old in France. Cost €300,000 at Arqana and the subject of positive stable vibes.

Abbyssial A four-time winner over hurdles last season, including a Grade 1 at Punchestown. This strapping son of Beneficial looks a ready-made chaser and Mullins is surely looking forward to exploiting his weight-for-age allowance.

Don Poli A stout stayer who looked wide open to improvement heading to Cheltenham last season and – like Sir Des Champs before him – stormed home to land the Martin Pipe. Surpassed that form at Punchestown with a close second to Beat That and looks a young chaser who can make a big impact this season.

Sure Reef Does nothing fancy but a Grade 2 winner over hurdles who showed in his time with Michael Halford on the Flat that he loves nothing better than running to the line. Could be the surprise package in the staying hurdle department.

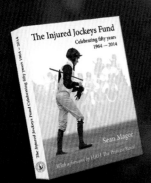

demand. If we don't give the money for that horse, somebody else will.

"We're buying the less obvious horse more and more – horses who are finishing second, third and fourth in France – because we can't compete with the prices for the winners. We're giving strong prices for horses and getting them, but most of the horses we have bought recently from France haven't won there. Trying to find horses for the top level is scary. Very, very scary."

The one factor that can perhaps soothe the bloodstock agent's fears is that the horses he buys are in the care of a man at the very top of this game.

"Willie is very much like his father in that he has his own unique way of doing things," says Ted Walsh. "You couldn't put it down on paper and I'd say if you asked him he'd struggle to put it in words. If you asked him why he did this or that, he might not be able to give you a reason – it's instinct. He just has it and Paddy was the same way."

Kirk agrees. "He's just brilliant at his job and he has a sixth sense that all of the top people have. All the top managers in the world have a sixth sense and there are times you query what he does, but 99 times out of 100 he's right. There are times that myself and Ruby might be saying to each other 'what's happening here?' but we'd end up having egg on our faces. He knows how to train bad horses to win ordinary races but he always knows how to train a very good horse. People used to tell me that anybody can train a good horse but I think you need a very good trainer to train a very good horse.

"It's something you're born with, and his father and his father's father probably had the same thing. But I think Willie is on a different level. He believes in himself and he believes in the people around him. He gives responsibility and he delegates. He believes in Ruby and his jockeys riding the horses, and he believes in me buying them."

COINCIDENCE or not, last season marked the renewal of the 'full-time' relationship between Mullins and Walsh, with the jockey quitting his plane-hopping role with Paul Nicholls. In a way it must have felt like Paul Scholes telling Sir Alex Ferguson he was quitting international football to extend his career at Old Trafford, and the results were spectacular.

"In my opinion Ruby is the best there has ever been, in terms of natural ability," Kirk says. "He needs no instruction, by instinct he could change his plan three times in a race and that's what makes the top jockeys."

In a season with some uncertainty – will these young horses step up to the

▶▶ Leader of the pack: (clockwise from top) Willie Mullins' high-class mare Annie Power heads the string after cantering; Mullins with Rich Ricci, whose wife Susannah's colours are carried by Faugheen and Vautour; stable jockey Ruby Walsh in a post-race debrief with the trainer

big league? – Walsh is a constant, a rock for Mullins to rely on. It has been that way for the best part of 20 years.

"The first of it was Willie was going to Leopardstown and he couldn't do the weight and he asked me whether Ruby would ride the horse for him," says Ruby's father Ted. "Ruby was only 16 and claiming 7lb but he rode the horse for Willie and won. First ride, first winner. After that I said to Willie that

the best thing Ruby could do was to go down to him for the summer. And they just clicked. He was champion amateur the first year he rode, he was champion amateur the second year and he's been champion jockey every year since except for the years when he got knocked out.

"They're on the same wavelength. Ruby will know a day that Willie might be in bad form and avoid him. And he knows when he's in good form and they just get on. Ruby would be a great timekeeper and a great worker, he'd be there on days when Willie might say there'd be no need.

"I wouldn't say 'father and son', but I'd say when it comes to asking his opinion and trusting him, he's as close to Willie as he is to anybody outside of me. Even when he got the job in England there was never any difference of opinion. Willie told him it was a great opportunity and maybe some day Ruby's knowledge of the tracks over there would come in handy. Willie would be thinking ahead, that's what has put him where he is today – at the very top."

With Faugheen, Vautour and all the rest coming along the production line, that is where Mullins intends to stay.

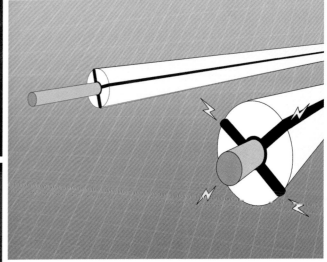

THE
BIGGER
PICTURE

Macgillycuddy's Reeks, the highest mountain range in Ireland, forms the spectacular backdrop at Killarney racecourse, County Kerry, as the runners head out of the back straight in the International Hotel Killarney Handicap Hurdle in May

**PATRICK McCANN
(RACINGPOST.COM/PHOTOS)**

UNSTOPPABLE

Tony McCoy turned 40 in May but he is as driven as ever and the records keep falling

By Alastair Down

PROLONGED proximity to the remarkable often leads to phenomenal achievements being taken for granted. After all, City commuters don't stop and gawp at the magnificence of St Paul's Cathedral each and every morning as they trudge into the office and, back in the 1960s after Arkle had become a household name, the locals around Tom Dreaper's yard in Greenogue would have got used to the sight of Himself ambling along the lanes as he did his road work in late summer and early autumn before the season's hard graft began in earnest.

St Paul's Cathedral? The incomparable Arkle? Just part of the day-to-day for some people.

To an extent we racing folk almost commit a similar sin of omission with AP McCoy. Virtually every day of the year he is out there somewhere gnawing his way towards the next target with all the inexorability of the ocean eroding the base of some mighty cliff. The vast majority of his unprecedented number of winners are racked up in a ceaseless criss-crossing of the country, often while the focus of the sport is elsewhere.

There are moments when he is lauded and superlatives are thrown his way. In 2010, having landed the Grand National on Don't Push It, he was named BBC Sports Personality of the Year. The milestone of his 4,000th winner at Towcester, hugely enhanced by John Hunt's soundbite dream of a commentary, made the national news in November 2013 and at the height of the jumps season when AP rides a big Saturday winner all eyes are on him.

But the grunt work behind McCoy's spiralling numbers is chiefly done far from the fleshpot meetings. When he completed his fastest-ever 100 winners on August 21 this year it was in the evening at Newton Abbot far from where the TV cameras and racing press were busy with four days of the York Ebor meeting.

We meet before racing at Uttoxeter – another typical workaday afternoon trying to pan gold out of the base metal of summer jumpers. It is the umpteenth time I have sat down to interview him but he has become ever more interesting with the passage of time and, having turned 40 in May, he is nearly unrecognisable from the almost haunted and detached figure of his early twenties.

He knows he has changed. "Looking back I'd say that between the ages of about 24 and 34 I was just like a robot because I was so wrapped up in myself," he says. "It is still about me but not nearly as much as it was, I'm pleased to say."

There is a widespread view that McCoy's riding has reached a new level. "He's riding better than ever, not least because he's riding cleverer than ever," his friend and rival Jason Maguire said in the summer. "He's as cute as a fox. There's no point getting older if you don't get wiser and that's exactly what he's done."

McCoy laughs when reminded of Maguire's observation. "I think that with experience you get more confident in your own judgement when it comes to choosing which risks or chances you can take. Am I riding better than ever? No, 2002 was when I was riding at my best because I'm a statistics man and that's what the numbers say."

In all frankness AP has a streak of nerdiness when it comes to his preoccupation with numbers but perhaps that comes with the territory of routinely rewriting records year in, year out. As well as his fastest 100, the latest year has seen him win his 19th British

jump jockeys' title – a competition he has never lost since he graduated to the senior ranks – and surpass trainer Martin Pipe's tally of 4,191 winners. That was more of a personal duel with the man who gave him so many winners, big and small, but it mattered to McCoy. Typically, having gone past Pipe, he immediately identified 4,500 winners as a target – "if I can still be competitive".

McCoy's grit-toughness is a given and it is an unspoken point of honour to him that he is the hardest man in the weighing room but, as well as particular injuries, the wear and tear of around 17,000 rides produces a cumulative clobbering as the seasons mount up. Already he has gone on much longer than champions such as John Francome, Peter Scudamore and Richard Dunwoody, none of whom rode on beyond their early to mid-thirties.

One of McCoy's most shocking recent falls was at Cheltenham in April 2013 from the moody Quantitativeeasing, which left a lasting legacy. "As a result of that one my chest is a mess. I punctured a lung, did five or six ribs and fractured my sternum." He then shows you where his broken sternum has gone walkabout and with your fingers you can feel a three- to four-inch protuberance of bone under his skin, rather as if someone has left the handle of a small saucepan there by mistake.

"I don't think I'm braver than I was 20 years ago and the thing that Cheltenham fall taught me is that the epidural is the greatest form of pain relief ever invented. I have stuff that I need to keep patching up but because jump jockeys are not that bright you think it won't happen again. But it does, of course.

"Mentally, you wouldn't want to
▸▸ *Continues page 40*

'Am I riding better than ever? No, 2002 was when I was at my best because that's what the numbers say'

▸▸ Family circle: McCoy with wife Chanelle, daughter Eve and son Archie on the final day of the 2013-14 British jumps season at Sandown, where he collected his 19th jockeys' title

STAR TURNS

Every year the perennial champion produces amazing rides. Here is just a small selection from 2014

Upswing *Newbury, February 8*
On heavy ground over 3m½f, Upswing looked dog-tired as leader Rydon Pines went five lengths clear going to the last. Slowly but surely, McCoy made up the ground and won by half a length

Taquin Du Seuil
Cheltenham, March 13
In agony after injuring his back the previous day, McCoy defied the pain to prevail in a three-way battle up the hill in the Grade 1 JLT Novices' Chase

Man With Van *Perth, May 15*
Three lengths down at the last, McCoy's mount wandered on the run-in but got up in the last stride to score by a head

It's A Gimme
Market Rasen, July 19
Big race, well-backed favourite: there seemed an inevitability about victory in the Summer Plate. But it only happened because of McCoy, who got him to the front with 50 yards to go

It Is What It Is and Barton Stacey *Worcester, August 27*
Part of a four-timer, these two wins were hard to separate for typical McCoy persistence. Odds-on It Is What It Is blundered badly at the 11th and again at the last but was driven back up to win by a short head; fifth two out, Barton Stacey traded at 90 in running on Betfair but won with a storming late burst

analyse it that much. It is hard for those close to you but Chanelle is much better at dealing with my injuries now. She knows that as long as it's not my head or spinal cord it isn't going to be that bad."

They say there was a time when Chanelle knew what sort of day her husband had endured at the office by the sound the car keys made when they hit the hall table on his return. But family life has suppressed most – though not all – of his selfishness gene and, at the risk of stooping into Hello! magazine territory, his daughter Eve and son Archie seem to have given him new eyes with which to look at the world.

Indeed, I can give you one

winning tip for this jumps season and that is to make for the paddock area whenever AP rides a winner at Cheltenham. Ignore him and keep your eye on the small figure of Eve somewhere around the weighing room because her celebrations are priceless. The six-year-old holds nothing back – an utterly uninhibited bouncing bundle of happiness and love for her dad.

Son Archie is rising 15 months and is fully recovered from issues that led to the harrowing process of heart surgery in March. "One of the many good things about the kids is that I can't – or don't – take a bad day home with me and inflict it on them," McCoy says.

"They have helped hugely because they snap me out of the bad bits and that makes them go quicker. It's something I never thought would happen. I always wanted kids but never understood – or even really thought about – just how much they could alter you for the better.

"Eve is more like her mum than her father – more outgoing, more pleasant and more approachable. Archie is going to be no jockey – he's a beast! There is a lot of McCoy in Archie – a bit of a temper and plenty of trying to get his own way."

There is no doubt family and fatherhood have introduced AP to an unimagined side of himself that is

▸▸ *Continues page 42*

all the more treasured by him for being unexpected. But none of his life off course has reduced the savagery of his hell-bent obsession with riding winners on course.

Indeed, there is an argument that the ferocity of his intent burns brighter than ever because he knows he cannot go on forever. "I appreciate things all the more because I know there's a lot more behind me than there is still in front. But enjoying it is all about being successful and going on riding winners. I'm not retiring today or tomorrow – when I start something I like to finish it and there's never going to be an easy time."

You can tell McCoy is slightly wound up by the way the media seems ever on the lookout for a sign that he is on the edge of packing it in. There is no air of goodbye when he talks about those who have helped him along the road from raw kid to sporting institution.

Having started close to home with Billy Rock in County Antrim, he moved south to the hard school of Jim Bolger. "His attention to detail and huge discipline almost seemed too much at the time, but it wasn't now that you look

HISTORY MAN
McCOY IN NUMBERS

Not all his numbers, just the significant ones of 2014 (and there are plenty of them)

1 Winner at the Cheltenham Festival (Taquin Du Seuil, JLT Novices' Chase), taking his overall total to 30

218 Winners in 2013-14 British jumps season, his joint-highest total of the past decade

19 Number of British jump jockeys' championships after winning his latest title by 63 from perennial runner-up Richard Johnson

4,192 Overall tally passed Martin Pipe's career total with victory on It's A Gimme at Market Rasen on July 19

100 Completed fastest century of winners with victory on Arabic History at Newton Abbot on August 21, beating his own record by 13 days and keeping him on course to beat his seasonal record of 289 set in 2001-02

▶▶ Man and superman: (clockwise from top) Tony McCoy signs an autograph on his way to the parade ring at Uttoxeter on July 16, the day he drew level with trainer Martin Pipe's total of 4,191 winners; with JP McManus after Jezki's victory in the Racing Post Champion Hurdle at the Punchestown festival; taking the Ice Bucket Challenge to mark his fastest century of winners at Newton Abbot in August; on his way to another dazzling victory on It's A Gimme in the Summer Plate at Market Rasen

back," he says. After moving to Britain, first becoming champion conditional in 1994-95 with a record (what else?) 74 winners, he has been helped by many benefactors – notably Toby Balding, Martin Pipe, Jonjo O'Neill and his employer JP McManus – and he is a great man for giving credit to all of them. When Balding died in September, he remembered: "Toby's help was invaluable. He was a huge influence on my career in so many respects."

There was a time when the only thing that frightened McCoy was the thought of retirement and, while he still hates the idea, you get the feeling the fear of it is less than of old. But the importance of choosing his own time is paramount. "I don't want to carry on for too long," he says. "I will know when the time has come and I have friends I respect who are good enough judges to tell me."

When he finally goes, McCoy will leave behind records that are likely to stand all tests of time. Enjoy the phenomenon while it is still out there illuminating the sport like nobody else has.

IN THE PICTURE

Maguire's scar a lasting reminder of the fall that almost cost him his life

It is often said an injury or suspension on the eve of the Cheltenham Festival is a jump jockey's worst nightmare, but Jason Maguire's fall at Stratford on March 10 was about much more than missing jump racing's biggest meeting.

For a time Maguire's life hung in the balance and the situation would have been perilous in the extreme at the racecourse if his own words had been heeded in response to the pain he felt from a fractured sternum.

"I was on the ground and couldn't get my breath, I just thought I was badly winded," recalled Maguire, 33, who had ridden 130 winners in the 2013-14 season and was on course for a personal-best total.

"The paramedics were trying to hold me quiet and ask me questions, but I just wanted them to give me morphine to take the pain away. They wouldn't, they didn't give me anything, and they were right not to because there was internal bleeding and they could have poisoned my blood."

That was the first of several interventions that saved the 2011 Grand National-winning jockey. Another was that by good fortune an air ambulance was already at the racecourse and he was quickly transferred to Coventry's University Hospital.

He was "a goner", he was told later, if the surgeons Peter McCullogh and Zaed Hamady had not operated straight away once he reached hospital. He had an emergency operation to remove part of his liver and stem the internal bleeding that quickly drained him of three litres of blood. When the festival started at Cheltenham the following day, Maguire was in an induced coma to aid his recovery.

The only physical reminder of the drama now is the long scar that once contained more than 40 staples. He could have returned to race-riding a couple of months after the fall but decided to delay in order to have surgery on a long-standing back complaint that was aggravated at Stratford.

In July he started a lengthy period of rehabilitation at Oaksey House in Lambourn, as well as working in his gym at home and road running. At the start of September he started riding out for Donald McCain, his main employer, and Kim Bailey. He also became a father for the first time when wife Lauren gave birth to a girl, Darcy Anne.

Finally, after six months on the sidelines, Maguire returned to action at Newton Abbot on September 19. He won on his comeback ride aboard the Bailey-trained Bonne Fee, coincidentally the same horse who had given him a winning return from a broken neck three years earlier.

Picture: EDWARD WHITAKER (RACINGPOST.COM/PHOTOS)

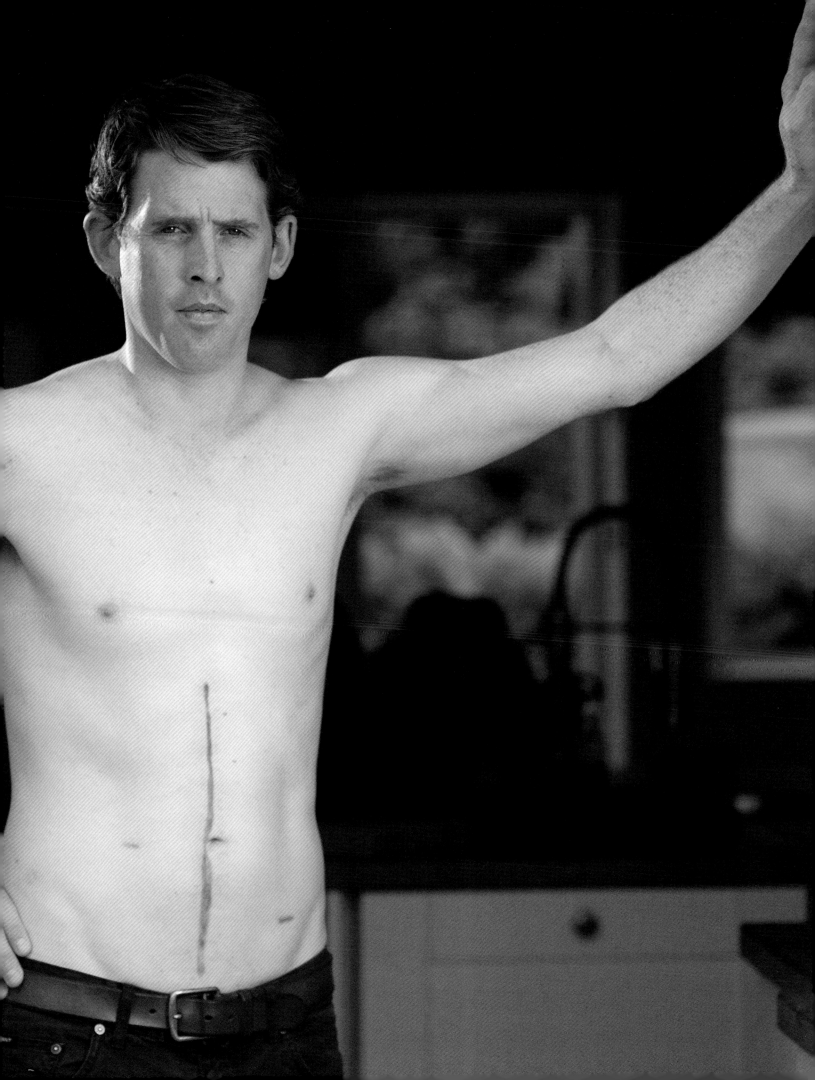

THE CHOSEN ONE

Australia fulfilled his destiny at Epsom, living up to his illustrious pedigree and his exalted reputation, before his career ended on a galling defeat

By David Jennings

D AY TWO of the Listowel harvest festival and Joseph O'Brien walks back to the weighing room after being narrowly denied aboard As Good As Gold in the opening fillies' maiden. He tries to fashion a smile but his lips won't budge. It is almost 48 hours since Australia was gathered in by The Grey Gatsby in the Qipco Irish Champion Stakes and O'Brien must have replayed the race in his head hundreds of times. Was he too far back? Did he stay too wide? Did he hit the front too soon? Only he knows the answers.

He agrees to stop and chat, as long as it's quick. We start on a positive note, drooling over the recent displays of Gleneagles and John F Kennedy. The middle ground is Leading Light, second to Brown Panther in the Irish St Leger, before the talk inevitably turns to Australia. "It's a pity to ride a horse like Australia and not make the most of him on every occasion

▸ *Continues page 48*

BIG HITTER
AUSTRALIA IN NUMBERS

5 Wins in eight starts

£2,090,503 Career earnings

3 Group 1 victories

2 Classic wins (Derby, Irish Derby)

129 Highest Racing Post Rating, recorded in the Juddmonte International

that you ride him. You live and learn," he says, stone-faced.

The Irish Champion would turn out to be Australia's last race, both horse and rider deprived of a shot at redemption on Champions Day at Ascot due to a hoof abscess that blew out through the bottom of his foot.

He had done the Derby double, beaten the Eclipse, French Derby and Hardwicke winners in the Juddmonte International at York and earned £2,090,503 in prize-money – all considerable efforts towards living up to his exalted reputation.

CONSIDER the comments made by Aidan O'Brien after Australia's steady workout at the Curragh on March 23. "Everyone probably knows we always thought he was the best horse we've ever had," he said. "I meant what I said after he won at Leopardstown in September. He's the second-best we've trained. The best we had wasn't even a Flat horse. It was Istabraq, who was head and shoulders above the rest as a hurdler."

Australia had a lot to live up to: he had to prove he had more class than Camelot, more determination than Dylan Thomas, a more powerful gallop than Galileo, a harder attitude than Giant's Causeway, more gears than Rock Of Gibraltar . . .

He was certainly bred to do all of the above. His parents – Galileo and Ouija Board – had won ten Group 1s between them. Daddy danced to Epsom Derby glory by an easy three and a half lengths while mammy left her six rivals for dead in the 2004 Oaks. No pressure then, son.

The level of expectation about his Classic campaign had been raised a few notches by his last performance as a two-year-old. Having been more workmanlike than wonderful when narrowly winning a Curragh maiden on his second start in July, Australia turned up for a Group 3 at Leopardstown the following month

to be part of the harmony group. Little did we know he would grab the microphone off Free Eagle and belt out a massive power ballad. It was note-perfect.

Reported to have done very well physically over the winter, Australia held firm in the market for the Qipco 2,000 Guineas despite Kingman doing a pretty good impression of Frankel in the Greenham. Toormore was in there too, rated 122 following his faultless juvenile campaign.

Fears that Australia might lack acceleration over a mile came to pass, but only just. Both Night Of Thunder (albeit drifting left close home) and Kingman came from the far-side group, leaving Joseph O'Brien to ponder what might have been had he been drawn in stall two rather than stall ten. "He ran a smashing race in the circumstances," he said, while looking forward to improvement over a longer trip.

Not just any longer trip: the mile and a half at Epsom would be his ultimate testing ground. Guineas glory would have been a bonus, just as it was for Camelot in 2012, but Australia was conceived with the Investec Derby in mind. His date with destiny arrived on the first Saturday in June.

It did not look a vintage Derby and Australia was 11-8 favourite. Next in the betting was the previous year's Racing Post Trophy winner Kingston Hill, who had finished eighth in the Guineas. The only other horse below 10-1 was True Story, whose best performance had been a seven-length victory in the Feilden at Newmarket's Craven meeting.

The race itself, as Joseph O'Brien described, was straightforward for Australia. "It went pretty much as planned. He travelled so well during the race and just idled a bit when he hit the front. They went a nice even pace and I was cantering the whole way. I got there too soon and he had a good look but I had to stay going."

Australia handled Tattenham Corner and the camber at Epsom just as well as his parents had. He glided to the front over a furlong out and kept Kingston Hill at bay from that point on. Maybe Aidan O'Brien was right; maybe this was something special. Afterwards the trainer reiterated his belief in the colt who had just become his fifth Derby winner, and the third in a row.

"We said what we thought about Australia when often the best thing is not to say it," he said. "He's a very special horse. The way he goes from

▸▸ Three in a row: (clockwise from left) Australia wins the Derby, Irish Derby and International Stakes

A to B so easily makes him unique. Horses who do that don't normally get a mile and a half. To get a mile and a half like that at Epsom, every sinew in his body was going to be tested. He had to settle, quicken, handle the hurly-burly and everything, but what makes him different is his natural pace."

The rest of us still needed more evidence that Australia was different, even unique. But it would not come at the Curragh in the Dubai Duty Free Irish Derby, which was ruined as a contest by lack of rain. With no Kingston Hill to test him again, Australia was sent off at 1-8 and cruised past his less esteemed stablemate Kingfisher. He won by two and a half lengths, which would have been closer to 12 and a half if Joseph had let the handbrake off. He did what he came to do but we learned nothing.

Ultimately, of course, Ballydoyle's best horses are playing to a small, select audience: the breeders

▸▸ *Continues page 50*

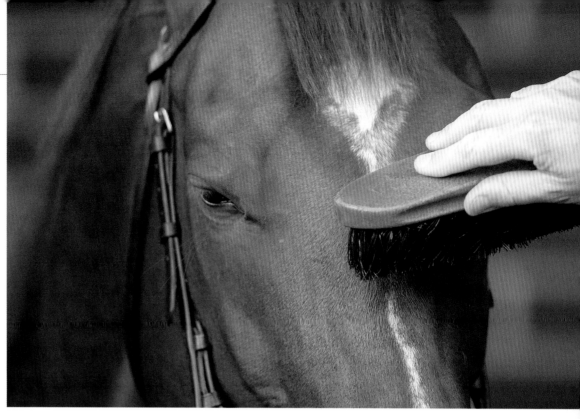

Coolmore hopes to attract once the racing stops and the more lucrative stallion career begins. Winning the Derby is as important as ever, but nowadays so is the versatility and speed that can be demonstrated in the top mile-and-a-quarter races.

Joseph O'Brien's comment after the Irish Derby – "I'd love to ride him over a mile and a quarter on fast ground, I think that would really be his thing" – implied we might never see Australia over a mile and a half again. That being the case, the natural next step was the Juddmonte International at York, which would be the perfect place to take on his elders for the first time.

THAT race did not come until late August, however, and Aidan O'Brien thought it was prudent to issue a warning about the Australia we could expect to see. "He's a good bit heavier than he was in the Derbys and I suppose that just makes you a little bit more anxious. We would imagine he would come on a lot from the run."

There was no need to worry. "A good horse becomes a great horse at York," proclaimed Channel 4 commentator Simon Holt as Australia powered to his third Group 1 victory. There was more substance to this success. A three-year-old may have chased him home but a four-year-old who had won the Hardwicke at Royal Ascot by seven lengths was third and a five-year-old who was stunning at Sandown when winning the Eclipse was back in fourth. The Grey Gatsby, Telescope and Mukhadram were good horses who were made to look ordinary. "I don't think he has a lot to prove to anybody now," said Aidan O'Brien.

A mile and a quarter was now believed to be Australia's optimum trip and Irish Champions Weekend needed a champion. They appeared made for each other, just as there is no point having the Champions League without Barcelona and the Ryder Cup would not be the same without Rory McIlroy. Here was a chance, too, for Australia to achieve something where his parents had failed: both Galileo and Ouija Board had been narrowly beaten into second in the Irish Champion.

Australia had devoured The Grey Gatsby and Mukhadram at York, despite not being 100 per cent fit, but both reopposed him. The sub-fertile Al Kazeem returned 12

months after being beaten in the race by The Fugue, while the previous year's Irish Derby hero Trading Leather added further substance to the contest. But this was Australia, the chosen one. Anything other than victory was out of the question. Paddy Power even paid out early.

Unlike at Epsom, the Curragh and York, Leopardstown did not go according to the pre-race script. Indeed, almost every single line was changed. "We were in a nice position but the pace steadied. He was on the outside of Al Kazeem and couldn't get in. He was trapped out there, so he had to go early," said a shocked Aidan O'Brien.

His son had tried to pinch the race on the home turn. Kicking three lengths clear should have been a sufficient lead but it wasn't. The man who regularly performs the role of supersub for Ballydoyle, the man who has given them so many Group 1 wins, had come back to haunt them. Ryan Moore, on board The Grey Gatsby, waited until Joseph O'Brien had taken in all the chips from the middle of the table before finally consenting to show his hand.

"I was confident that I'd pass five of them," Moore said. "I just wasn't quite so confident about the sixth." The sixth horse was Australia – the 30-100 favourite – but The Grey Gatsby got to him and edged a neck clear at the line.

Asked to describe Australia in three words earlier in the year, Joseph O'Brien replied with "a jockey's dream". Unfortunately for him, the

THIRD TIME UNLUCKY

Australia's defeat in the Irish Champion completed an unwanted hat-trick for his family, as he followed his parents Galileo and Ouija Board by losing in unsatisfactory circumstances

Galileo was unbeaten in six races – including the Derby, Irish Derby and King George – when he turned up for the 2001 edition. He was sent off at 4-11 but lost by a head in a desperate battle with Fantastic Light, amid accusations of team riding by Godolphin. While Fantastic Light had a dream run on the inner when his pacemaker Give The Slip moved out rounding the home turn, Galileo lost crucial ground by being forced to run wider.

In 2006 there was another thrilling battle, but no such controversy, when Ouija Board went down by a neck to Dylan Thomas. Ouija Board took the lead a furlong and a half out and there was a feeling that was too early, as it gave an inspired Kieren Fallon time to stoke up Dylan Thomas for a stirring fightback.

Australia's neck defeat by The Grey Gatsby meant his parents and their most illustrious son had lost their three attempts at the Irish Champion by a cumulative distance of less than a length.

Finishing touch: Australia is groomed by Aidan O'Brien before winning the International at York

dream became a nightmare at Leopardstown. "The Irish Champion didn't work out for him," he said. "If he'd had the same trip as The Grey Gatsby he would have easily won three or four lengths, and if I had the race back I would have ridden him differently. No doubt he was the moral winner but that isn't good enough in the end, is it?"

There was to be no chance of revenge or redemption. A month later came the announcement of Australia's retirement, after he developed a problem in his right hind hoof, and Aidan O'Brien paid one last tribute. "Because of what he showed us at home, every race he ran in was always eagerly anticipated," he said. "Every time he worked or raced we knew great things were possible. We always regarded him as an exceptional racehorse."

Bred to be exceptional, Australia fulfilled his destiny at Epsom, added a second Classic at the Curragh and then reached his highest level against his elders at York. Everything was heading in the right direction until that unfortunate and slightly bitter defeat on his final outing. Australia retired with a Racing Post Rating of 129, short of the 132 achieved by his father. In the end, he was not even the best horse in his own family.

THE
BIGGER
PICTURE

Snow Fairy (left) and Ouija Board, both Oaks winners for Ed Dunlop in their racing days, enjoy some winter sun in their paddock at Stanley House Stud, Newmarket, in January. There was more Classic success for Ouija Board this year when her son Australia, by Galileo, landed the Derby and Irish Derby

**EDWARD WHITAKER
(RACINGPOST.COM/PHOTOS)**

WAITING GAME

Roger Varian had a frustrating summer with Kingston Hill before Classic success finally arrived in the St Leger

By Julian Muscat

PATIENCE is a virtue that would have been instilled in Roger Varian from a young age by his mentor, the late Michael Jarvis, and how he needed it this year. In Kingston Hill he had a colt with the quality and robustness to compete in all three British Classics for which he was eligible – a rare occurrence nowadays – and yet whose opportunities were restricted by the weather on more than one occasion.

Varian did not panic, did not rush, and above all did not take chances with his precious commodity. Eventually, after much frustration, the perfect moment arrived and he was rewarded with Kingston Hill's barnstorming victory in the Ladbrokes St Leger. It was a first British Classic for the 35-year-old trainer, as he neared the end of his fourth season since taking the reins at Kremlin House Stables, Newmarket, where he spent ten years as Jarvis's assistant.

At the season's dawn the St Leger seemed the most unlikely Classic-winning opportunity for a son of the miler Mastercraftsman, yet Varian always maintained the mile and six and a half furlongs of the Doncaster Classic was the least of his concerns. He was more preoccupied with the dry summer. Forecast rain did not materialise for the 2,000 Guineas and Derby, compromising Kingston Hill's chance, and opportunities to contest the Irish Derby and Great Voltigeur Stakes were both spurned due to fast conditions. There had even been a doubt about Kingston Hill's participation in the St Leger,

"Throughout the season I must have put everybody to sleep by talking so much about the ground," Varian says. "I don't think the decision to run a horse is any harder whether they are good horses or slow ones. With a good one you just feel you are being watched a lot more closely."

St Leger day dawned with the going just on the quick side of good at Doncaster. Having deemed the surface suitable, if not exactly favourable, Varian set about resolving another conundrum. Kingston Hill was drawn low and, in pre-race discussions with jockey Andrea Atzeni, he emphasised one detail. "The most important thing was to make sure we didn't get stuck on the rail, or in a box behind a wall of horses," Varian says. "The last thing I said to Andrea was: 'Do your utmost to get off that rail'."

Atzeni heeded those instructions but in consequence Kingston Hill was stationed towards the rear of the 12-runner field early on. "It was probably further back than we'd have liked but I was glad he was where he was, rather than closer up but where we didn't want to be," Varian says. "He's the type of horse who doesn't pick up instantly when you ask him. To have to suddenly take a gap on the inside when one became

says. "To win them both proved to us and anyone else watching that we could deliver in the highest class."

A sense of justice also accompanied Kingston Hill's triumph. "It would have been disappointing on several fronts if we'd gone all year without winning a Group 1 race – especially with a horse like him in the yard. So it was a great day and a great moment. I probably hadn't allowed myself to think what it would be like to win my first Classic. You only set yourself up for disappointment, but when it happened it was very special – with a bit of relief thrown in as well."

Extra pleasure came from the friendship between Varian and Paul Smith, who purchased Kingston Hill for 70,000gns as a yearling. Mastercraftsman is close to Smith's heart: the horse carried his father Derrick's colours to win the Irish 2,000 Guineas among four Group 1 triumphs for the Coolmore syndicate.

Varian and Smith now had some thinking to do. Kingston Hill's abbreviated campaign meant they had a relatively fresh horse. Should they pitch him back into the furnace of the Qatar Prix de l'Arc de Triomphe 22 days later? The portents were mixed. Alleged posted his first Arc victory in 1977 after his St Leger defeat by Dunfermline. But the fact remained that no St Leger winner had ever taken the Arc in the same season, a detail doubtless influenced by the close proximity of the two races.

One thing played in Kingston Hill's favour: connections knew he took his races well. "As a two-year-old we didn't expect him to win a Group 1 race [the Racing Post Trophy] only five weeks after he'd won his maiden at Newbury," Varian says. "But that's part of his attitude and constitution, which I think is incredible. It's hard for older horses to do that, never mind two-year-olds."

With Kingston Hill having rebounded robustly from Doncaster, the Arc was given the green light. Again, however, circumstances conspired against Kingston Hill when he was given a shocking draw – stall 20 among 20 runners. And with the Indian summer showing little inclination to relent, Atzeni had plenty to ponder on the way to post. "We couldn't control the state of the ground or the draw," Varian reflects. "We just had to make the best of it."

The best of it they made, too,

available would not have played to his strengths. He takes a bit of organising to find his stride. We wanted him to come with one clear run on the outside."

That run was a while in coming. Atzeni prompted Kingston Hill soon after turning into the long home straight but the response was minimal. Then, just as Varian had anticipated, the horse got rolling and was suddenly challenging for the

lead approaching the final furlong. Romsdal dug in to match the grey's initial surge but he foundered when Kingston Hill conjured extra momentum in the last 100 yards.

All manner of emotions ran through Varian's mind in the aftermath. As well as his first British Classic, Kingston Hill had also given him a personal-best in terms of prize-money won. But there was so much more. In the St Leger build-

up, despite healthy seasonal returns, the trainer had lamented his failure to win a Group 1 race in 2014. Of course, having won the first, he would wait just 24 hours for a second, courtesy of Cursory Glance's triumph in the Moyglare Stud Stakes at the Curragh.

"What pleased me most about that weekend is that we went into both races with fancied horses, and that brings a bit of extra pressure," Varian

▶▶ Continues page 56

with Kingston Hill advancing to track pacemaking Montviron after a couple of furlongs. Turning for home, Atzeni, like so many other jockeys, must have felt victory was not an unrealistic proposition – until Treve rediscovered herself to burst clear of a chasing pack headed by Flintshire.

Nevertheless, Kingston Hill rallied manfully in the closing stages. He ran hard all the way to the line, which he reached in fourth place, three-quarters of a length behind Oaks and King George heroine Taghrooda. "I thought he ran a mighty race in the circumstances," Varian says. "We were all very proud of him."

Kingston Hill signed off after the Arc, five months after opening an exclusively Group 1 campaign in the Qipco 2,000 Guineas over a mile on fast ground, when he finished eighth. "We were disappointed at the time," Varian admits, "but on reflection the race was obviously a very hot one. And the way his season panned out, he was never going to be a miler. After that we went to Epsom for the Derby. We had a canter round the course nine days before at the Breakfast with the Stars gathering, when the ground was heavy. But by Derby day it had dried right out."

Nevertheless, Kingston Hill ran a huge race from his prominent early position. He led at the two-furlong pole before Australia caught up with him. Even then, in a demonstration of the fighting qualities that would later carry him to Classic success, he rallied to make a race of it with what many felt was a superior Derby winner.

"We had very mixed feelings that day," Varian says. "In two or three years' time you don't get remembered for finishing second in the Derby. But it was one hell of an experience to be involved and run so well."

Kingston Hill's other run of a five-race campaign saw him finish fourth in a highly tactical renewal of the Coral-Eclipse Stakes. Varian feels his colt ran another good race in circumstances where a small group of horses including the winner, Mukhadram, poached a clear lead they would maintain to the finish.

In his debrief from the saddle, Frankie Dettori, who replaced the unavailable Atzeni, was adamant the mile-and-a-quarter trip was insufficient. Subsequent events would endorse Dettori's view, so

▶▶ Worth waiting for: Kingston Hill and Andrea Atzeni after achieving Classic success at the third attempt in the St Leger at Doncaster

much so that a colt who started the season with stamina doubts over a mile and a half is now seen as one for whom that trip is imperative.

While fellow Classic winners Australia and Taghrooda have been retired, he will race on. "He has shown himself good enough for us to look at the fancy middle-distance prizes next season," Varian says. "We know he stays further but he has enough class to be one of the best over a mile and a half, so we'll be looking at races like the Coronation Cup early on. And I'd dearly love to get him back to Longchamp at the back end."

Next season might also be kinder in delivering Kingston Hill's optimum racing ground, especially in the autumn. "You have to be careful complaining about the ground when he won the St Leger on a decent surface," Varian says. "He handles good ground perfectly well but we never encountered ground with some cut in it, like he had as a two-year-old [when he won all three of his starts]. So we close the season with an exciting feeling. He had a fabulous year but we know what's left in the locker."

A Classic campaign, followed by the Arc, was also an instructive experience for Varian. "As a young outfit, we have learned certain things about having a big horse in the yard," he says. All of which suggests 2015 cannot come soon enough.

OWEN SCORES

Irish St Leger triumph for former England striker

In a year with a host of Classic firsts, one of the more notable was Michael Owen's breakthrough with his homebred Brown Panther in the Palmerstown House Estate Irish St Leger.

The former England footballer brings a wider audience to the sport, as well as significant investment at Manor House Stables in Cheshire, and his Classic victory at the Curragh was greeted with rare fervour.

Brown Panther has been Owen's flagbearer, with a Royal Ascot success already to his credit, but this was a first Group 1 victory for both horse and owner. "That was very special," said Owen, close to tears. "He's the apple of my eye, as everyone knows, and he was pretty spectacular out there today. He's a superstar."

The six-year-old, who won by six and a half lengths, was also a first Classic winner for trainer Tom Dascombe, who is based at Manor House, and jockey Richard Kingscote.

Classics are rarely won so emphatically and Kingscote was widely praised for his enterprise in kicking on early in the straight and leaving Leading Light, the odds-on favourite, with too much ground to make up. "Our horse benefited from a very good ride. The others never looked like catching him," Dascombe said.

Just like Owen in his footballing prime, Brown Panther left them all trailing.

EL FAMILY
A *VISUAL* CLIMAX

Your eyes, which are well-trained in spotting rare bird species, have already enabled you to enjoy many wonderful sights. But if you increase your visual acuity using SWAROVISION technology, you'll get the most out of every birding experience. The EL family takes long-range optics to a new level. The field flattener lenses in every pair of these binoculars ensure perfect edge-to-edge sharpness, and the HD optics impress with brilliant, lifelike colours. And thanks to their unique wrap-around grip, the EL binoculars fit perfectly in your hands – no matter what size binoculars you choose. Enjoy moments even more – with SWAROVSKI OPTIK.

SEE THE UNSEEN
WWW.SWAROVSKIOPTIK.COM

SWAROVSKI
OPTIK

GREY AREA

The Grey Gatsby was a dual Group 1 winner and conqueror of Australia but judging his merit was not always as simple as black and white

By Nick Pulford

THE GREY GATSBY can be seen as the Sire De Grugy of the Flat racing world. He does not hail from a yard seen as the natural home of a championship contender and success did not come easily to him from day one, rather it has been earned on a steady but sure climb towards the top.

Even when success started to flow, people were apt to find other reasons beyond the horse's own ability – an astute piece of jockeyship, perhaps, or perceived underperformance by a main rival. It is the sort of thing that must begin to grate after a while, especially for a trainer who has always been able to see the ability in his horse and has invested time and skill to bring it out.

By the end of the season, which had brought victory in the French Derby and the Qipco Irish Champion Stakes, Kevin Ryan was tired of having to defend The Grey Gatsby's reputation. Surely the proof was in the results.

"I don't have to bleat on about what a good horse he is," Ryan says. "I've stopped talking about that, it's past tense now. The horse has done his own talking. Everyone can see what he's done, it's there in black and white."

The form book identifies a progressive three-year-old who ended the season close to the top of his division. On the six occasions in 2014 when he ran on ground that included his preferred 'good' in the official description, The Grey Gatsby's chronological performances on Racing Post Ratings were 109, 110, 112, 119, 125 and 126.

That last mark put him just 3lb behind divisional leader Australia, with Kingman the only other three-year-old rated above him. Unlike that pair, The Grey Gatsby will be back in 2015 and his profile gives every encouragement he will be better still as a four-year-old.

Ryan has no doubt. "Yeah, he's going to be. He has improved throughout this year, whenever he has run, and he's going to get stronger again over the winter. He's going to mature."

The Grey Gatsby's best performances have been over a mile and a quarter but Ryan expects that with maturity will come more options. "Next year will sort itself out once he's back in training but I'd say he'll start off at a mile and a quarter and there's every chance he'll step up to a mile and a half as the season goes on."

This year The Grey Gatsby became a mile-and-a-quarter specialist and it was the trip that persuaded Ryan to take him to Chantilly for the Prix du Jockey Club rather than go to Epsom for the Derby. He had won the Dante at York but, in a theme that would become familiar, Ryan felt he had "not got the credit he deserved" for winning that Derby trial. Possibly that had something to do with The Grey Gatsby hanging across the track in the closing stages and having to survive a stewards' inquiry.

Ryan Moore, who rode The Grey Gatsby for the first time in the Dante, was much more positive and told Ryan the French Derby was the right target. "Ryan has a great feel for a horse and after he rode him in the Dante he held the horse in high regard," the trainer says.

Moore played a big part in the victory at Chantilly, masterfully weaving through the 16-runner field before unleashing The Grey Gatsby for a three-length win. Prince Gibraltar, the 2-1 favourite, had no luck in running but finished well in third, catching the eye of those who wanted another reason to crab The Grey Gatsby's form.

That could not diminish the trainer's enjoyment of a first Classic win. Reflecting at the end of the season, he says: "It meant a lot. We try to compete on the big days and it's fantastic to have a horse like him to win us a Classic."

Defeat followed in the Grand Prix de Paris but was easily excused by the very soft ground. Conditions were much more favourable back at York for the Juddmonte International but this clash of the Derby winners was seen as a one-sided affair, with Australia 8-13 and The Grey Gatsby 12-1, behind older rivals Telescope and Mukhadram in the betting. Although The Grey Gatsby outran his odds to finish second, Australia's two-length winning margin seemed decisive.

Richard Hughes, who had taken over on The Grey Gatsby with Moore on Telescope, thought differently. He believed a significant factor was that Australia got first run and Ryan took on board that view, as well as his own sense that The Grey Gatsby was still improving, in deciding to supplement for the Irish Champion Stakes at a cost of €75,000.

Some questioned Ryan's boldness in reopposing Australia, but he had Moore back on board at Leopardstown and Moore had a plan. The jockey envisaged a scenario where they would go fast up front and decided he would wait at the back of the seven-runner field. "Turning in I was thinking 'Oh God, he's got a lot of ground to make up'," Ryan admitted afterwards, "but in fairness to Ryan he was saving ground while Australia had to go wide."

While Australia used up precious gas, Moore had conserved The Grey Gatsby's fuel for one last thrust and he got home by a neck. "I was confident I'd pass five of them," Moore said. "I just wasn't quite so confident about the sixth."

Amid the praise for Moore's masterclass and question marks over Joseph O'Brien's riding of Australia, The Grey Gatsby was somehow lost again. In the winner's enclosure, Ryan said: "I've felt all along he's never had the credit he deserves and if he doesn't now it will be unbelievable. He's a great racehorse and I'm very proud of him."

Ryan always felt the €120,000 breeze-up purchase could turn into something valuable. "The first time he worked you could tell he was very good, the question was how far he was going to go," he says. "We knew he was smart but he was also weak and backward." While he was developing physically, The Grey Gatsby lost five of his first six starts and that may have coloured judgement of his ability.

Next year the battle to prove the doubters wrong will start all over again.

QIPCO 2000 Guineas	QIPCO 2000 Guineas	QIPCO 2000 Guineas	QIPCO 2000 Guineas	QIPCO 2000 Guineas	QIPCO 2000 Guineas	QIPCO 2000 Guineas
14	13	12	11	10	9	8
WAR COMMAND	TOORMORE	THE GREY GATSBY	SHIFTING POWER	OUTSTRIP	NOOZHOH CANARIAS	NIGHT OF THUNDER
JOCKEY: RYAN MOORE	JOCKEY: RICHARD HUGHES	JOCKEY: JAMIE SPENCER	JOCKEY: FRANKIE DETTORI	JOCKEY: MICKAEL BARZALONA	JOCKEY: C. SOUMILLON	JOCKEY: KIEREN FALLON
	TRAINER: RICHARD HANNON	TRAINER: KEVIN RYAN	TRAINER: RICHARD HANNON	TRAINER: CHARLIE APP	TRAINER: ENRIQUE LEON PENATE	TRAINER: RICHARD HANNON
	MIDD...PARK RACING	MR F. GILLESPIE	MS ELAINE CHIVERS & POTENSIS LTD		GRUPO BOLANOS GRAN CANARIAS S.L.	MR SAEED MANANA

1 Fashion with a difference on Irish 1,000 Guineas day at the Curragh

2 Miss France (Maxime Guyon) wins the 1,000 Guineas at Newmarket to complete the full set of British Classics for trainer Andre Fabre

3 Racegoers arrive for Oaks day at Epsom

4 Paul Hanagan celebrates his first Classic success aboard Taghrooda in the Oaks

5 Australia's saddlecloth for the Irish Derby, which he won at odds of 1-8 to follow up his Derby triumph at Epsom three weeks earlier

6 Andrea Atzeni after riding Kingston Hill to victory in the St Leger at Doncaster – a first British Classic for the jockey and trainer Roger Varian

7 Night Of Thunder (Kieren Fallon) after winning the 2,000 Guineas to give trainer Richard Hannon a Classic success at his first attempt

8 Australia and Joseph O'Brien after winning the Derby

9 Racegoers view the 1,000 Guineas roll of honour at Newmarket

10 Jockeys line up before the 2,000 Guineas. It was a strong field: Night Of Thunder won that day and further Classic victories followed for Kingman (Irish 2,000 Guineas), Australia (Derby and Irish Derby), Kingston Hill (St Leger) and The Grey Gatsby (Prix du Jockey Club)

SUPER POWERS

Eddie Lynam took control of the British midsummer sprints with Sole Power and Slade Power, both dual Group 1 winners

By Jonathan Mullin

CALL it lazy, call it what you want, but when you're known as 'Eddie', there is a chance people will add the prefix 'Fast'. And when you train the winners of four Group 1 sprints in one season and dominate the sphere in a manner rarely seen at that level, the odds on picking up a lackadaisical nickname contract. That's what happened with Fast Eddie Lynam.

On one particular day in June, his nickname could have described the beating of his heart. Lynam stood half a furlong from the winning post on the first day of Ascot's royal meeting, in among the photographers, waiting for the runners in the King's Stand Stakes to rush past. He admits he is wracked by nerves when he watches his big race runners, but at least that patch of ground was familiar to Lynam; he had stood there before and felt it lucky for him. And what he saw dissipated all worry and took his fast-beating heart back towards normal. He was convinced victory was in the bag for Sole Power.

"I saw Richard [Hughes] take a pull at the furlong pole, so I turned and walked towards the winning post," Lynam said. "I knew he had won. And he was still nearly last. That's how sure I was."

Sole Power's success, by a length and a quarter, was more decisive, less nerve-jangling, than his neck victory in the same race 12 months earlier. And this time, rather than being the high point of Lynam's season, it was merely the beginning.

Trainers spend their careers evolving with the horses staring out at them every morning, working with the material they have and doing their best to turn out winners. As the old Irish expression goes, you can only dance with the ladies in the hall.

Lynam's evolution has seen him first pigeonholed as a trainer of two-year-olds, then as a trainer of fillies. Not so long ago his exploits on Friday nights at Dundalk saw him nicknamed 'king of the sand' before the racing world settled on 'Fast Eddie'.

"I'm training failed milers to run in sprints," is a typically self-deprecating verbal hand-off from Lynam, and if that's all he was doing he did it pretty well in 2014, but of course there was more to it than that.

When Lynam eyed up his sprint team for 2014 he would have known there were no failed milers in this bunch. First on the team sheet last spring was the stable mainstay, Sole Power. A sprinter who is best when fired like a slingshot, he was the established Group 1 performer and at the age of seven he showed no sign

▸ Continues page 64

of slowing down. He had carried the flag for Lynam ever since his 100-1 Nunthorpe upset win as a three-year-old, but this time he would have back-up.

In the same red and white colours of Sabena Power, matriarch of a Power family so synonymous with bookmaking, Slade Power was also togged and ready for the season. Two years younger than his illustrious stablemate, he had finished second to Gordon Lord Byron in the Group 1 Sprint Cup at Haydock the previous autumn and then won the British Champions Sprint. Although well beaten in Hong Kong on his final start of 2013, while Sole Power went agonisingly close to victory, he was clearly ready for a full-on Group 1 campaign.

Yet, whereas you could ride Sole Power down to the shops and leave him standing at the door while you grabbed some groceries, Slade Power is a different animal altogether. A horse psychologist would probably conclude that his enigmatic ways were the product of a confusing upbringing: Slade Power's mother, Girl Power, rejected her foal, while his first foster mare wasn't that keen on him either.

"Yer man's a bit of a clown," said Lynam this summer. "And the trip to Hong Kong made him. Even though he didn't run particularly well on the day it made a man of him and I found the international trips away with both horses made them."

When discussing Slade Power in 2013, Lynam was always happy to put on record his belief that another winter would turn his caterpillar into a sprinting butterfly. The beauty of it all for the trainer was that they were easy to keep apart: Sole Power, all speed, was best at the minimum trip, while Slade Power could go for the six-furlong prizes. And so they turned up for Royal Ascot at opposite ends of the meeting: Sole Power in the King's Stand on the Tuesday and Slade Power in the Diamond Jubilee on the Saturday. Lynam badly wanted to win with both of them, for different reasons.

RUMOURS around Sole Power's King's Stand victory of 2013 had dragged their bad smell into 2014, in a tale so bizarre that it almost defies retelling. A video, distributed online, originating in South Africa and accompanied by damaging rumours, purported to tell a fancy story, the rumours accusing Johnny Murtagh of using a 'buzzer' to prompt that explosive final burst from Sole Power – but that was not the only layer heaped on the pile. Murtagh was then supposed to have passed the buzzer to Lynam's daughter Sarah in the winner's enclosure after the race.

Slow down anything on video and you will find it difficult not to look at it through a sinister prism and these slow-motion replays were presented in such a way as to suggest wrongdoing. A BHA inquiry found no basis in the claims and, as Lynam and Murtagh knew all along, this was nothing but a cruel ruse.

It irked Lynam greatly and it bubbled just below the surface right through the spring and early summer. If there was one blessing it was that the whole episode was behind them by the time Sole Power lined up for the King's Stand but, of course, there was no escaping the fact that another victory would be a slap in the face of the rumour-mongers.

Sole Power, brought to a perfect pitch by Lynam, was on song. Held up at the back by Hughes, bang in the centre of a 16-strong field, occasionally his white face could be seen bobbing up and down, as if the horse himself wondered just when he would be permitted to run.

Hughes crept up on the field like a sheepdog at the trials, dabbled with going left, a slight shift like a winger faking left to go right, but by the time it came to press the button on Sole Power he darted right towards the rail. If a swoop could be trademarked, this would be the one. Brilliant and bold, he quickly put distance between him and the rest and by the line Hughes was back low in the saddle, perfectly poised for the winning photos.

The bizarre background was not easily forgotten. "He won the King's Stand last year and at the time it was my greatest success but rumours about the buzzer were floating around when I was out in Dubai last January and it turned out that Johnny Murtagh had already heard about it," Lynam said.

"What I found horrible was that

▶▶ Life in the fast lane: (clockwise from top) Sole Power sets the tone for the season with victory in the Palace House Stakes at Newmarket in May; Slade Power and Wayne Lordan win the Diamond Jubilee at Royal Ascot; jubilant connections celebrate Slade Power's July Cup; Sole Power with Richard Hughes and Eddie Lynam after winning the King's Stand at Royal Ascot; (previous page) Lynam with Sole Power (left) and Slade Power at his County Meath stables

our integrity and Johnny's integrity had been brought into question. The BHA was right to have a proper investigation, but whoever posted that or was behind it, they were faceless. I felt very bad about being called a cheat and it was a constant stone in my shoe.

"It has never left my mind. You can call me a moderate trainer and I'll shrug my shoulders and say fine. But if you call me a dishonest trainer, I will be very upset. And as for Johnny Murtagh: what a career he has had and then the rumour mill started 'this is one of the reasons he quit' and all this rubbish. It left a bit of a sour taste."

But there was nothing sour about Lynam's Royal Ascot experience, for Sole Power's victory was followed by a Queen Mary win for Anthem Alexander [beating Tiggy Wiggy] and then the red and white of Sabena Power was back to the fore

▶▶ Continues page 66

'He's brilliant, he's made for me. When I was 14 or 15 I dreamed of riding horses like this and winning like that'

in Saturday's Diamond Jubilee, a race that Lynam faced with supreme confidence.

"I think if you go to Royal Ascot with four horses and one of them wins, it's a success. If you go with four and two of them win, it's brilliant . . . but if Slade Power had lost on Saturday I'd have been sick," he laughed afterwards.

But there was scarcely a worry as Slade Power and Wayne Lordan first chased a strong pace set by Astaire and Gordon Lord Byron, and then just simply took over, bullying a Group 1 field into submission despite idling in the closing stages.

"Slade would pull up in front, that's the downside with him," said Lynam, with affection. "It's the one kink in his armour. He's not ungenuine, but he just wonders when he gets to the front 'what's next?'"

Where there had been an element of personal vindication with Sole Power's win, the need for victory with Slade Power was driven by commercial and professional considerations. Unlike his older comrade in arms, he was bred as well as owned by the Powers and moving him into the Group 1 bracket had a dramatic effect on his value in the breeding shed.

"You have to think about the next one, and we needed him," said Lynam, in reference to the Diamond Jubilee win. "We bred him and that win makes him a proper stallion, gives him huge potential. And he's only our second individual Group 1 winner even though we had won three before. Sole Power carried me."

BY JULY some rain had fallen on Newmarket's July course and few sprinters around are as effective as Slade Power over six furlongs on ground with cut. Punters thought so anyway and backed him into 7-4 favourite for the Group 1 Darley July Cup. Again, in contrast to his stablemate who likes to turn every canvas into a beauty, Slade Power kept it simple, everything went like clockwork and he was a length and a half too good for the rest.

Just a few days before, the financial significance of that Royal Ascot Group 1 success had been made clear with the news that Slade Power had been bought by Sheikh Mohammed's Darley operation to stand at Kildangan Stud. The July Cup made him a dual Group 1 winner and that was the last we would see of him in Europe. From next year, he gets to live the playboy's life for real.

The focus now turned back to Sole Power, with Britain's next Group 1 sprint – the Coolmore Nunthorpe Stakes – being held over his ideal distance of five furlongs. Perhaps smarting at having to share the attention at Lynam's County Meath yard, he had plenty of drama up his sleeve.

The dash down York's straight was simply sensational and this was a reminder that, while Lynam tore his hair out in the spring thinking about nailing down a regular jockey for Sole Power to replace the retired Murtagh, the answer could not have been more obvious. Those final, nail-biting seconds of the Nunthorpe taught us that.

Fully ten horses were within a length or so of each other at the furlong pole, all theoretically in with a chance of landing the Group 1 prize, but the eye was drawn to one horse and one man. You were compelled to hold your breath for just a second or two as Hughes, with a double handful on Sole Power and the patience to match, waited for a brick to fall from the wall of horses in front of him and nipped through the gap to win by the most audacious half-length.

"He's brilliant, he's made for me. When I was 14 or 15 I dreamed of riding horses like this and winning like that," Hughes smiled afterwards.

"The one thing you'd have to admire about a horse like that is that he doesn't hide, he doesn't shirk. We're not making excuses for him ever, you can set your clock to him, he turns up," Lynam said.

With Sole Power beginning the drift towards veteran status – though

▶ Sole Power and Richard Hughes after their spine-tingling victory in the Nunthorpe Stakes at York

that is often far from a hindrance for a sprinter – and Slade Power starting life as a stallion, things will be different now. The Power family – with an album book of memories – may be reduced to an ageing three-time Group 1 sensation, but Fast Eddie could be ready to play for high stakes with a new generation.

He has Agnes Stewart, the Park Hill winner, and in his sprint team there is the small matter of Anthem Alexander, the Queen Mary winner. The racing world begins to shrink when you think that Anthem Alexander's sire, Starspangledbanner, was the superstar sprinter stunned by Sole Power's 100-1 Nunthorpe success in 2010, a critical juncture in his trainer's career.

In Lynam's ever evolving world of big-race victories, the big wheel keeps on turning. But the summer of 2014, with its four Group 1 victories, will be hard to match.

LANE'S END

12X LEADING STUD FARM

THE LEADER IN 2014

7 GRADE 1 WINNERS
32 GRADED STAKES WINNERS
71 BLACK-TYPE WINNERS
$49,000,000 IN EARNINGS

More than any farm in North America

CANDY RIDE (ARG)	LEMON DROP KID	SMART STRIKE
CITY ZIP	MINESHAFT	STEPHEN GOT EVEN
CURLIN	MORNING LINE	THE FACTOR
DISCREETLY MINE	QUALITY ROAD	TWIRLING CANDY
LANGFUHR		UNION RAGS

Versailles, KY 40383 | p (859) 873.7300 | f (859) 873.3746 | lanesend.com

*TDN Stats as of 10/8/14

FAST TRACK TO SUCCESS

Rising star David O'Meara made his Group 1 breakthrough with G Force and quickly followed up with Move In Time

By Nick Pulford

DAVID O'MEARA'S horses, along with their trainer, were going places fast in 2014. Like Eddie Lynam with the Power pair, the North Yorkshire trainer had two Group 1-winning sprinters in his yard as he landed the Betfred Sprint Cup with G Force and the QNB Prix de l'Abbaye with Move In Time.

Those victories came little more than four years after O'Meara's entry to the training ranks and confirmed him as a fast-rising star. After 25 winners in his debut season, which began only in June 2010, the former jump jockey almost doubled his tally of winners in his second season, in the third he went up another 50 per cent and in 2013 he virtually doubled again to a phenomenal 136 winners – behind only Richard Hannon snr, Mark Johnston and Richard Fahey in numerical terms.

Another century duly followed in 2014, but more notably so did the big-race winners. The 37-year-old trainer had a first Royal Ascot success with Louis The Pious in the Buckingham Palace Handicap and then made his Group 1 breakthrough with G Force and Move In Time. Just for good measure, in between the two Group 1 winners, Louis The Pious added the Ayr Gold Cup to his spoils.

All three horses bore the O'Meara hallmark of rapid improvement once they joined his yard, not least G Force. He was bought for 25,000gns out of the Hannon yard after just one maiden run as a two-year-old in 2013 and had a mark of 87 on his handicap debut for O'Meara in May but, having won then, he progressed quickly into Listed, Group 2 and finally Group 1 company in the Coolmore Nunthorpe Stakes at York, where he suffered bad luck in running and was sixth.

With a smooth run just over a fortnight later in the Haydock Sprint Cup, G Force delivered a first Group 1 for the Irishman by three-quarters of a length from Gordon Lord Byron, the previous year's winner. "I'm still shaking," an emotional O'Meara said in the winner's enclosure. "I'm delighted for everybody who has put so much time into helping build our yard. We've always said this horse was very good. He hasn't had the rub of the green a couple of times this year, but we had every faith he would be able to go and do this one day."

Less than a year earlier, only one man – Nick Bradley of Middleham Park Racing – had that sort of conviction about G Force. The ownership group's racing manager was in a near deserted sale ring at Tattersalls when he made the winning bid for the once-raced two-year-old. "There was one bid and I bought him," he recalled. "I said after I bought him it was a no-brainer. He ran such a good race on his debut for Richard Hannon and I don't know why they sold him."

O'Meara quickly discovered there was plenty of talent in the Qatar Racing cast-off. "In late March we took him for a bit of work with a horse rated in the mid-90s," Bradley said, "and David said 'he is about 30lb better than that one'. We thought 95 plus 30 is 125 – so we should be in business."

Making good on that promise with Group 1 victory at Haydock was a clear demonstration of O'Meara's own talent and Bradley said: "It was a great result for David. He's a trainer going places. Hopefully this will make people notice how good a trainer he is."

If they hadn't then, O'Meara gave them another hefty nudge just four weeks later with Move In Time's Abbaye victory. The six-year-old has been with O'Meara for two seasons and, although on the whole he seemed a consistent but lower-level Group sprinter, the trainer had set his sights high. "Hopefully he'll end up in the Abbaye at the end of the year," he told the Racing Post in April.

When Move In Time did indeed turn up at Longchamp he was a 31-1 shot on the pari-mutuel and 25-1 with British bookmakers but, just as Louis The Pious had proved with his 33-1 win at Royal Ascot, it was a mistake to underestimate O'Meara. Sole Power, having won the season's previous two five-furlong Group 1 contests, was 6-4 favourite but on this occasion he could not find a clear passage and was only eighth. Move In Time, meanwhile, was produced perfectly by Danny Tudhope to prevail in a tight finish, with a head the margin between each of the first four.

"I can't believe it," said Tudhope, whose star has risen in conjunction with O'Meara's. "I managed to get a gap and when it came I went for it. It's difficult to know where the line is here but it worked out well."

G Force had been Tudhope's Group 1 breakthrough too, confirming the 28-year-old jockey's remarkable climb back from the depths of just six winners in 2010. The following year he linked up with O'Meara and they quickly clicked. "Luckily I got off to a good start with David and things went on from there," Tudhope said in a Racing Post interview after G Force's win. "It was the break I needed. Every jockey needs a bit of luck – there are lots out there who would do well if they were attached to a big yard. It's very hard to make it work without that kind of backing."

Like O'Meara, Tudhope has made the most of every opportunity. After a memorable Group 1 double in 2014, their success together shows no sign of slowing down.

IN THE PICTURE

Viewpoint a historic winner as racing is held on Good Friday

One of British racing's long-standing taboos was broken in April when meetings were held on Good Friday for the first time.

History was made at Lingfield on April 18 with the running of the coral.co.uk All-Weather Championships Apprentice Handicap at 1.45pm, the first event of a £1m raceday that drew a capacity crowd of 8,777 at the Surrey track. The ground-breaking race was won by the Richard Hannon-trained Viewpoint (pictured right, orange and black), ridden by 17-year-old Cam Hardie.

Twenty-five minutes later, Musselburgh joined the party with the opening event on its eight-race card. The attendance there was more modest, with 2,875 racegoers going through the turnstiles.

David Thorpe, chairman of Arena Racing Company, which owns Lingfield, hailed the day as "highly successful for racing, a great historic moment" and the major bookmakers were also delighted. Ladbrokes spokesman David Williams said: "The bare numbers are terrific. We saw a great uplift, with another 50 per cent or so in turnover compared to standard Fridays."

Until 2008 the law prevented racecourses from even contemplating the staging of meetings with bookmakers present. Even thereafter racing's leaders ensured the turnstiles remained locked, not principally out of respect for religious sensibilities but due to the annual open days that are held in Lambourn and Middleham.

The fixtures at Lingfield and Musselburgh were sanctioned by the BHA despite strong opposition to Good Friday racing in several sectors of the sport, notably from jockeys and stable staff, although the move was widely accepted as inevitable in the end.

One source of grievance for the jockeys was the removal of a blank day after their annual awards ceremony, the Lesters, which was traditionally held the night before Good Friday. The Lesters have been moved to December 22, now that the only blank days in the British racing calendar are December 23, 24 and 25.

The open days, which raise a combined sum of around £70,000 for charity each year, remained in their Good Friday slots. Despite fears that attendances would be hit by having race meetings on the same day, Lambourn attracted a record crowd of between 11,000 and 12,000, while Middleham's attendance was estimated at 4,000 – around 40 per cent higher than the figure at Musselburgh's race meeting.

Bookmakers were quick to call for the addition of a third meeting on Good Friday, but the BHA said it would like to analyse data from more than just one year before committing to any expansion of the programme.

Picture: EDWARD WHITAKER (RACINGPOST.COM/PHOTOS)

LAST GASP

Lord Windermere snatched an unlikely victory in a breathtaking finish to the Cheltenham Gold Cup that lifted trainer Jim Culloty from despair to delight

By David Jennings

JIM CULLOTY described the stewards' inquiry after the Betfred Cheltenham Gold Cup as the worst few minutes of his life. The first two and a half miles of the race had not been not much better for the trainer's nerves. But this was the Gold Cup where expectations would turn upside down more than once and judgements made one moment would have to be revised the next. By the end, after a wild finish on the famous hill, Lord Windermere reached the line first, leaving a trail of what ifs and maybes behind him. Even then, it wasn't quite over.

The first judgement about Lord Windermere was Culloty's and, as we know now, it was worth heeding because he knew his horse best. The trainer had long been convinced he had a Gold Cup winner in his Churchtown stable in County Cork. Success in the 2013 RSA Chase made us realise he was not talking complete gibberish, but still there was the question of whether Lord

Windermere would have won if Boston Bob had not fallen at the last when in front.

"Some people are in the camp that Boston Bob would have won. I'm not," Culloty says. "Between the third-last and second-last Lord Windermere nearly fell over a road crossing. That cost him a couple of lengths and momentum. Even so, he challenged on the outside and winged the last two, not like a tired horse. I think he'd have won even if Boston Bob had stayed up."

Others concluded that Lord Windermere's victory had more than an element of fluke. Finishing 22 lengths behind Triolo D'Alene in the Hennessy at Newbury the following November, 11 lengths adrift of Bobs Worth in the Lexus at Leopardstown and 26 lengths behind Last Instalment in the Irish Hennessy were hardly ringing endorsements of Culloty's claim that he was a Gold Cup winner waiting to happen.

Yet Culloty filled Davy Russell, his big-race rider, with confidence all through Gold Cup week. "I thought he had a decent each-way chance myself but Jim was convinced he was coming to himself," Russell says. "Every morning I'd be on the gallops giving something a blowout and I'd meet Jim up the chute and he said to me every time: 'I can't wait for Friday, I just can't wait for Friday.' He knew he had him where he wanted to be."

Russell was not where he wanted to be in the early stages of the race, however, and Culloty's confidence in Lord Windermere began to look as misplaced as Fifa's decision to take the 2022 World Cup to Qatar. As early as the fourth fence, commentator Mark Johnson drew attention to the purple and yellow colours of Dr Ronan Lambe. "Lord Windermere is slightly detached at the rear of the field and was just nudged away from that fence by

Davy Russell," he said. Two fences later, he was back on Lord Windermere's case: "Again, just niggled away from that fence is Lord Windermere. He's surrendered four or five lengths on the main body of the field."

Betfair punters now made their judgement. Having started at 20-1, Lord Windermere would hit 480 in running. If anyone had asked Culloty's opinion at that point, he would have agreed it did not look good. "I'd told Davy to take his time but halfway round I wondered what he was doing – I wanted to sack him," Culloty says. "I told him to take his time and ride the horse to get a place but he exaggerated the waiting tactics a bit too much."

Russell admits it was not the ideal start. "He got very anxious in the parade and sweated up a bit on the way to the start too," he explains. "Then there were a couple of false starts which didn't help him either.

Over the first couple of fences it was a case of staying as close as I could to them and trying to find a nice position, but the position I got was a little bit further back than I would have liked to have been."

UP FRONT, the race was going pretty much to script. Bobs Worth and Silviniaco Conti, the reigning title-holders of the Gold Cup and King George VI Chase respectively, were well placed to deliver a victory by one of the main fancies, which is what happens most years. Last Instalment, their only rival sent off at less than 10-1, departed at the 17th fence but he was back-pedalling at the time and his exit seemed merely to reduce the list of probable winners to two.

Silviniaco Conti, whose stamina shone through when winning the King George, was sent to the front

▶ *Continues page 74*

by Noel Fehily with four to jump. Bobs Worth was hot on his heels and had just two lengths to retrieve on the home turn. Everything was in place for the heavyweight bout to commence. But, when the bell sounded, there were more than two fighters inside the ropes.

Silviniaco Conti started up the run-in a length in front of Bobs Worth, but then he began to get lonely. First he wandered left, then he wandered right. Now was not the time for wandering. He reached a low of 1.7 in running but the money of his backers, as well as his jockey's dream, was about to disappear in a matter of seconds. "I didn't sleep a lot on the Friday night. I was absolutely sick," Fehily reflected later, still reeling from the what might have been. "I thought he was the best horse and that he would gallop all the way to the line. I think he likes a little bit of company."

Bobs Worth could not keep straight either, uncharacteristically lugging to his left and throwing away any chance of holding on to his crown. He traded at 1.42 on Betfair, money piled upon faith that he would conquer the Cheltenham hill, as he had done on his five previous visits to the track. But not this time.

Silviniaco Conti was cooked. Bobs Worth was beaten. The main action

was now unfolding down the centre of the wide, uphill finish as Lord Windermere, Willie Mullins' On His Own and the David Bridgwater-trained The Giant Bolster all found their second wind. Johnson, as any good commentator should, had noted Lord Windermere's progress from just before the home turn. Though still eighth, Russell's mount had "never been closer than he is now" and approaching the last he had moved into a challenging fourth. "Still Lord Windermere continues to stay on."

As the drama unfolded, Fehily was not the only one who would cast a rueful glance back at the final moments. On His Own and The Giant Bolster, who would end up second and third, had bumped in midair over the second-last. "We were virtually stopped on our feet but the ground he made up was phenomenal," recalled Simon Hunt, The Giant Bolster's owner. "I will always have that great sense of pride in the achievement. However, I will also always have that pain of coming so close to the impossible dream. I think the best staying chaser in England sits in the Cotswolds in Bridgie's yard."

The interference didn't stop there. As Silviniaco Conti drifted to his right up the run-in, he seemed to

▸Golden glow: (clockwise from top left) Lord Windermere (left) challenges Silviniaco Conti (centre) and Bobs Worth at the last; Jim Culloty with his Gold Cup winner at his Churchtown yard the following day; Culloty is congratulated at Cheltenham; Davy Russell celebrates as he arrives in the winner's enclosure

intimidate Lord Windermere, who in turn carried On His Own and The Giant Bolster towards the middle of the track. Lord Windermere was a length clear 100 yards out, half a length up 50 yards out, a neck, a head, a short head, the line. Lord Windermere had won the 2014 Cheltenham Gold Cup. Or had he?

The head-on replay did not do him any favours. "I felt at the time I was going to get up on top with a straight run," argued David Casey, On His Own's jockey, in the stewards' room. "I was actually upsides, I think, at the line, or just after the line, and two strides after I am in front. I felt that, with a straight run, I would have won the race. I felt all the way up the straight I was being impeded."

This was no ordinary inquiry. Not
▸ Continues page 76

LOW LEVEL

Lord Windermere was not a vintage Gold Cup winner – far from it. In a bunched finish and a relatively ordinary time, he posted a Racing Post Rating of 170, which was the lowest since The Fellow achieved the same figure in 1994.

The recent standard was set by Kauto Star with an RPR of 185 in his second Gold Cup win in 2009. That was part of a vintage run of four consecutive winners with RPRs in the 180s.

Bobs Worth, an above-average winner in 2013 with an RPR of 181, was well below that mark in his title defence as he finished fifth behind Lord Windermere with an RPR of 167.

LAST TEN WINNERS

Year	Horse	RPR
2014	Lord Windermere	170
2013	Bobs Worth	181
2012	Synchronised	173
2011	Long Run	181
2010	Imperial Commander	182
2009	Kauto Star	185
2008	Denman	184
2007	Kauto Star	175
2006	War Of Attrition	173
2005	Kicking King	177

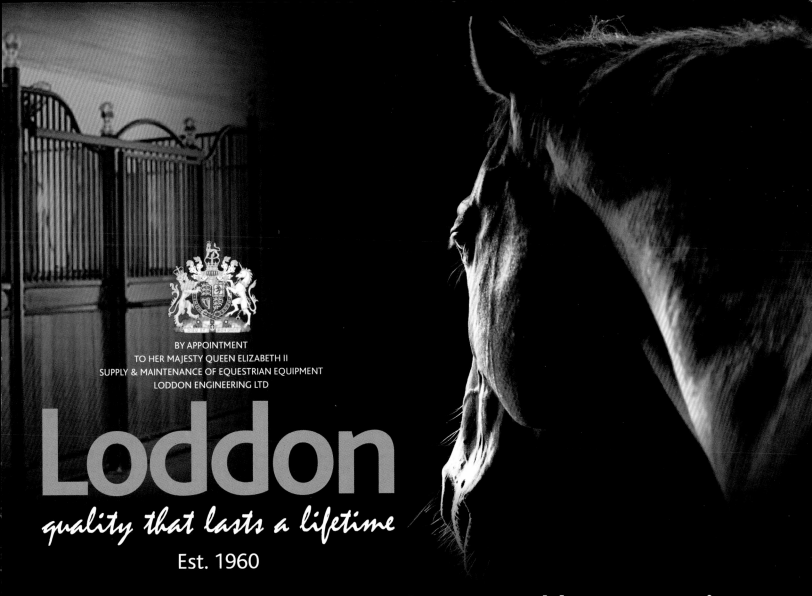

DOUBLE UP

Jim Culloty, who partnered Best Mate to three consecutive Gold Cup victories in 2002-04, became the fifth man (and fourth Irishman) to win the Cheltenham Gold Cup as both a jockey and a trainer in its 90-year history.

The first, Danny Morgan, became the only jockey to beat Golden Miller in the Gold Cup when triumphing on Morse Code in 1938, thus thwarting the great champion's attempt at a six-timer in the race. He trained Roddy Owen to a lucky win in 1959 when the leader, Pas Seul, fell at the last and badly hampered his two closest pursuers.

Pat Taaffe, revered as the jockey of triple winner Arkle (1964-66), also rode Fort Leney in 1968 and trained Captain Christy in 1974 when that champion became the most recent novice to triumph.

Fred Winter, the only Englishman to do the double, rode consecutive winners Saffron Tartan and Mandarin (1961-62) but had bad luck as a trainer apart from his victory with Midnight Court, when the race was postponed to April in 1978. Winter also won the Champion Hurdle and the Grand National as both jockey and trainer.

Jonjo O'Neill won the Gold Cup on Alverton (1979) and Dawn Run (1986), and trained 2012 winner Synchronised.

only was it for the most prestigious prize in jump racing but the two jockeys sparring in the stewards' room were the best of friends. "Myself and David have sat beside one another in the weighing room for a long, long time now and, if I didn't win it, he would be one of the ones I'd love to see winning it," Russell says.

But now was not the time for friendship. Russell and Lord Windermere had won the Gold Cup and now they had to keep it. "Without a doubt, I am on the best horse in the race," Russell told the stewards. "I am never going to be passed the whole way. If I had continued going aggressively, I was never going to be passed. My horse is very idle and was pricking his ears. There's no doubt I was on the best horse."

The stewards agreed and after 20 long minutes – the worst minutes of Culloty's life – the placings remained unaltered. The following day Mullins said there would be no appeal from the On His Own camp, despite many thinking they had a strong case.

On the day Culloty was convinced the result would be reversed in the stewards' room. "I thought we were certain to lose it given my luck," he says. "They were the worst few minutes of my life. He just idled in front. He doesn't go a stroke sometimes when he's in front but Davy got him over the line in front."

But just how did a horse who was

'There were days when I couldn't be bothered riding them out. The horses just weren't right. I was in the doldrums for a long, long time and started to wonder whether I could actually do this job'

beaten 26 lengths in the Irish Hennessy get over the line in front in the Gold Cup less than five weeks later?

"I rode him at Leopardstown and I knew going out that I was riding him the wrong way but I wanted to see what would happen if he was in a Gold Cup when he was in the thick of things and whether it would suit him," Russell explains. "The first thing I said to Dr Lambe and Jim when I came in was 'don't worry, he's just a horse who needs to be dropped in.' Jim was of the same opinion and the Hennessy was a fact-finding mission. We learned a lot that day."

IF ADVERSITY is a valuable teacher, Culloty also learned a lot last season. Spring Heeled's success in a novice chase at Killarney in the final week of August was his last winner before the Cheltenham Festival. He had endured six and a half months of torture. Disappointment after disappointment. He questioned his ability and wondered whether it was all worth it.

"There were days when I said I couldn't be bothered riding them out," he admits. "The horses just weren't right. Things have been tough since I decided to train. I was in the doldrums for a long, long time and started to wonder whether I could actually do this job.

"I was ringing up everyone for advice. I called Paul Nicholls and Victor Dartnall, who I used to ride

for and who I think is a brilliant trainer. I was quite low at one point and I started thinking about getting a proper job. We tried to change everything – routine, feed, gallops – but we found out it was a fungus problem. As soon as that was sorted, we've never looked back."

Once the fungus was found, Culloty's crop began to bloom. After no winner in six and a half months, he had two in the space of two days at the Cheltenham Festival as Spring Heeled landed the Kim Muir 24 hours before Lord Windermere bagged the big one.

It was a case of love at first sight when Culloty first caught a glimpse of Lord Windermere, who was rising five years old, at the sales in December 2010. "I wasn't looking to buy anything that day but as soon as I saw him, I fell in love with him," he says. "I was bidding on him in the ring and I didn't know that the vendor was behind me. Someone else was bidding as well but all of a sudden they stopped and I was able to get him." The price was £75,000.

"I called Dr Lambe afterwards and he asked me if I liked him. I told him I loved him and so he decided to take him. Everything this horse has done suggested the Gold Cup was the perfect race for him."

When Lord Windermere finally got to the race, it did not seem so perfect for a while. But in the end Culloty had the perfect result. And the perfect way to shake off the season from hell.

GO RACING IN IRELAND 2015

Wherever you are in Ireland, you're never far from a race meeting and if you want to understand one of our country's great passions, choose from over 300 race meetings at any of the 26 racecourses around the country and have a day you'll always remember.

2015 RACING FESTIVALS

LEOPARDSTOWN
BHP Irish Champions Hurdle
25th January

CORK
Easter Festival
4th - 6th April

FAIRYHOUSE
Easter Festival
5th - 7th April

PUNCHESTOWN
National Hunt Festival
28th April - 2nd May

KILLARNEY
Spring Festival
10th - 12th May

CURRAGH
Guineas Festival
23rd - 24th May

CURRAGH
Irish Derby Festival
26th - 28th June

BELLEWSTOWN
July Festival
2nd - 4th July

KILLARNEY
July Festival
13th - 16th July

GALWAY
Summer Festival
27th July - 2nd August

TRAMORE
August Festival
13th - 16th August

KILLARNEY
August Festival
19th - 22nd August

LEOPARDSTOWN & CURRAGH
Irish Champions Weekend
12th - 13th September

LISTOWEL
Harvest Festival
13th - 19th September

DOWN ROYAL
Northern Ireland Festival of Racing
30th - 31st October

FAIRYHOUSE
Premier Jumps Weekend
28th - 29th November

LEOPARDSTOWN
Christmas Festival
26th - 29th December

LIMERICK
Christmas Festival
26th - 29th December

HORSE RACING IRELAND

To plan your day at the races or for a FREE racing information pack, please call the **Marketing Team on + 353 45 455 455** or visit **www.goracing.ie**

f facebook.com/goracing twitter.com/@goracing

goracing.ie
The Horse Racing Ireland Website

THE
BIGGER
PICTURE

Get Me Out Of Here leads Jonjo O'Neill's string on the gallops at Jackdaws Castle in February. Perhaps the unluckiest horse in training, Get Me Out Of Here was beaten a short head in the Coral Cup the following month – the fourth time he had finished runner-up at the Cheltenham Festival

EDWARD WHITAKER
(RACINGPOST.COM/PHOTOS)

Credit where it's due

Sire De Grugy was a popular hero after winning the Queen Mother Champion Chase for his enthusiastic owners and hard-working trainer but did not always get the respect he deserved

By Peter Thomas

AS the dust settled on the jumps season, in which the name of Sire De Grugy was inked into the record books as winner of the Queen Mother Champion Chase and the best two-mile chaser of 2013-14, Gary Moore was left with a smile on his face but a nagging doubt on his mind.

"The best horse I've ever trained" had done all that could have been asked of him and then some, but in the final analysis the trainer could have been forgiven for wondering what it all meant. On the one hand, he had warm memories of a hero with a bright

▸▸ *Continues page 82*

future; on the other, his stable star was described by some critics as "the best of a bad bunch" and rated a full 18lb inferior to a rival he may never meet in anger.

Sire De Grugy earned championship honours with six wins from his seven runs, including four Grade 1 triumphs, but in some eyes he was the poor relation who profited from the infirmity of the reigning champion and remained no more than a pretender to the throne of the great Sprinter Sacre.

Having had the summer to digest the slights on Sire De Grugy's achievements, Moore seems undecided between being mortally wounded and not giving two hoots before summoning a display of admirable belligerence. "Handicappers? They're the worst judges in the world," he states, with no expectation of an argument. "I'd like to see Sprinter Sacre try and give mine 18lb in a handicap, but I bet Nicky Henderson wouldn't.

"Nicky said to me at the end of the season that he'd see us in the Tingle Creek, and I'd love to give him a go somewhere along the line. Sire De Grugy may not be as imposing as Sprinter Sacre, but it's not a beauty contest and if you can't take the strains of training, you're weak."

AT Cisswood Stables in the West Sussex village of Lower Beeding, Sire De Grugy looks ready for a scrap as he gears up for a new campaign. He has had his short summer break and come in itching to get back to his working routine. Two small scars on each ankle – reminders of an operation to remove chips of bone that may have been displaced by his efforts on the lively Cheltenham turf – are the only visible signs of the efforts that culminated in a repeat success in Sandown's Celebration Chase on the final day of the season.

Inside, he seems to be his old, dangerous self – the same horse who broke his trainer's shin two years ago with a flailing hoof and still strikes fear into vet and blacksmith alike. "He'd never bite you, but he'd kick your head off," says Moore affectionately, rolling up a trouser leg to show the scars of battle. It may have hurt at the time, but it was a sign of the fighting spirit he has channelled into the eight-year-old's efforts on the track. And what an effort it was to defeat the best two-mile chasers that could be mustered on that glory day at the Cheltenham Festival.

Sire De Grugy's season had begun well enough, as he followed up the previous term's Celebration Chase win with an impressive, if routine, handicap

victory in the soft at Chepstow. It was in the back of Moore's mind to plot a course back to Sandown the following April, but little could he have dreamed of what was to follow in the intervening months, especially when Sire De Grugy had his colours lowered by Henderson's Kid Cassidy – a horse rated 19lb his inferior – in Cheltenham's Shloer Chase, a mere Listed race.

It was a loss that not only put a temporary spoke in the wheel of Sire De Grugy's progress but also raised doubts about his effectiveness on the track where he had already suffered defeat by Henderson's Captain Conan in 2012 – doubts that would linger until he dispersed them with March's flash of brilliance.

Undeterred, Moore sent his emergent stable star to Sandown for the Tingle Creek Chase, where he slammed Somersby and Captain Conan and incontrovertibly proved he had metamorphosed from a hurdler who had reached his handicap ceiling to a chaser who belonged in Grade 1 company.

'He seems to be his old, dangerous self – the same horse who broke his trainer's shin and still strikes fear into vet and blacksmith alike'

Moore's son Jamie had been instrumental in the buying of Sire De Grugy, dashing to France to roadtest the unraced horse and returning with tales of a gallop in which he had readily picked off horses who had started a field in front of him.

By now, the rider's judgement had been vindicated and his faith in the formerly nervy and fragile beast remained equally intact. "He'd still boot you if you did anything silly," he said, "but when it comes to working he'll do anything for you and he's much more relaxed. His best attribute, though, is his heart and that will be important in the Queen Mother.

"The Cheltenham debate doesn't really bother me at all. I don't know why he does it but he's always been a bit too exuberant there and taken off a stride too early, and perhaps he just hasn't been quite right on those two days, but I honestly wouldn't swap him for anything else in the race, including Sprinter Sacre."

The bandwagon was rolling, but

THE PEOPLE'S CHOICE

The racing public voted with their hearts in choosing Sire De Grugy as Horse of the Year

The combined minds of the official handicappers made Silviniaco Conti the best chaser of the 2013-14 season, but there was no doubt hearts were won by Sire De Grugy's exploits.

King George VI Chase winner Silviniaco Conti was given an official rating of 174, 2lb ahead of Sire De Grugy in the Anglo-Irish classifications unveiled in May. Those figures were well behind recent vintage champions Kauto Star (190 in 2009-10) and Sprinter Sacre (188 in 2012-13), leading many commentators to conclude it was a disappointing season.

With several of the major prizes going to smaller stables, however, there was widespread enjoyment of the more open competition and in Sire De Grugy the racing public found a hero.

Michael McSherry, from Farnham, Surrey, summed up the majority view of Sire De Grugy's Cheltenham success in a letter to the Racing Post. "What a breath of fresh air to see Sire De Grugy win the Queen Mother Champion Chase," he wrote. "I fully endorse Gary and Jamie Moore's view that the horse hasn't had the credit he deserves – it's been all Sprinter Sacre this, Sprinter Sacre that."

Recognition duly arrived at the end of the jumps season when Sire De Grugy was named the public's overwhelming choice as Horse of the Year, with more than 70 per cent of the votes cast on racingpost.com.

Many Racing Post social media users expressed their approval. Paul Hodson, on Facebook, said: "If this horse was in the Henderson or Nicholls yard he'd have been revered as a genuine superstar. He's a great advert for our sport."

Rebecca Wade, also on Facebook, said: "The most heartwarming story. He has made a dream come true for the Moore family and is a fairytale for the owners."

On racingpost.com, the user course-specialist said: "Sire De Grugy has been the star of this jumps season both for his exploits and how he has thrust his enthusiastic but modest connections into the spotlight."

Other social media users hailed "well-deserved recognition of a great horse" and the "feelgood story of the year".

For many jump racing fans, Sire De Grugy was all about following the heart.

---

there was still one major obstacle in the road: the champ, Sprinter Sacre, widely regarded as unbeatable. He was the 2-9 favourite for the Desert Orchid Chase at Kempton at Christmas and, while Sire De Grugy arrived in great form to take him on, the script said Moore's challenger would finish second at a respectful distance.

The script, however, was shredded when Barry Geraghty pulled up Sprinter Sacre after the seventh fence, leaving Sire De Grugy to score a success that was never likely to earn him any credit at all from the sidelines.

As if Moore could care less. With another £45,000 safely stuffed into the horse's saddlebags, the team headed off to Ascot, where the 5-4 shot dismissed his inferiors with ease (£59,000 this time) in the Clarence House Chase (his second Grade 1 of the season) and returned to Lower Beeding to kick a vet or two and put in the hard yards that would ensure he arrived at Cheltenham in winning fettle.

"Luckily, he's a great worker who's

▶▶ Sire on the march: (clockwise from top left) Sire De Grugy gallops to his first Grade 1 success in the Tingle Creek; in the winner's enclosure after the Tingle Creek; winning the Desert Orchid Chase at Kempton after Sprinter Sacre was pulled up; another Grade 1 victory in the Clarence House Chase at Ascot; with Jamie Moore after winning the Queen Mother Champion Chase; on his way to victory in the Celebration Chase at Sandown

never happier than when he's galloping," says Moore. "If I turned him out now he'd wander off, wander back, have a roll and stand by the gate wanting to come in. He doesn't like being turned out. He's a professional racehorse."

THIS is music to the ears of owner Steve Preston, who has watched the Sire De Grugy story unfold with a sense of wide-eyed amazement, having drifted into racehorse ownership only at the insistence of family and friends who were keen that his long-standing dream be realised.

They clubbed together and chipped in a couple of thousand pounds for his 50th birthday, to start the ball rolling, leaving Preston himself with the shock of having to find the remaining €48,000 that was required to secure his new best friend. At Preston's insistence, Moore retained a 25 per cent share – to keep him on his toes – and the former south London boy (by now relocated to Runcorn and running a sporting goods business in Holland) set about

watching his red and blue silks advertise the charms of Crystal Palace FC on the nation's racecourses.

Come February, with Cheltenham on the horizon, the ownership group officially listed as The Preston Family and Friends (incorporating father, sons Sean, Liam and Ryan and pals Neil McNulty, Barry Lockett and Dave Simpson) were already gearing up for the biggest day of their lives. Preston had found a company in Leicester that produced bespoke knitwear and was happy to turn out a small wardrobe-load of team scarves that would ensure the Palace colours appeared in front of their biggest crowd in decades.

With 'Sire De Grugy' slap bang in the middle and the legend 'Sire's on Fire' emblazoned alongside, the scarves identified and unified the excited band of pals. Little did Preston know they would soon become sought-after collector's items, with one finding its way around the regal neck of the Duchess of Cornwall in the most
▶▶ *Continues page 84*

coveted winner's enclosure in jump racing.

"We had 18 going for the big day and we could have had 80," recalls the still giddy head of the partnership. "Cheltenham very kindly allowed us all in the ring and we set our stall out to make sure it was a day of celebration, come what may, because just getting to the race was wonderful in itself.

"We were continually worrying why everybody seemed to think he wasn't good enough and he kept drifting in the betting, but the trainer told us he was fine. There was the monkey on his back about the course but we were reasonably hopeful in spite of everything and the race itself was one of the most surreal things I can remember.

"Our entire group watched on the big screen in the parade ring and it was a nervous time, but in among all the doubts the race itself went completely to plan, to the point that he got a slice of luck when Baily Green fell and brought Hinterland down, while we skipped through on the inside. For tuppence he could have fallen the other way and it would have been us that came down, but it was our day.

"It was wonderful. We gave him a big roar home and we've been embarrassed many times by the TV pictures of us jumping around like fools. It couldn't come true but for once it actually did."

HAVING stayed in the paddock to avoid getting caught up in the crowds, Preston was quick out of the blocks as Sire De Grugy passed the winning post six lengths clear of Somersby, with Module and Sizing Europe chasing them home. He bounded down the horsewalk to greet the homecoming heroes and led them in to a rapturous reception.

It was a proper festival moment, marked by a flurry of red and blue and accompanied by the biggest cheer of the week, for a first-time owner and a trainer whose hard graft against the odds had earned him many admirers since he jacked in a tough career as a journeyman jump jockey to begin an even tougher one as a dual-purpose trainer.

"As a jockey I never achieved anything really," says the battle-scarred 58-year-old, still amazed that Sire De Grugy didn't kick anybody in the post-race melee, "so to train a Champion Chase winner and for Jamie to have ridden it meant as much as you could ever want. It meant everything, but the trouble is now you want to do it again, and there's no reason why you shouldn't, but you're expected to."

Preston has now had time to

digest the win and come to similar conclusions, but in the heat of the moment he struggled to take in the heady swirl of emotions and alcohol.

"When the jockeys gave Jamie a huge fanfare when he came in, it seemed that for the Moore family and the Preston family we were simultaneously having the best day of our lives," he enthuses in lingering disbelief. "The experience was second to none, although after that it becomes slightly blurry because we went straight back into the Lawn Bar and started buying massive bottles of champagne.

"Everybody in the town was brilliant with us later on when they saw us in our regalia. We got the courtesy bus from the track to the town centre and we had everybody singing along with us, Sire De Grugy this and Crystal Palace that,

▶▶ Dream come true: the Cheltenham winner's enclosure is a riot of red and blue as joyous connections celebrate Sire De Grugy's victory in the Queen Mother Champion Chase

then we went straight into the bar we'd organised for ourselves.

"We'd told them to expect us, win, lose or draw, and we were received with open arms. They roped off an area for us but after a couple of hours we went into the main bit, where everyone was in good spirits, and there was drinking and music until we dragged ourselves away at about two o'clock, managed to get taxis back to the hotel and nursed our headaches the following day.

"It was such a warm feeling and the day of a lifetime, and we had another party back at Gary's local pub, the Wheatsheaf, that really capped the season."

The aptly named Celebration Chase was never likely to scale the same heights of emotion, and when Sire De

▶▶ *Continues page 86*

Nothing but the BEST!

MAXIOS

Monsun - Moonlight's Box (Nureyev)

Winner of 5 group races, including **2 Gr.1 wins**

Son of the outstanding **Champion sire MONSUN**, who has **19 Gr.1 winners** among them in 2013 **FIORENTE, NOVELLIST, ESTIMATE, SILASOL** and **MAXIOS**

Half-brother to the Arc-winner **BAGO** out of a daughter of the **Gr.1** winner **COUP DE GENIE**, half-sister to **OCEAN OF WISDOM** and **MACCHIAVELLIAN**

Out of the direct dam line of world-class sires **NORTHERN DANCER** and **DANEHILL**

CAMPANOLOGIST

Kingmambo - Ring of Music (Sadler's Wells)

Winner of 4 Gr.1 races by the world-class miler **KINGMAMBO**

Outstanding pedigree: Out of a half-sister to **SINGSPIEL** and **RAHY**

Has won over **7 – 12 furlongs**

Has beaten more than **50 individual Gr.1 winners**

Excellent first book with numerous top mares, such as the dams of **Gr.1 winners EARL OF TINSDAL** and **DURBAN THUNDER**

PASTORIUS

Soldier Hollow - Princess Li (Monsun)

Germany's Champion 3yo 2012 and winner of **3 Gr.1** races

Classic winner and group winner at 2yo

By Champion sire **SOLDIER HOLLOW**, one of the best sons of the sire of sires, **IN THE WINGS**

Out of the dam line of **Champion sires LOMITAS** and **LAGUNAS** and Derby winner **LAVIRCO**

His dam is by the **Champion sire MONSUN**, who records **19 Gr.1 winners**, and is a granddaughter of the **classic winner PRINCESS NANA**

FÄHRHOF

Daniel Krüger · Mobile: +162 733 2 339 · krueger@faehrhof.de · www.faehrhof.de

Al Co's National makes Moore the merrier

Sire De Grugy was not the only high-profile winner for Jamie Moore in a season to remember. Just a month after Sire De Grugy gave him his first Cheltenham Festival success, he landed another big race with Al Co in the Scottish Grand National.

Sire De Grugy's triumphs were the sweetest – a family affair with the jockey along for the ride all the way – but victory on Al Co advertised Moore's skills away from the familiarity of father Gary's string.

Having had barely a moment's concern aboard Sire De Grugy in the Queen Mother Champion Chase, Moore needed supreme horsemanship to survive a hair-raising run-in at Ayr. Not once but twice, the Peter Bowen-trained Al Co threatened to throw away victory by jinking and almost unseating Moore, and it was only the jockey's quick reactions that kept the partnership intact.

After coming home a length and a half clear of Godsmejudge, the previous year's winner, a relieved Moore said: "He spooked at something. I honestly nearly fell off twice, and thank God I didn't. I don't know what caused it – billboards, cameramen. Maybe he saw someone he didn't like."

Al Co was a 40-1 outsider for the Ayr marathon but not unfancied by Bowen. "I told everyone to back him each-way, I thought he had a big chance," he said. "He was in the best form we've ever had him. This race has always been the plan and he runs well fresh."

Bowen's plan for Al Co this season is the Grand National at Aintree, in which the Welsh trainer finished second with Mckelvey in 2007. After his Ayr success – and other odds-defying efforts such as Take The Stand's second place at 25-1 in the 2005 Cheltenham Gold Cup – Bowen is not a trainer to take lightly. "I think Peter is capable of anything, so if he thinks he is a National horse he might be," Moore said.

It was a season that proved Moore is more than capable, too, and the respect in which he is held was clear from the guard of honour formed by his fellow jockeys at Cheltenham to greet him after Sire De Grugy's victory. "It proves what a popular person he is. It's probably not been done for a long time," said his proud father after the accolade from the weighing room.

Giving credit to the role played by his jockey son in Sire De Grugy's rise to the top, the trainer added: "Jamie knows what he's doing."

Nobody can be in any doubt of that after the season of Moore's life.

» Mission accomplished: owner Steve Preston receives his prize at Cheltenham from the Duchess of Cornwall and greets winning trainer Gary Moore

Grugy returned home from Cheltenham moving like anything but a champion, there were doubts about his making what had been planned as the season's finale. He came right again, however, and headed to Sandown for a regulation Grade 1 win that was rated some way inferior to what he had done at Cheltenham.

"He wasn't the same horse to saddle at Sandown as he had been at Cheltenham," explains Moore. "He was stressed and I think the problems with his joints might have been in the back of his mind that day. We had him bone scanned before he went away for the summer and two hot spots came up, so we had him operated on and he's come back big and strong and maybe ready to improve a little bit more."

The plan is to head for the Tingle Creek, from where all roads lead back to Cheltenham. For Moore, a clash with Sprinter Sacre is high on the agenda, and he's not as sure as most people about the likely result.

"Nicky's horse is gorgeous, but he really only beat the same horses we beat," he reasons. "He might have beaten them more easily, but that's the kind of horse he is, and it would be great to have a crack at him."

Preston, meanwhile, is less sure of what is to be gained from such a showdown. "We won't avoid him," he says, "but if we take him on and he beats us, it will confirm he's better than us and if we beat him people will just say he's not back to his best, so I think it's an argument we'll never win.

"But it doesn't matter. All that matters is that we had the right horse at the right time and we'll always have the memories of that great day."

1

2

THE DAWN RUN STAND

4

5

7

10

1 Fingal Bay (far side) and Richard Johnson on their way to victory in a tight finish to the Pertemps Network Final. The first four in the three-mile handicap hurdle were separated by a nose and two necks, with subsequent Grand National winner Pineau De Re in third place

2 The winner Present View (Brendan Powell) races away from the third-last fence in the Rewards4Racing Novices' Handicap Chase with the rest of the field in hot pursuit

3 Barry Geraghty is congratulated by trainer Jonjo O'Neill's wife Jacqui after winning the World Hurdle on More Of That

4 Racegoers enjoy the opening-day action in the Dawn Run Stand

5 Cameras focus on Western Warhorse (nearside, No9) and Tom Scudamore as they jump the fourth fence in the Racing Post Arkle Chase. The David Pipe-trained 33-1 shot went on to win by a head from Champagne Fever

6 Tony McCoy drives Taquin Du Seuil (centre) between Uxizandre and Double Ross after jumping the last in the JLT Novices' Chase. Taquin Du Seuil went on to win by three-quarters of a length from Uxizandre (far side)

7 Arriving at the races the old-fashioned way as the steam train pulls into the racecourse station

8 The Cheltenham Gold Cup is captured on a smartphone

9 A racegoer studies his paper at a foggy Prestbury Park on day three

10 Runners in the Coral Cup make a long line as they head away from the stands. The race was won by the Nicky Henderson-trained Whisper, a first festival winner for jockey Nico de Boinville

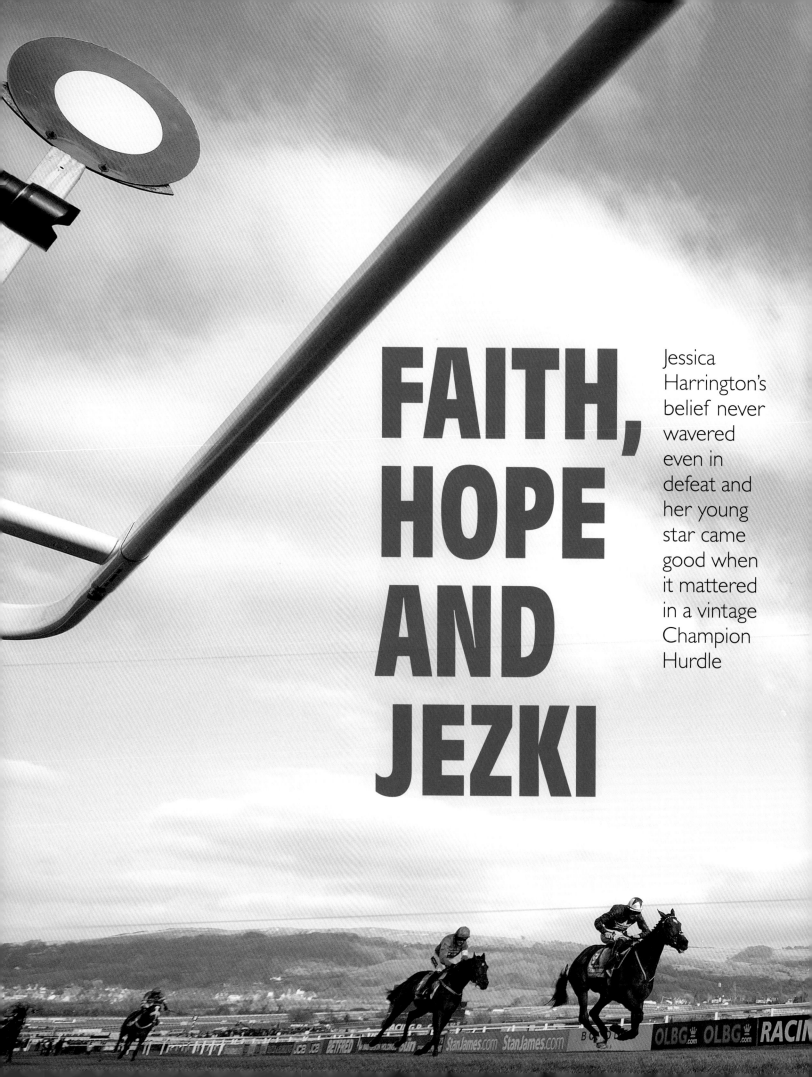

FAITH, HOPE AND JEZKI

Jessica Harrington's belief never wavered even in defeat and her young star came good when it mattered in a vintage Champion Hurdle

By Steve Dennis

HOPE springs eternal, but faith endures. Hope can be short-lived, easily extinguished, readily replaced with whatever the antonym for hope is – despair, probably. But faith is unwavering, unaffected by minor reversals of fortune, unbroken by adversity, reinforced by affirmation. Many men and women merely hope that this horse or that might be a champion but Jessica Harrington had faith that Jezki would be.

"I've always had faith in Jezki, all through his life," says Harrington, trainer of the six-year-old who won a notably strong edition of the Champion Hurdle at Cheltenham in March. That faith had been thoroughly tested throughout the previous 12 months and occasionally doubts had been voiced, yet the spring brought glorious vindication.

In last year's Racing Post Annual, Harrington discussed the bay gelding with the white-splashed face in the manner of a mother slightly bemused by her son's school report. His homework had indicated an 'A', but the big exam had returned a 'B+'. "I'm still mystified about why he ran so badly at Cheltenham," she said, considering Jezki's third-place finish in the Supreme Novices' Hurdle behind Champagne Fever and My Tent Or Yours. The first three had drawn well clear of the fourth, however, and time would tell that all three were top-quality jumpers.

On his next outing Jezki redeemed himself with a 16-length victory in a Grade 1 at Punchestown, with Champagne Fever a toiling third, and went away for the summer as a valid contender for top honours in his second season. Trouble was, there was a whole host of valid contenders in what would develop into a vintage crop of two-mile hurdlers, and at that point Jezki's prospects were best viewed through the rosy prism of hope. Harrington, though, studied him with the clear-eyed and steady gaze of faith.

"His first two outings last season were muddling affairs and he won them both without being suited by what happened during the races," she says. "At Down Royal there was no pace but he still did it all very easy, and it was a very strange race at Fairyhouse over an extra half-mile [the Grade 1 Hatton's Grace Hurdle]. Diakali went off 20 lengths in front and turned into a sitting duck, and Jezki picked him off well."

The Racing Post's analysis of the Hatton's Grace is instructive: "He's likely to fall just short at Champion Hurdle level this season, but . . . a hard nut to crack in a race like the Aintree Hurdle. Interesting times await." There are undertones of the old Chinese curse 'may you live in interesting times' and overtones of a gradual external loss of faith in Jezki that would gather pace as the season progressed. Harrington, though, could see what no-one else could see.

"He does everything so easily at home, he's very relaxed," she says. "When he gets to the racecourse, though, he likes to get on with it and that's why we decided to put a hood on him for Cheltenham, just to help him settle better, to help him cope with the buzz there. It was Barry's idea [Geraghty] after Punchestown, when he said Jezki didn't drop the bit until the second flight."

The pre-Christmas exchanges are often inconclusive skirmishes in comparison to the major battles ahead and Jezki's true position in the broader picture had yet to be inked in. However, even the flimsiest of flaws are seized upon as being incontrovertible evidence of not possessing 'the right stuff' and when Jezki was weighed in the balance he seemed to be found wanting. Most observers, swift to pigeonhole, lost their faith in Jezki after two runs at Leopardstown within a month. Not Harrington, though, even if she reverts to the status of a mother trying to read between the lines of a bewildering half-term report.

"His two defeats did surprise me – apart from that Cheltenham run, they were the only times he's been beaten over hurdles," she says. "I knew they weren't a true reflection of his ability and even though I was surprised by them I wasn't disheartened.

"The horse goes on all ground, although he's definitely better on good ground because he has such speed and soft or heavy ground does blunt that. So the ground at Leopardstown didn't show him in the best light and neither race panned out how I'd have liked."

The two races – the Ryanair Hurdle and Irish Champion Hurdle, both Grade 1s – instead turned the

▸ Continues page 92

spotlight on to the old guard in the shape of dual Champion Hurdle winner Hurricane Fly, apparently as good as ever at the age of ten. This, in turn, made the road towards the Cheltenham Festival a more compelling journey than in many years, for here we had the old champ matched against an army of young challengers who were throwing down the gauntlet from all quarters.

Hurricane Fly, in pursuit of the grail-like third crown, seemed to have cast-iron credentials following his defeat of the Dessie Hughes-trained Our Conor – a jaw-droppingly easy winner of the Triumph Hurdle the previous season – and a lacklustre Jezki in the Irish Champion. In Britain, the ranks were led by My Tent Or Yours and The New One, who had fought out an exhilarating finish to the Grade 1 Christmas Hurdle at Kempton. Each horse had his share of vociferous support – The New One was a Cheltenham specialist and had plenty of stamina, My Tent Or Yours had a quirk in that he had to be produced very late but had dazzling acceleration when so ridden, Our Conor was rolling to a boil after just two starts, both very creditable ones behind Hurricane Fly, and Hurricane Fly was, well, Hurricane Fly.

Jezki was shoved to the margins, perceived as a promising novice who had not progressed as excitingly as had been hoped. Hope had blossomed and died, its petals trodden underfoot by seemingly better horses. Faith, though, was in the root, and isn't spring the time for roots to flourish?

"I was very happy with Jezki going into the Champion Hurdle, everything was right, he was fit, he hadn't been overraced, he'd strengthened up and put on a bit of weight through the winter," says Harrington, who was utterly unflustered by AP McCoy's decision to partner My Tent Or Yours in preference to Jezki, yet another demonstration of failing faith in the six-year-old with both horses running in the green and gold silks of owner JP McManus. "Why wouldn't he ride My Tent Or Yours? He'd always ridden it and the horse was second favourite," she says.

Barry Geraghty was recruited to renew a partnership with Jezki that had hitherto brought immaculate returns of four wins in four races, and Harrington was ready for

▶▶Hero's welcome: Jessica Harrington greets jockey Barry Geraghty and Jezki in the Cheltenham winner's enclosure

HAUL OF FAME

Victory with Jezki was another milestone moment for Jessica Harrington in a life that has defied barriers

The 67-year-old became only the second female trainer to land the Champion Hurdle – joining Mercy Rimell, successful with Gaye Brief in 1983 – and now has two of the three monuments of the Cheltenham Festival to her credit, having won the Queen Mother Champion Chase twice with Moscow Flyer in 2003 and 2005. Victory in the Cheltenham Gold Cup would give her the full set and she admits that is the jumps race she would most like to win.

Henrietta Knight – who won the Gold Cup three times with Best Mate (2002-04) and the Champion Chase with Edredon Bleu (2000) – is the only other woman to have won two of Cheltenham's big three races.

Harrington, who has joined Jenny Pitman as the joint-winningmost female trainer at the Cheltenham Festival with eight successes, has also made her mark at the highest level on the Flat, having won the Group 1 National Stakes in 2010 with Pathfork. Before taking out a training permit in 1989, she was a highly successful three-day event rider, having represented Ireland at three European and one world championships.

Having made such indelible marks in fields often seen as the preserve of men, Harrington did not need to think too hard when she was asked 'what's the worst thing anyone has said to you?' in the RP Sunday questionnaire in August.

Her reply? "'You can't do that, you're a woman' – but I proved them wrong."

Cheltenham. Sadly, though, this year there had been a darker thread woven into the narrative, with Harrington's husband Johnny in the final stages of a brave struggle with cancer.

At this remove Harrington is phlegmatic about the situation – "You take what you get dealt in life," she says – but her resolve would have been tested on more than one front as those four days in the Cotswolds drew nearer.

Johnny's illness must have lent a different cast to the usual preparations – Champion Hurdle or no, it's still only a horse race – but the Harringtons' faith in Jezki buoyed them in the darker moments. "The horse gave Johnny a great lift, kept him going," says Harrington, and the same might have applied to her.

On the big day Jezki was only fifth choice in a field of nine. Hurricane Fly was favoured in a frenzy of fractions over My Tent Or Yours and The New One, with Our Conor close up in the market.

▶▶ *Continues page 94*

2015 Racing Dates

Saturday 3rd January

Cork's RedFM Student Race Day
Thursday 26th March

Racing Home for Easter Festival
Saturday 4th to Monday 6th April

Monday 20th April

Friday Evening Racing - BBQ
Friday 8th May

Friday 22nd May

Sunday 14th June

BBQ
Friday 10th July

Monday 3rd August
Tuesday 4th August

Sunday 30th August

Saturday 17th October
Sunday 18th October

The PaddyPower Cork National
Sunday 1st November
Sunday 15th November

The Kerry Group Hillyway Chase
Sunday 6th December

Get your heart racing...

- Premium Level Restaurant Package
- Premium Level Barbeque Package
- Social Package
- Premium Level Admission
- General Admission
- Children go FREE

Book your tickets today

 **BUY NOW ONLINE**

www.corkracecourse.ie

t: +353 22 50207

corkracecourse.ie

Cork Racecourse MALLOW

 @corkracecourse

 **facebook**
Cork Racecourse Mallow

Yet Father Time beats them all in the end and the telling statistic that no horse of Hurricane Fly's age had won the Champion Hurdle since the great Sea Pigeon more than 30 years earlier was frequently raised against him. Youth must have its day; this was that day.

For a great many, the race was wrecked as a spectacle by the fatal fall of Our Conor at the third hurdle, a sorrowful shadow cast across the race and the four-day meeting. Yet the race was there to be won, and the better ground, faster pace and the calming hood were all in Jezki's favour, and he went to the front at the second last. The New One's chance had gone when he had been hampered by the ill-fated Our Conor and Hurricane Fly began to cry enough on the sprint to the last. There was to be a new name on the roll of honour and Jezki withstood the late thrust of My Tent Or Yours under a no-doubt-cursing McCoy to win by a neck.

"Oh, it was very satisfying indeed," Harrington says. "The Champion Hurdle is one of the great old races, a fantastic race to win, and even though Johnny wasn't able to be there he was celebrating like mad at home. We were lucky to have a very sound, very healthy horse, who has been a really nice horse ever since his bumper days. We'd always believed in him."

Johnny Harrington lost his fight a month later and it was a poignant moment when Jezki underlined his arrival at the top of the tree by beating Hurricane Fly at Punchestown in May, recording his sixth Grade 1 win and emphasising the transfer of power in the two-mile hurdling division. With Hurricane Fly unlikely to recapture his former place as the central player and My Tent Or Yours ruled out for the season, Jezki has assumed a leading role and his campaign is likely to be drawn on identical lines.

"I think he'd still improve a little bit – he's rising seven and many horses tend to peak between seven and eight, so there might be more to come," Harrington says. "If we can keep him sound and healthy we'll hope for the best."

Hope, of course, once again irrepressibly bubbling to the surface. When the bubbles burst, faith is what remains. They say it can move mountains; it certainly helped Jezki to reach the peak.

Numbers up for Hurricane

Hurricane Fly lost his crown in the Champion Hurdle but still added to his record-breaking career in another remarkable season

Sporting history is written by the victors. Where the Champion Hurdle line-up provided a riot of possibilities and colour – the blue of Hurricane Fly, the red of The New One, the green and gold of My Tent Or Yours and Jezki, the yellow and blue of Our Conor – the end result was recorded in black and white. There was Jezki, the vaunted winner, and the vanquished.

Our Conor, of course, lost everything; a life of high promise and high achievement extinguished with a fall at the third hurdle. The ones who made it across the line behind Jezki merely lost a horse race, and they lived to fight another day.

Yet, in sporting terms, it seemed like the end of an era. Until that day, Hurricane Fly had been unassailable against his younger rivals in Ireland, twice defeating Jezki and Our Conor, and an exalted place among the greats beckoned. Victory at Cheltenham would have made him the sixth to land three Champion Hurdles and the first winner in the double-figure age bracket since Sea Pigeon in 1980 and 1981.

Instead, after finishing fourth at Cheltenham and later second to Jezki at Punchestown in May, Hurricane Fly appeared to be yesterday's horse by the end of the season.

After all his achievements, it was a cruel judgement. In the build-up to Cheltenham, he had taken sole possession of the world record for Grade 1 wins, raising his score to 19 and going three clear of steeplechasing great Kauto Star and American Flat racing legend John Henry. He equalled Istabraq by winning a fourth Irish Champion Hurdle (to go with his two Champion Hurdles) and stretched his hurdling prize-money record to £1,637,556.

Cheltenham, though, counts like nothing else and in that respect Hurricane Fly failed. Willie Mullins put it into perspective on Champion Hurdle day, as he reflected

on Our Conor's fall. "As disappointed as we were after the Champion Hurdle, it's nothing to the disappointment Barry Connell [Our Conor's owner], Dessie Hughes [trainer] and Danny [Mullins, jockey] must be feeling. There's disappointment and then there's that. All our sentiments go to that team."

As for Hurricane Fly, Mullins remained defiantly optimistic as the season drew to a close. "He's only ten and he's still a relatively young horse in National Hunt terms and he is injury free. I think he's still got one or two Grade 1s left in him and we might just go up in trip.

"He might have lost the dash he needs against younger horses at shorter trips but I would have no problem going up in trip with him.

"I certainly wouldn't be writing him off just yet."

THE
BIGGER
PICTURE

Nick Gifford waits at the end of the gallop with his dogs Freddie and Walter on a work morning at Downs Stables in Findon, West Sussex, in March
ALAN CROWHURST/GETTY IMAGES

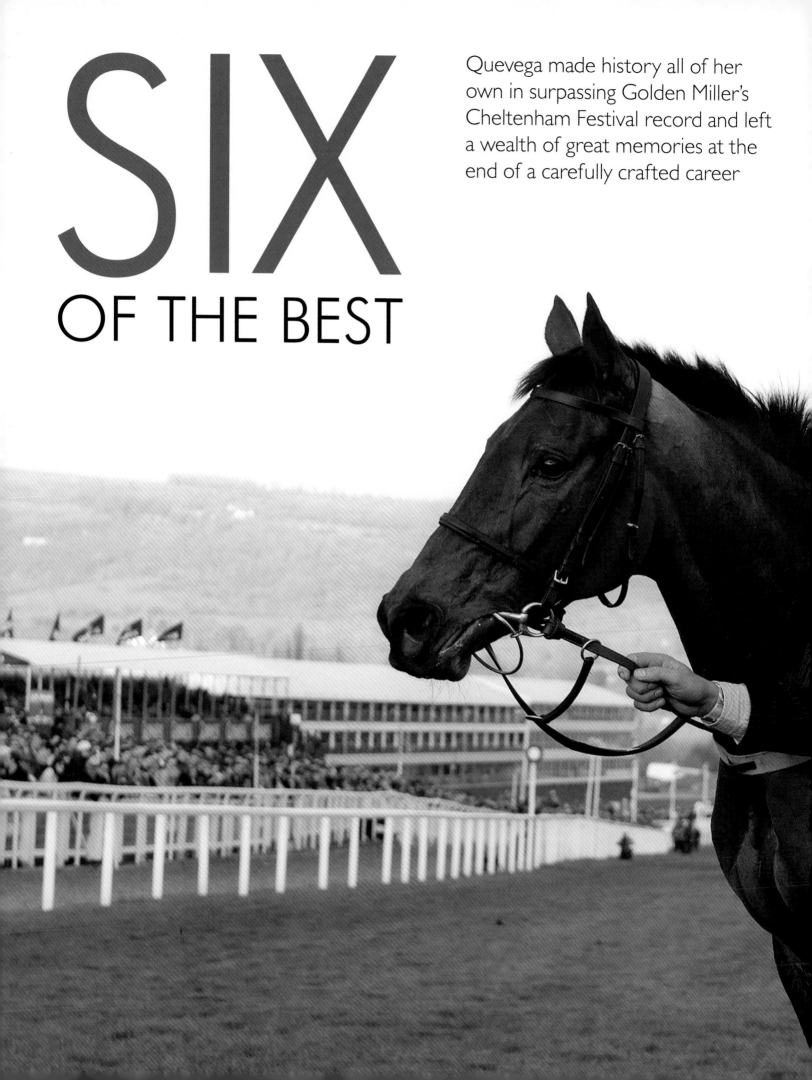

SIX
OF THE BEST

Quevega made history all of her own in surpassing Golden Miller's Cheltenham Festival record and left a wealth of great memories at the end of a carefully crafted career

By Nick Pulford

RECORD books are important but they never tell the full story, nor even come close to it. When, in the years and generations to come, Quevega's name appears in black and white as a six-time winner at the Cheltenham Festival she will be recognised for her outstanding and historic feat, and with every reason.

In winning her sixth consecutive Mares' Hurdle, Quevega surpassed even five-time Gold Cup winner Golden Miller for the longevity of her reign at the Cheltenham Festival. As it took almost eight decades for Golden Miller to be caught and finally overhauled, Quevega's record may never be matched. Truly, she was a once-in-a-lifetime horse for trainer Willie Mullins, jockey Ruby Walsh, her band of owners and for all those lucky enough to have been there for even one of her historic six.

Yet the clinical list of results will not reveal the yearly struggle to keep her sound and get her ready for Cheltenham, the dramatic moments when she appeared beaten and fought back, the deep affection in which she was held and the rousing receptions she received year in, year out. As fresh as those memories are now, they will fade with time.

Nor, from mere race results, will future generations know how close Quevega came to having her Cheltenham destiny snatched away. History is not simply about names and dates, it comes alive through the stories of the people involved; the devil is in the detail. In the moment of triumph after her sixth success, as emotional scenes erupted all around him, Mullins composed himself to record for posterity his thanks to an unsung hero of the story.

In doing so, he went back to Quevega's salad days. She already had one Mares' Hurdle in the bag – won in devastating fashion in 2009 when she annihilated her 20 opponents by 14 lengths – but it might have ended there. Two months after her first Cheltenham victory, she suffered a serious tendon injury that threatened to curtail her racing career at the age of five.

As he related at Cheltenham, Mullins turned to Ned Gowing, the respected Curragh vet. "Veterinary advice was telling us to put her to stud," he said. "I sent her up to Ned Gowing and said I wanted her back as a racemare and he told me what to do. He treated her and told me the way to train her, so a lot of this achievement is down to him. He put her right for me and we just follow the same procedure every year."

The 'procedure' involved an extremely spartan campaign, reminiscent of Nicky Henderson's careful handling of three-time Champion Hurdle winner See You Then in the 1980s. Quevega would turn up each year at the Cheltenham and Punchestown festivals, and nowhere else, as Mullins heeded Gowing's advice and devised a plan that he would execute with singular brilliance.

Ten months after suffering her injury, and without a prep run, Quevega went to Cheltenham for the second time and won the Mares' Hurdle again, this time by four and a half lengths. That cemented a superiority over her own sex that would endure for the rest of her career. In all, 87 different mares would take her on at Cheltenham and every one would come up short.

The mould had been set. After going on to her first World Series Hurdle success at the Punchestown festival at the end of that season, Quevega would not be seen again until the next Cheltenham Festival. In sticking rigidly to that programme, Mullins kept in mind another piece of advice that would help frame Quevega's achievements. "The breeder told me when she was five that she would get better with age and that her mother wasn't at her best until she was nine," he recalled.

Quevega did indeed mature like a fine French wine and for four seasons in a row she compiled a perfect record at

▸ Continues page 100

▶▶ Joy of six: (clockwise from left) Quevega in the Cheltenham winner's enclosure after her sixth victory and with Ruby Walsh and Willie Mullins

the two festivals. As well as her annual domination of the Mares' Hurdle, she completed a four-timer in the World Series Hurdle – a significant feat in itself because the Punchestown race carried Grade 1 status, whereas the Mares' Hurdle was only Grade 2, and these wins on home soil came not only at the highest level but against male opposition.

Cheltenham, though, was where she made her name and made history. For years Quevega and Big Buck's raced alongside each other as multiple winners at the festival but when the four-time World Hurdle hero suffered a serious tendon injury himself at the end of 2012 and found age had caught up with him on his return, Mullins' marvellous mare spurted ahead.

Some had wanted Quevega to take on Big Buck's in his prime – rather than stick to the much easier task of the Mares' Hurdle – but she was not quite in that class. Her best Racing Post Rating was 162 and this year there was even a better mare in her own stable – Annie Power, who did go for the World Hurdle and recorded an RPR of 164 in finishing second to More Of That.

Yet that in no way detracts from the scale of Quevega's achievement in the Mares' Hurdle. Nothing could stop her, not even at the age of ten when she went for outright ownership of the Cheltenham Festival record ahead of Golden Miller. As had become the custom, she was odds-on for the 2014 Mares' Hurdle as she lined up against 15 younger rivals – some only half her age, including second favourite Cockney Sparrow. But this would not be the procession of her younger days; to make history all of her own she would have to fight all the way.

Coming off the home turn, Quevega was a close third but Walsh was sending out urgent signals for her to keep tabs on stablemate Glens Melody, who was travelling well in front. The position worsened on the run to the final flight as Glens Melody kicked again and L'Unique loomed up on the inside, with Walsh pushing hard on Quevega.

Glens Melody jumped the last a length in front and for 100 yards, as Quevega struggled and L'Unique

faded, it seemed as if this was the end of an era. But this was the hill Quevega and Walsh had climbed so many times together and it was not going to beat them now. Glens Melody's one-length lead became three-quarters of a length, half a length, a neck and then, to a great roar, Quevega was in front.

Before the line Walsh was rising tall in the saddle, confident victory was in the bag once more. Number six had not been easy, three-quarters of a length the margin over the gallant Glens Melody, but it was mission accomplished. Mullins, fresh from the disappointment of Hurricane Fly losing his crown in the Champion Hurdle three-quarters of an hour earlier, was ecstatic.

"I'm delighted for Glens Melody and connections," he said, "but I would never have been as disappointed at having a winner at Cheltenham if she had beaten Quevega. It was fantastic the way she turned it around over the last 200 yards. She put down her head and is so brave – she keeps pulling it out. She is never beaten. It's way up there with all of my festival winners.

"She's just something else. She's got stamina, speed and everything. I'm so pleased for her and she has her own place in history now."

Sadly, the ending at Punchestown was not so glorious. In her attempt to add the World Series Hurdle to Cheltenham success for the fifth year in a row, Quevega lost – yes, lost –

by a length and a quarter to Jetson, Jezki's full-brother. That stopped her winning run at nine, a sequence that stretched back almost five full years, and Mullins quickly announced she would stop entirely.

The trainer was close to tears in the unsaddling enclosure at Punchestown. "She has nothing more to prove," he said. "She has been a fantastic servant and a history maker. We'll always be trying to buy one like her but we'll find it very hard to replace her."

Perhaps, one day, Quevega herself will help to produce one in her own image. Unlike the male jumps stars who have no opportunity to pass on their genes of greatness, Quevega has gone on to another career in the breeding paddocks and she has been covered by Beat Hollow, whose jumps progeny include 2012 Supreme Novices' Hurdle winner Cinders And Ashes.

The Quevega family line could endure on the racing scene for years, even decades, and her offspring will help to prompt reminiscence of a special jumps mare. Ah yes, we'll say to the next generation, those were the days.

SIX HITTER
QUEVEGA IN NUMBERS

6 Wins in the Mares' Hurdle (2009-14)

4 Wins in the World Series Hurdle (2010-13)

£749,280 Career earnings

4 Grade 1 victories

13 Wins in 16 races in Britain and Ireland

162 Highest Racing Post Rating, recorded in the 2013 World Series Hurdle

LUCKY LION • a BBAG graduate

1. Großer Dallmayr-Preis, Gr. 1
1. German 2.000 Guineas, Gr. 2
2. German Derby, Gr. 1

FEODORA • a BBAG graduate

1. German Oaks - Gr.1

SIRIUS • a BBAG graduate

1. Großer Preis von Berlin, Gr. 1

Sales dates 2015

Spring Breeze Up Sale: 5th June

Yearling Sales: 3rd and 4th September

October Mixed Sales: 16th and 17th October

 www.bbag-sales.de

BIG
ACHIEVER

Age and his rivals finally caught up with Big Buck's but he left a rich legacy as he headed into retirement

By Lee Mottershead

PAUL NICHOLLS considered Big Buck's to be slightly mad. Andy Stewart was at one point left thinking Nicholls was rather bonkers due to his plans for the horse. Yet both trainer and owner were agreed that Big Buck's was completely magnificent. On the day he paraded around the Cheltenham winner's enclosure for the final time, the feeling seemed to be unanimous.

We had, of course, been hoping to see him parade around that winner's enclosure as the winner. It was what we had become used to, not only at Cheltenham but also at Aintree, Ascot and Newbury. Big Buck's had long since become a winning machine but in the December of 2012 the machine became broken and thereafter nothing was ever again the same.

He came back from the tendon injury to race twice more but he was older and slower. Suddenly, in a most unusual turn of events when it came to the greatest long-distance hurdler of all time, others were faster and better. Crucially they were also younger. Time's winged chariot had finally caught up, but what fun we all had while it, and all those unfortunate enough to be rivals of Big Buck's, gave forlorn chase.

Ah yes. Chase. A crucial word in the Big Buck's story, although one could equally apply the synonym 'fence'. Try as they might, Nicholls, Ruby Walsh and the members of Team Ditcheat had been unable to turn their French recruit into a chaser. At the final fence of the 2008 Hennessy Gold Cup, Sam Thomas had the same problem. Having ended the previous season by winning Aintree's Mildmay Novices' Chase, the then Cheltenham Gold Cup aspirant was expected by many, not least his trainer, to start the new season by landing Newbury's signature jumps prize. Had Walsh been aboard, Nicholls believes the then five-year-old would have won, but Walsh was injured, Thomas was his deputy and at the Hennessy's final fence the deputy, when his mount was a dangerous third, fell off. Thomas, under

▶▶ *Continues page 104*

huge pressure at the time, walked away in tears. Nicholls walked away in fury.

It is a story that has been told so often, but it is a story so crucial to what came thereafter. Nicholls decided Big Buck's needed Walsh but Walsh was needed for Kauto Star or Denman, depending on the venue and the day. Even with Walsh on his back, the dual Auteuil winner had never impressed as a natural chaser. The solution, therefore, was to switch the French-bred son of Cadoudal to hurdles. It was at this point, when told of the trainer's plan, that Stewart decided Nicholls was bonkers. He did, though, go along with the plan. Bonkers has never been so brilliant.

What followed was the most remarkable career ever accomplished by a staying hurdler. There would be 20 more runs, all of them over hurdles. He won the first 18, with Walsh in the saddle for all but two of them. The first came in a New Year's Day Cheltenham handicap, secured off a mark of 151. After that it was an upgrade to the Cleeve Hurdle, in which Nicholls had forecast success in his Racing Post Saturday column. By this point he had already backed Big Buck's to win the World Hurdle at 20-1. The bet was landed, although by raceday Big Buck's was just 6-1, with France's 10-11 favourite Kasbah Bliss a well-beaten fourth.

Odds-on favouritism then became the norm for the horse christened Bucky Boo by devoted groom Rose Loxton. In the rest of his winning run, with that familiar sheepskin noseband on his head, he was never sent off bigger than 5-6 and for one success, the final success as it transpired, the bookmakers returned him at 1-12.

You could understand the layers' caution. With Big Buck's – Bucky Boo seems to diminish some of his deserved gravitas – it was all rather predictable. You knew he would win and you knew he would do so readily, while probably having hit one of his trademark flat spots. For a few strides he would seemingly lose concentration and come under a shove from Walsh. At least that's how it looked. Nicholls suggested Walsh was telling a visual lie in order to give opposing jockeys a misleading impression. Walsh himself said he purposely allowed the horse to find one of the flat spots to help

ensure he did not hit the front too soon. That so, perhaps Big Buck's was more straightforward than we thought.

Or perhaps he was not. The reason Nicholls described him as mad was not because of what he did on the racecourse but at home. Big Buck's was not so much a box walker as a box galloper. His master eventually gave in to the inevitable and, after discovering the spinning stayer had worn away an inch of his stable floor, laid down a lovely rubber surface. Big Buck's nevertheless continued to go round and round and round, so much so that when in a racecourse stable Loxton had to keep a hold of him all the time.

Not that any of it was the poor animal's fault. He had been relatively normal back in France but that was because he lived with a goat. During the journey to Britain customs confiscated the goat. Stewart bought Big Buck's a new goat but Big Buck's wanted his old goat and snarled at the imposter. After that a rubber floor turned out to be a better solution.

FINAL SCORE
BIG BUCK'S IN NUMBERS

4 Wins in the World Hurdle (2009, 2010, 2011, 2012)

£1,309,055 Career earnings

10 Grade 1 victories

18 Straight wins between January 2009 and December 2012

1-12 Shortest starting price, when winning the 2012 Long Distance Hurdle at Newbury

178 Highest Racing Post Rating, recorded in the 2011 Liverpool Hurdle at Aintree

160 Racing Post Rating in his last two races, when he was defeated in the 2014 Cleeve Hurdle and World Hurdle

6 Jockeys who rode him in Britain (Ruby Walsh, Sam Thomas, Tony McCoy, Sam Twiston-Davies, Nick Scholfield and Liam Heard)

5 British racecourses he raced at (Aintree, Ascot, Cheltenham, Newbury and Warwick)

▸▸ A life less ordinary: (clockwise from left) Big Buck's with Paul Nicholls at Manor Farm Stables; a birthday treat from Nicholls' head lad Clifford Baker; after his comeback run in the Cleeve Hurdle at Cheltenham in January, when his 18-race winning streak came to an end

Many of those who sought to embarrass Big Buck's were made to look like goats. New pretenders to his crown came along season after season but the likes of Punchestowns, Grands Crus and Dynaste were all put in their place. It was at Aintree, where he won four Liverpool Hurdles, that he arguably produced his most dominant displays, but when winning six times at Newbury (two Long Walk Hurdles and four Long Distance Hurdles) he was also superb, as he was when landing a third Long Walk at its usual Ascot base. But it is Cheltenham with which he will be

▸▸ *Continues page 106*

One of Danzig's Best Sons

Exchange Rate is the sire of more Grade 1 Winners, Stakes Winners, and Winners in 2014 than Danzig's son War Front.

Sire of 11 Stakes Winners in 2014.
Sire of 11 Stakes Winners in 2013.

Exchange Rate

trade up

THREE CHIMNEYS
859.873.7053 | www.threechimneys.com
@three_chimneys

EGR, LLC 2014 | Statistics through October 14, 2014

forever associated, for it was there he achieved his most memorable feat when doing something no horse had ever done in the World Hurdle, or the Stayers' Hurdle that preceded it, by triumphing on four occasions.

Four might well have become five had fate not intervened. Less than three weeks after cruising to his 18th win on the bounce Big Buck's was found to have a tiny tear in a tendon. Immediately he was ruled out for the rest of the 2012-13 campaign. That meant another horse, Solwhit, won the World Hurdle, which seemed a bit odd. By this stage Big Buck's had proved himself to be the best there had ever been in his division, which has enjoyed a golden age in the new millennium. Baracouda never surpassed a Racing Post Rating of 176, Inglis Drever, a three-time World Hurdle hero, reached 174, but Big Buck's got to 178. That falls some way short of the marks hit by stable companions Kauto Star, Denman and Master Minded, with whom Nicholls insisted the hurdler was equal. The problem Big Buck's faced was there was not much more he could do against contemporaries who were by some margin inferior.

Sadly, when the now 11-year-old Big Buck's emerged from injury in January 2014 there were more juniors than contemporaries and the leading lights among them were not inferior. Walsh had decided to make Willie Mullins his main man, which meant he was unavailable when Big Buck's returned in the Cleeve Hurdle and then went on to the World Hurdle. With future stable jockey Sam Twiston-Davies preferred for the hallowed seat over then current stable jockey Daryl Jacob, Big Buck's gave encouragement for the festival by finishing third in the Cleeve. On the figures he then ran exactly the same race in the World Hurdle. It was not enough. He finished fifth, the contest won by More Of That, which is what we had wanted from Big Buck's. The truth is we had already been spoiled.

Nicholls and Stewart had previously decided that whatever happened in the race, win or lose, it would be their champion's last. When reporters approached Nicholls in the winner's enclosure, where his Zarkandar had headed after finishing fourth, he seemed desperate to impart the retirement news. He was not a sad man, a disappointed man or a dejected man. He was a proud

▶▶ Final act: Big Buck's, with Sam Twiston-Davies in the saddle, goes to post for the last time in the World Hurdle at Cheltenham in March

man, relieved as well that a loyal and trusted ally had bowed out in one piece. News of the retirement spread even before it had been announced and, once the winner and placed horses had enjoyed their applause, a louder, longer and more loving reception was given to Big Buck's. It was no more than he deserved.

He went back to Ditcheat and a few months later on to Dorset and a new life with Lucy Tucker. She gave him a fresh nickname, Bert, and for a reason only Bert knows, he never once walked his box. Whereas once he hurtled incessantly like a mad man around his home, here he stayed still. By now he surely knew his running days were over.

'A PHENOMENAL JOURNEY'
WHAT THEY SAID ABOUT BIG BUCK'S

Big Buck's has been an amazing horse and I'm very lucky and honoured to have trained him, just like Kauto Star, Denman, Master Minded and Neptune Collonges. I've always said they were the horses of a lifetime *Paul Nicholls, trainer*

When I was riding him I always knew there was loads in the tank. He had some ability and was a great horse, right up there with the best horses I've ridden. His record was outstanding *Ruby Walsh, jockey*

It's been a phenomenal journey, with the highlight his fourth World Hurdle win. People love him. Last year he got nearly 200 Christmas cards. Forget the prize-money, he has given so much enjoyment *Andy Stewart, owner*

My favourite moment was winning the fourth World Hurdle, because of what it meant. Others had won three but winning four meant Big Buck's was the best of all. That's the race we wanted him to win more than any other *Clifford Baker, head lad*

Head and shoulders above the opposition in more ways than one. His 2014 efforts aside, Big Buck's has set the standard for future World Hurdle winners to aim at, but we won't see one like him again for years. A credit to all connected with him *Racing Post reader Mark Kelly*

When I first got to look after him I was told he was high maintenance but he has always been nice, kind and polite – a very friendly horse. You prepare yourself for the day he will get beaten and I was sad when it happened. I was more upset than I thought I'd be *Rose Loxton, assistant head girl (right)*

THE
BIGGER
PICTURE

Seamster (green) makes the early running in the opening event of Laytown's famous beach races, first held in 1868. The Richard Ford-trained Seamster, the 3-1 favourite, went on to win the six-furlong race by a length and three-quarters under Colin Keane

MICHAEL STEELE/GETTY IMAGES

Like father, like son

By Lee Mottershead

Classic success at the first attempt set the tone for a seamless transition as one Richard Hannon took over from another at Britain's biggest Flat stable

NOTHING really changed, not even the name on the licence. For more than four decades it had been Richard Hannon in charge and it continued to be Richard Hannon in charge. Masses of horses continued to be trained, masses of winners continued to be sent out and masses of fun continued to be had by all those associated with an operation that enjoyed Classic success in 2013 and did so again in 2014.

It might be unfair to describe Night Of Thunder as the new Richard Hannon's first Classic winner, because Sky Lantern was in many ways not really the old Richard Hannon's last Classic winner. The dashing grey filly was very much under the control of the younger Hannon throughout her 1,000 Guineas-winning preparation, so much so that the elder Hannon had stayed away from Newmarket on the afternoon of her coronation. He did so again 12 months later on the first Saturday in May, overseeing business down at the afternoon's second meeting, Goodwood, just as any decent assistant should.

His son had been a very decent assistant himself, a trainer in waiting, for what seemed like an awfully long time. He had been working under, and then alongside, his father from pretty much the moment he left university. The long-time boss had been in charge since taking over from his own father, Harry, with just 12

horses in 1970. Over the years that followed there were some difficult times and some enormous financial risks but many more rewarding, triumphant days at the races, with the last of five championships coming in what turned out to be his final year at the helm. On November 21, 2013, coincidentally his heir's 38th birthday, Hannon let slip, with a little gentle encouragement from the Racing Post, what he described as the "worst-kept secret in racing". The baton was to be passed on January 1.

"He'll be an enormous act – maybe an impossible act – to follow," was the son's reaction at the time. Now, looking back on a succession

completed peacefully and without any sense of revolution, he says: "We had spoken about it for a couple of years beforehand but he had been enjoying training more than ever and he was being more successful than ever. When I was 29 and 30 I was itching to get on with it and very keen to take over, but then as I got older I realised it was better with two than one. Dad wasn't in a massive rush to retire and I wasn't really in a rush, either, but last year we had some nice young horses and he had a few health issues, so it seemed the logical time to do it. He hasn't really retired, though. There is room for both of us and there always will be."

Fortunately, across the glorious, sweeping greenery of Herridge, the Hannons' main base in Wiltshire, there is plenty of space for both of them as well. On New Year's Day they stood together on some of the best morning turf in Britain – "I arrived on the gallops, saw him and asked him what he was doing there," the son recalls. By this point it had been decided Richard Hannon jnr would become Richard Hannon, while his father became known as Richard Hannon snr. In a very generous late Christmas present, the son was bestowed with around 250 horses, making his first-season string the biggest in Britain. Among its

LIGHT AND SHADE

Kieren Fallon was centre stage with Night Of Thunder in the 2,000 Guineas but then his star waned again

It was a strange race in what was a strange season for the man who rode the winner. The 2,000 Guineas of 2014 will be remembered as much for the men who trained and steered Night Of Thunder as much as for Night Of Thunder himself. Try as you might, it is hard to rate the 40-1 outsider as a vintage winner of Britain's first Classic. Indeed, as the season progressed it was evident the horses he beat into second and third were clearly superior animals. As talented a horse as he undoubtedly is, Night Of Thunder's star waned in the immediate aftermath of his Newmarket triumph. The same was sadly true for Kieren Fallon (below, with Night Of Thunder after the Guineas).

This was the year in which Fallon came in from the cold, enjoyed a spell in the sun and then found things getting a little chilly once again. After a torrid 2013 in which only 62 winners were ridden he spent the winter months in Dubai, hoping to reignite his career. Fallon subsequently said he expected to retire after riding Saeed Bin Suroor's Prince Bishop in the second round of the Maktoum Challenge but he won the race and thereafter kept winning more races for the trainer – so many, in fact, that in the British spring he took over from Silvestre de Sousa as Bin Suroor's unofficial number one.

The announcement came on 1,000 Guineas day, 24 hours after Night Of Thunder veered across the Rowley Mile close home but still managed to overhaul the subsequently unbeatable Kingman. Australia, who raced on the other side of the track and finished third, later confirmed he was not unbeatable but he did win the Derby and Irish Derby on his next two starts. The Guineas form was not bad at all.

The race was not, however, won by the best horse who ran in it. No matter. This was a first Classic victory for Richard Hannon, whose stable jockey Richard Hughes understandably chose Toormore (who finished seventh) despite having a soft spot for Night Of Thunder. It was also a first British Classic in eight years for Fallon but, although he continued to ride for Bin Suroor, the Godolphin opportunities came along much less frequently.

Towards the end of the year Fallon was looking to the United States for salvation. "I've always wanted to go there and kind of stay there but there was always something here for me to come back to. Now there doesn't seem to be a lot to come back to."

At 49 Fallon became a Classic winner once again. He showed it is never too late but, as a 50-year-old, there might need to be another comeback.

band were Group 1-winning milers Toronado, Olympic Glory and Sky Lantern, the 2013 champion two-year-old Toormore, a clutch of other potential Guineas candidates and a vast squad of two-year-olds, quite a few of whom would turn out to be very good indeed. But before he could race any of them, Hannon, who also had no less than the Queen as one of his owners, first had to go to Wolverhampton.

It was a winning trip. Unscripted, who probably was not, stormed to a ten-length victory: winner number one was on the board. That was just the first of many. By the time May started the new licence-holder

already had 25 winners. Two of those strikes had been achieved in trials for the 2,000 Guineas, with Toormore collecting the Craven Stakes in workmanlike fashion and Shifting Power coming out on top in a blanket finish to the European Free Handicap. Also in the mix was Night Of Thunder, who had been run over by Kingman in the Greenham Stakes but was still described as "very good" on a sun-kissed April morning when all three Newmarket-bound colts worked in front of members of the press. Hannon would have many more press mornings as the year went on but this was the first and his

▸▸ *Continues page 112*

father felt he needed to offer some guidance.

"He sent me off to change my trousers," explained an embarrassed Hannon. "I'm nearly 40 years old and he sent me off to change. I told him we had the press coming over and he told me my trousers were too smart. He said to me: 'Where are you going? You look like you're off to bloody London.' I asked him if he had nothing else to worry about apart from what I was wearing. As I walked off I said to him: 'No, you haven't!'"

Hannon then sought the advice of his always reliable mother, Jo, who confirmed to him that his preferred trousers were indeed too smart. Hannon then changed his trousers.

Not that Hannon followed his parents' established way all the time. Far from it. A trip to Herridge now is very different to a trip to Herridge in the not so distant past. Towards the end of his father's reign the then assistant oversaw the building of a stunning new office complex. On its top floor is a large room with sofas, comfortable chairs, trophies, a kitchen and balcony that overlooks the trotting ring in which horses limber up before facing the gallops. Next door is the office itself, where the main wall has five huge electronic screens that list in alphabetical order every member of

the stable with accompanying details that include a horse's owner, age and official rating. It is like a scene from Heathrow airport's Terminal 5.

"We needed somewhere nice we could take the owners," says Hannon. "My parents were retiring, so we didn't want to be sitting in the house they live in here all the time. We've got a new office, new facilities and we're expanding one of the gallops to make it a little bit longer. We've also got the screens now. The guy who owns Ivawood had his company put them in and people love them. I just felt we needed to be well organised and slick."

Ivawood, a stunningly fast two-year-old colt, would prove to be one of the stars of the season, as would Tiggy Wiggy, a stunningly fast two-year-old filly. They made significant contributions to a prize-money haul that enabled Hannon to outpace championship rival John Gosden and take the title in his first year. So, too, did Night Of Thunder, who proved Hannon right in thinking him very good by reversing the Kingman Newbury form with a 40-1 victory in the Guineas.

"Winning the Guineas made it a lovely start," says the now Classic-winning trainer, who then went on to enjoy a successful Royal Ascot, landing the Queen Anne Stakes with Sheikh Joaan's Toronado (whose Al

▶ Success story: (clockwise from top left) Richard Hannon with Ivawood after winning the Richmond Stakes at Glorious Goodwood; exciting two-year-old filly Tiggy Wiggy lands the National Stakes at Sandown; Toronado wins the Queen Anne Stakes at Royal Ascot

Shaqab-owned stable companion Olympic Glory had earlier won the Lockinge Stakes and later won the Prix de la Foret) and the Norfolk Stakes with the same team's Baitha Alga.

Over the months that followed the big wins kept coming, at home, in Ireland, France and even Turkey, where Pether's Moon picked up an impressive £150,000 for taking the Bosphorus Cup under champion jockey Richard Hughes, whose continued presence on the yard's horses was another feature of the seamless transition.

And it truly was seamless. This was a magnificent first season and with a tremendous team of two-year-olds set to become exciting three-year-olds there is the inevitable expectation of a magnificent second season as well.

"I've thoroughly enjoyed it," Hannon says. "Yes, it has been

stressful at times but I'm a very lucky boy. We've won some massive races and, although there have been some disappointments, that's life. It won't do me any harm as a person to go through the odd setback. Overall we're going from strength to strength. The more success you have, the more you want it. You need to be young, energetic and ultra-ambitious in this business. You need to be more than just enthusiastic."

Although no longer young, Hannon snr, 69, is certainly enthusiastic and certainly still part of the team. "Dad takes things easier these days but he is enjoying what we're doing as much as anyone," Hannon says. "He now likes to come to my house for breakfast. He enjoys being able to leave behind a mess and not be told by Mum to clean it up. He heads up to the office at about 11am and if we've got owners here he often looks after them while I go to the races. There is room for both of us. We couldn't run a business like this on our own. There needs to be two of us."

The two of them are doing extremely well. There has been a Richard Hannon in the top division of British racing for many decades. That remains the case. As the old year turned into the new, all that really happened was we lost a junior and gained a senior.

IN THE
PICTURE

Warwick stages final Flat meeting after management opt to go jumps-only

More than 300 years of Flat racing came to an end at Warwick on August bank holiday Monday after Jockey Club Racecourses (JCR) decided it was viable only as a jumps venue.

Speculation had been rife for two years that the course, leased by the local council to JCR, was destined to lose Flat racing and concern grew when the meeting on May 20 had to be abandoned after two races following the fatal fall of Artful Lady on the dogleg bend at the merger of the sprint and round courses.

The last two Flat meetings at Warwick, on July 4 and August 25, were restricted to sprint races but JCR decided remedial work on the bend would not help the viability of the track, which struggled commercially as a dual-code venue.

Ian Renton, JCR's regional director for Warwick, said: "It's not a decision we've taken lightly but I feel we have left no stone unturned. Warwick can now benefit from a clear identity and significant investment as a top-quality small jumps course."

Warwick followed tracks such as Worcester in 1966 and Aintree in 1976 in dropping Flat racing to become an all-jumps course. The news meant the loss of another turf Flat track following the conversion of Kempton, Southwell and Wolverhampton to all-weather, with Newcastle hoping to follow suit, and the closure of Folkestone in 2012.

JCR said trainers had been consulted over Warwick's future, but still many were upset at the closure. "It's another to knock off the list and I'm very disappointed," said Clive Cox, while William Muir, who had a winner on the final Flat card with Caffeine, commented: "I thought I'd be long dead before they closed Warwick. The bend can get slippery, but then so can the bends at Bath and Goodwood. Are they going to close them for the same reason?"

Tony Carroll, who trains 20 minutes away, was another to have a final-day winner with Serenity Spa (fourth left, blue) and he could not understand the reasons for the closure. "It's a good course for Flat racing," he said. "The facilities are nice and they've built a new stable block."

Warwick, which was the first course to stage jump racing in Britain in 1831, will hold 17 such fixtures in 2015. JCR said it would invest "several million pounds" in Warwick in the coming years, through reservoir expansion, enhanced irrigation systems and prize-money. The Flat course will be used to provide an extra facility for spring or autumn jump racing, in addition to the existing winter track.

Picture: EDWARD WHITAKER (RACINGPOST.COM/PHOTOS)

Final flourish

By Nicholas Godfrey

After a career that varied between brilliance and bad luck, The Fugue had one more burst of glory at Royal Ascot before heading into retirement

SELDOM can a racehorse have been as subject to the caprices of Dame Fortune as The Fugue. Hugely talented, immensely popular and blessed with a lightning turn of foot, this estimable mare rarely finished out of the first three in a long career in which she habitually competed at the sport's apex.

No fewer than 14 of her 17 career starts came at Group or Grade 1 level – yet while she won four of them, The Fugue ran into so much trouble over the years that her connections were often left ruing what might have been. "There have been few top-class fillies on whom the gods have frowned with such random frequency as The Fugue," suggested Alastair Down in the Racing Post, and it was hard to quibble.

Although the daughter of Dansili completed 2013 with three Group 1 successes on her CV, that campaign ended in total frustration after a couple of notorious near-misses in America and Hong Kong. Such was the agonising nature of these reverses that her connections must have been tempted to throw in the towel and send the beautifully bred filly to the paddocks at

▸▸ Continues page 118

Watership Down Stud, the famous Berkshire establishment run by her owner-breeders Lord and Lady Lloyd-Webber (the emphasis very much on the 'Lady', by the way, as Andrew Lloyd Webber has no pretensions to equine expertise and it is his wife Madeleine, a former three-day-event rider, who is the driving force of the racing and breeding operation).

It wasn't to be, though, as The Fugue had a spot of unfinished business. The star mare was duly kept in training as a five-year-old in 2014, when her connections were to be rewarded with a breathtaking performance as she downed the exalted Arc winner Treve at Royal Ascot, breaking the track record in the Prince of Wales's Stakes. For trainer John Gosden it was the highlight of a memorable season; for the mare, it was the defining effort of a long career during which she raced in five different countries. Apart from a troubled run a couple of weeks later in the Eclipse, it was also to be her swansong.

NO appreciation of The Fugue's season can start without a bit of context. While she had three brilliant Group 1 victories to her name by the end of 2013 – the Nassau at three, the Yorkshire Oaks and Irish Champion at four – she plainly had more than her fair share of narrow defeats. Usually this was entirely down to her preferred style of running, which often left regular jockey William Buick a hostage to fortune: in order to utilise her tremendous powers of acceleration, The Fugue had to be held up, which often resulted in a less than straightforward assignment for the man on top.

What is more, she also needed fast ground and a fast pace to make the most of her fast finish. Granted those, mind you, and her turn of foot was the most potent weapon. "When she gets a clear, uncomplicated run and the others come back to her she is lethal," Buick said.

He knew better than most how tricky it could be to harness that huge talent. As a three-year-old The Fugue was a beaten favourite in the Oaks, going down by less than a length in a Classic she would surely have won but for being severely hampered before charging down the outside. She was beaten by a vastly inferior filly, Was, in the kind of luckless defeat that was to be repeated more than once.

Witness, for example, the following year at the Breeders' Cup, where The Fugue was stuck on the inner off a steady pace in the Filly & Mare Turf and never found room to challenge behind Zagora until it was far too late. That she was the best filly in the race offered cold comfort. Defeat was not her rider's fault, incidentally; the race simply was not run to suit.

Then, after a glorious late summer marked by a couple of Group 1 victories, she ended 2013 with another pair of crushing disappointments, chinned by less than a length in both the Breeders' Cup Turf and the Hong Kong Vase. In America, Buick was left in tears after she kicked on earlier than usual only to get run down by Magician; reverting to type, The Fugue met trouble at Sha Tin and went down to local star Dominant in yet another race she might have won with a clear passage. One could not help but feel for Buick: damned if he did, damned if he didn't, it seemed.

Kept in training, The Fugue's five-year-old campaign also started in far from auspicious fashion when she was struck into when well fancied for the Dubai Duty Free. Despite

the obvious excuse, Royal Ascot, where she had been beaten twice before, must have looked a long way off when she could finish only 11th of 13 behind impressive Japanese winner Just A Way.

Indeed, the Prince of Wales's Stakes wasn't on the agenda at all until The Fugue dazzled in a gallop a week before, convincing Gosden she was ready to take on a field of the highest calibre featuring Treve, soon-to-be Eclipse winner Mukhadram, her old nemesis Magician and Dank, both of whom had been victorious at the Breeders' Cup. Such was the strength of the opposition that The Fugue was sent off an 11-2 shot

– only once had she been a bigger price since she was fourth over an inadequate trip in the 1,000 Guineas more than two years previously.

Be that as it may, everything else was left trailing in the wake of The Fugue, who produced an utterly authoritative performance. For once, it all seemed so simple: The Fugue picked up the leaders in the straight and quickened away to score by a length and three-quarters from Magician, with a troubled Treve never able to land a glove on her in third.

Connections had every reason to feel a few wrongs had been righted as The Fugue indisputably confirmed her place among the elite with an emphatic and richly deserved triumph. "She's been an absolute star for me and everybody back at the yard," Buick said. "She proved today what she can do against top-class horses. It means everything to everyone involved."

The Lloyd-Webbers were cock-a-hoop – though the female side of the partnership admitted she hadn't really wanted her husband present. "Andrew has never seen her win before," she said. "He's the kiss of death – I hoped he'd have a cold today and not come!

"It's the best day of our lives and this is absolutely what she deserves,"

she added. "She has finally done it on the biggest stage. It's all very well going around the world trying to pick up these prizes but the stages are not as big as Royal Ascot. Whatever anyone likes to say, the Hong Kong Vase is not the same as Royal Ascot."

Personal jinx dismissed, Lord Lloyd-Webber expressed similar delight. "We are completely thrilled," he said. "She has proved she is the best in the world. We've always thought she was but she has had awful luck."

Such an exhilarating victory provided the highlight of a glorious Royal Ascot for Gosden, who also scored with Kingman (St James's Palace), Richard Pankhurst (Chesham) and Eagle Top (King Edward VII). "We trained her in the winter and she was like a little bud that went tight, but now she's flowered and she looks great. Her last piece of work left her spot on, cherry ripe," explained the trainer.

"I think Treve is unbeatable over a mile and a half with cut in the ground in the autumn. We wouldn't go near her then, but I thought we had half a chance meeting her on good to firm ground over a mile and a quarter in midsummer. I felt we might just do her for that little bit of toe.

"I walked down before the race

with the Princess Royal. I said to her: 'Look at this race. It's all girl power.' It was as well. The Fugue is a magnificent filly and we are lucky to have her."

Gosden was soon mulling over the Eclipse less than three weeks later. "It comes up quite soon but she didn't have the hardest race," he said. "William was under strict instructions he could flick her but no more than that because she is a filly who will give you her all without being asked."

IN the event, The Fugue did turn out again at Sandown, where a late shower hardly helped her cause and she could finish only sixth of nine to her Ascot victim Mukhadram, recording his first Group 1 success under a brainy tactical ride from Paul Hanagan.

The Fugue had also flopped in the previous year's Eclipse and while connections initially blamed the ground – "loose on top," said Gosden – a more obvious explanation was soon to emerge. The Fugue had suffered a knock at Sandown, sustaining a leg injury: she was retired to Watership Down amid glowing tributes from her adoring connections.

"The Fugue has been a pleasure

▶▶ Crowning glory: (from left) The Fugue produces the performance of her life to win the Prince of Wales's Stakes under William Buick; trainer John Gosden congratulates Buick; Lady Lloyd-Webber savours the moment in the Royal Ascot winner's enclosure

'It's the best day of our lives and this is absolutely what she deserves. She has finally done it on the biggest stage'

to train and to be around for all of us here and never ceased to amaze us with her courage and athletic ability," Gosden said. "She had such extraordinary acceleration off a strong pace and she's been at the top level for a long time. We were thankful for all the good days – she ran a wonderful race on her favourite ground to break the track record at Ascot, which was the highlight of our year."

Lady Lloyd-Webber added: "It's impossible to describe how much fun The Fugue has given us over the last two and a half years. She's taken us to 14 Group 1s all around the world, culminating in the highlight of her career when she beat the track record in the Prince of Wales's Stakes at Royal Ascot. We feel incredibly privileged and lucky to have bred and owned such a magnificent filly and we look forward to her coming home to the stud for her second career."

Having scored on her debut as a two-year-old at Newmarket in October 2011, The Fugue finished her career with a record of six wins and seven places from 17 starts. For a while, it looked as if she was destined to be remembered more for her defeats than her victories; after Royal Ascot, there was little danger of that.

THE
BIGGER
PICTURE

The field in the 2m5½f maiden hurdle won by
the Neil Mulholland-trained Carole's Destrier
jump the final flight on the first circuit at
Huntingdon in January
**EDWARD WHITAKER
(RACINGPOST.COM/PHOTOS)**

Richard Newland's 12-horse stable hit the jackpot at Aintree with Pineau De Re and he celebrated in style with family and friends. Now the trainer is dreaming of a Grand National repeat next April

PARTY TIME

By Nick Pulford

THE call came about 11.30am on the day of the Crabbie's Grand National. It was the call that could have changed everything. At the time Richard Newland was just arriving at Aintree, looking forward to his first National runner and doubly excited because he thought Pineau De Re would run a big race. For a few minutes after he answered the phone, all his hopes and dreams hung in the balance.

On the other end of the line was Carolyn White, one of Newland's trusty band of five staff at his small Worcestershire stable. She had travelled up with Pineau De Re to Aintree that morning and the journey had gone smoothly, but now there was a problem. Newland recalls: "Carolyn said: 'Don't panic, but you need to come quick to the stables because they've failed him on his trot up.'"

Every National runner is trotted up in front of the on-course vets to make sure they are sound – part of the stringent procedure in place for the most high-profile race of the year – and without their approval Pineau De Re would not be allowed to run. "The first vet was all for having him withdrawn," Newland says. "Imagine that – the National had been the plan for a long time and we had 41 family and friends in our party who had come to watch the race. It was obviously a bit of a sweaty moment.

"One vet thought he was slightly lame, the second vet thought he was all right but wasn't sure, and the third vet said, 'Well, let's get Dr Newland to have a look.' So when I got there we all looked at him. He's an older horse and he'd just walked off the lorry, maybe he was slightly stiff, but there was nothing there at all. He trotted up and I said: 'He's fine, put him in his box.'" The vets agreed; disaster was averted.

Pineau De Re was a 25-1 shot and few among the audience of millions would have missed him if he had not lined up in the National. Who would have realised that a Grand National winner had been denied his place in history? Dr Richard Newland, that's who. Well, he could not have been sure, of course, but he would have felt a strong chance of National glory had been snatched away from him.

Newland, 50, may be a doctor who trains, but he is no ordinary doctor and no ordinary trainer. He set up Birmingham's first private GP service and has other medical businesses dealing with areas such as foot and ankle surgery and long-term care. One of his companies, CHS Healthcare, employs more than 200 people nationwide. While his responsibilities elsewhere make him a part-time trainer, he is

▸▸ Continues page 124

very much hands-on: he feeds the horses, organises the work and schooling schedule, harrows the gallop every morning, oversees almost all the important work days and spends his weekends, alongside wife Laura, mucking out and taking the horses in and out of the fields at their stables in Claines, near Worcester.

The good doctor is also highly successful in training. Burntoakboy gave him a Cheltenham Festival win in his first season, 2006-07, and his string – which numbers no more than 12 at any one time – habitually operates at a strike-rate of 20 per cent or more. If Newland fancied Pineau De Re – and he did – this was a challenger to take seriously.

"You can never allow yourself to believe you're definitely going to win but I thought we had a massive chance," Newland says. "I know it's a corny thing to say but if you'd asked me before the race whether I would swap my horse for anything else I'd have said no. So I did have expectation, I had thought through the possibility that we might win. I guess I'd have been horribly disappointed if he hadn't won."

Imagine, then, the depth of Newland's disappointment if Pineau De Re had not been allowed to run at all.

THIS was not the first time Pineau De Re had been close to missing out on the National. Newland, who specialises in reviving horses from other stables, had bought him the previous May and gone into partnership with John Provan, his oldest racing friend. They met when Newland's first GP placement after medical school took him to the Derbyshire village where Provan still lives and they started going to the Cheltenham Festival as part of a bigger group before switching their "boys' trips" to Aintree.

The pair had dreamed of one day owning a National runner and Pineau De Re, who would carry Provan's colours, was their opportunity. There was just one small problem: his handicap mark of 137 was almost certainly too low to get him into the race. Newland's intention was to win with him to push his handicap mark into the 140s and then ease off and prepare him for the National. It was easier said than done.

After more than six months of trying, events had conspired to such an extent that Pineau De Re had failed to win in eight runs for his new yard and his mark had dropped to 133. With the National weights due to be published in February,

time was fast running out and virtually the only option seemed to be the West Wales National at Ffos Las, which is prone to being run on bottomless ground or even abandoned. Neither scenario would help Pineau De Re.

Then came the stroke of luck that every National winner is supposed to need. Owing to a spate of abandoned meetings, an extra veterans' chase was scheduled at Exeter for January 14 and Newland spotted the opportunity. "I entered him quickly and I thought we had to have a go. It was two weeks sooner than I wanted to run him but he seemed fine. He hacked up, he won beautifully, and then we knew he was in the National."

When the National weights were published, Pineau De Re was 51st in the list off his new mark of 143. To all intents and purposes he had secured his place and on the big day he was number 29 in the field of 40, carrying a handy 10st 6lb.

IF IT seemed Pineau De Re was somewhat fortunate to have made the line-up, it was certainly true of jockey

▶▶ National joy: (clockwise from left) Pineau De Re jumps the last; jockey Leighton Aspell with his family; Richard Newland at the centre of celebrations; owner John Provan (centre) with Newland and Aspell at the presentation; the new village sign in Claines; Newland with staff members (from left) Carolyn White, Chris Ward, Charlie Hammond and Amanda Pettit; the morning after at the yard; (below) the Racing Post front page on April 6

Leighton Aspell, who had retired in the summer of 2007 before returning to the saddle after an absence of more than 18 months. Now 37, Aspell had got the ride on Pineau De Re only after Sam Twiston-Davies was called on to partner topweight Tidal Bay for Paul Nicholls. He had never ridden Pineau De Re in a race but had schooled him over National-type fences in Lambourn and picked up on Newland's excitement about their chances.

Aspell, a strong but thoughtful horseman, was perfect for Newland's race plan, which the trainer summarises in a few words: "Take a pull, take a pull, conserve, conserve, conserve." Expanding on his thinking, he says: "I was concerned about the four and a half miles. Even though you can't be too far away in the National, we had a clear view that he should just hunt round for the first circuit. Pineau has plenty of speed and the key is not to use up the petrol too early. If you can hang on to him and keep filling him up, he can inject that little bit of pace that burns the others off, and that's what he did."

Aspell had a few hairy moments, notably towards the end of the first

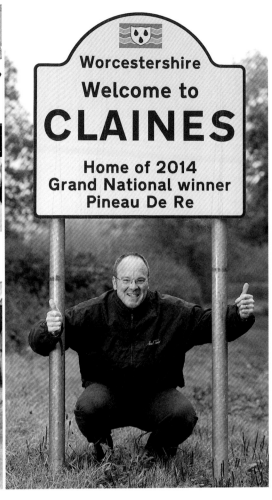

Worcestershire
Welcome to
CLAINES
Home of 2014
Grand National winner
Pineau De Re

circuit at the 13th when Pineau De Re was knocked sideways and the jockey lost one of his irons. "Tidal Bay had unseated at the Canal Turn and he made his way through the field and coming to the 13th he got upsides me," Aspell recalls. "Then he came across me just at the wrong time and we nearly parted company. Pineau De Re seemed a bit more nervous for a few fences after that. At the water he was sloppy and at the first fence on the second circuit he guessed a little bit. But from there on I was very happy with his jumping."

After all those boys' trips to Aintree, Newland thought he knew the National. Watching from the owners' and trainers' stand, in line with the winning post, Newland found it was a totally different experience with his first National runner.

"As the race went on it was becoming more random with horses falling and we were swerving around and I was thinking 'oh my God, this isn't like a normal race'," he says. "He made that mistake at the 13th and then he didn't jump the water very well. On the second circuit I started to relax but then Leighton went up the inside at Becher's.

'I had been watching through my binoculars but they got a bit shaky. I put them down and we all started screaming'

I was almost laughing, saying 'what's he doing that for?'"

The sense of hysteria was about to reach a whole new level, while out on the course Aspell was forcing himself to remain calm. "From Becher's second time I was in a close fifth and I could have taken up the running at any point," he says. "When we got to the Canal Turn I had a lot of horse underneath me. That was the most nervous part of the race. It really hit home that I had a real chance of winning. I was very conscious over the next line of five fences to make no mistakes and to follow the right horses."

Back in the stand, Newland was aware of mounting excitement around him as Pineau De Re threw down his challenge. Their party of 41 followers was scattered in various locations but his small group included the middle of his three daughters, Felicity, and one of her friends, as well as Provan and one of his daughters. "There was a great moment three out when me and John caught each other's eye – we both realised 'my God, we're running a big race here' and I looked at him and gave a little tap on my heart. I get very emotionally wound

up watching the horses and it's fair to say I got pretty excited.

"On the big screen they show the numbers of the leaders and number 29 came up and I had these hysterical girls around me shouting 'fourth . . . third . . .' I had been watching through my binoculars but they were getting a bit shaky and in the end I put them down and we all started screaming.

"After he jumped the last and he hit the Elbow, I turned away and started celebrating because I knew he wasn't going to lose it from there unless he did a Devon Loch. That's very unusual for me, I wouldn't normally do that."

Then Newland was off and running, down the steps from the stand and out to greet his winner. "Someone once said to me: 'When you have a good winner, lead that horse up, be with that horse.' That's why I ran out to see him. What I didn't realise was that they walk the winner back in front of the stands, so by the time I got to him I'd run about half a mile."

If Newland was tired, Aspell was exhausted. People wondered why he didn't celebrate more exuberantly but he

➤ *Continues page 126*

How the flying doctor took a tip from McCoy

▶Local hero: Pineau De Re outside The Mug House, where the celebrations of his victory went on long into the night
Picture: CHRISTOPHER HUGHES

In Grand National week Richard Newland listened to a radio programme reliving Tony McCoy's victory with Don't Push It in 2010 and was interested to hear that the champion jockey had to take a helicopter to the races the day after, having first fulfilled his duties at the traditional Sunday morning parade of the National winner.

That got Newland thinking about what would happen if Pineau De Re won the National. "We had three runners at Market Rasen the next day and I wanted to be there, but I was aware that if we won the National there would have to be an open morning at the stables for the media and then there wouldn't be enough time to drive to Market Rasen.

"This tells you something about what a good chance I thought we had because, after listening to that radio programme, I googled 'helicopter hire' and rang up to see how much it would cost to go from the stables to Market Rasen and how long it would take. Then I said, 'Well, this is a really unusual request. I'd like to book the helicopter but I only want it if my horse wins the Grand National.' At which point, instead of saying 'don't be ridiculous', he said, 'Certainly sir, what's the name of the horse?'

"I told him and then left it that I would ring him after the race. Well, after we'd won, I was so distracted by all the interviews that it got to about a quarter to six before I rang him back. I thought he'd have left the office by then but I managed to get hold of him and told him I definitely needed the helicopter. And he said, 'Yes, I know, we all backed it!'

"So we had this magical thing where we did the open morning and then a helicopter arrived and whisked us off to Market Rasen — me, John [Provan] and Rod [Trow, his assistant trainer]. We had a bottle of champagne on the way and it was fantastic. And I had two winners at Market Rasen."

was overwhelmed by his efforts – both physical and mental – and by the mayhem that had suddenly engulfed him. "I was elated but from the Canal Turn I really fancied my chances and I was concentrating very hard, so when I got past the line I was pretty tired," he says. "Then you get a wave of congratulations from all the other jockeys and the media are there, so you get very little time to take it all in."

NEWLAND'S party didn't hold back in the winner's enclosure and, for all the professionalism with which he approaches training, the unbridled joy of a small stable having a National winner was there for all to see. "My wife and all my daughters [Amelia, 22, Felicity, 20, and Annabelle, 17] were there. It's very unusual for all of us to be at the races at the same time. Felicity had been on holiday and we paid for a flight to bring her back early. It would have been a real shame on a personal level if one of them had missed out. John was the same, all his daughters were there."

It was the same for Aspell, whose wife Nicola had travelled all the way from West Sussex to Aintree by train with daughters Lucy, 6, Niamh, 4, and Kitty, 2. "The family usually only get the opportunity to go to the local meetings, like Fontwell, and it was great that they could make it," the jockey says. "It made it even more special. My parents were there and they were so proud."

Afterwards the Newland and Provan clans all made their way back to Worcestershire. The destination was The

Mug House, Newland's local and famous as one of only two pubs in Britain that stand on consecrated ground in a churchyard. The church bells had already been rung in honour of the new local hero by the time Newland arrived shortly after 9pm to be greeted by a multitude of well-wishers that had grown tenfold from their original party.

"The pub had 400 people – friends and family and quite a few locals. I stood up and made a little speech and then I paid for a free bar until two o'clock in the morning. It was magical, you've got to catch the moment, these things don't happen – ever."

Yet it had happened, and Newland is more than hopeful that it could be repeated. "There was a big story about Leighton Aspell and his comeback, quite a story about a small trainer winning the National, the doctor angle, but the bit that was missed out is how good Pineau De Re is. I think he's seriously good and that's why I'm pretty optimistic about him doing it again. The second and third [Balthazar King and Double Seven] were well handicapped and I thought Pineau beat them pretty easily.

"It wouldn't surprise me at all if he does it again next year. It's a hell of a challenge to take on, but it gives us something to dream about over the winter."

▶Flight of fancy: (from left to right) Rod Trow, Richard Newland and John Provan ready for takeoff

MADE IN BRITAIN

CHARLES OWEN

THE LEADER IN EQUESTRIAN SAFETY

www.charlesowen.co.uk

THE
BIGGER
PICTURE

Nina Carberry and Be Positive (second left) clear 'Ruby's Double' on their way to victory in the Kildare Hunt Club Fr Sean Breen Memorial Cross Country Chase on the first day of the Punchestown festival in April. Four days later, attempting a second festival win in the Irish Field Cross Country Chase, the pairing were beaten a neck into second place by Sizing Australia

ALAN CROWHURST/GETTY IMAGES

Quick change

Paul Nicholls says the trainers' title is not such a major motivation these days but his 2013-14 success was a sign that his stable is rising again after a period of upheaval

By Nick Pulford

MISSION IMPOSSIBLE? Not quite, but Paul Nicholls was pleasantly surprised at managing to wrest back the British jumps trainers' title from Nicky Henderson in another season of transition, albeit one that was highlighted by Silviniaco Conti's victory in the William Hill King George VI Chase.

"We'd lost a few of our older horses and Nicky had such a fearsome squad that it looked on paper near impossible at the start of the season for us to beat him again," says Nicholls, reflecting over the summer on a job well done in the 2013-14 campaign. "We were having a bit of change with staff and jockeys and we genuinely thought it would be a year or two before we got back to where we were, but it went a lot better than we thought."

Nicholls' eighth title in nine seasons was not secured in the all-conquering manner of old, more by steady accumulation over a long winter where many of the big prizes went to smaller stables – Jim Culloty's Gold Cup with Lord Windermere, the Queen Mother

Champion Chase for Gary Moore's Sire De Grugy and the Grand National for Dr Richard Newland and Pineau De Re. Silviniaco Conti was seventh in the prize-money list in Britain and Ireland, the only Nicholls representative in the top 25.

"One feature of the season was that I had one winner at Cheltenham and still won the trainers' championship and Nicky had one winner there too – the whole season doesn't have to revolve around Cheltenham," Nicholls says. "There's massive prize-money and big races every weekend through the winter. Lots of horses in the middle range won a lot of races for us and kept adding to the prize-money. It shows you can win it without having a mega-Cheltenham."

Without the big money in the pot, Nicholls' £2,469,892 in win and place prize-money was the third-lowest winning total in the nine seasons since his first title and only a slight improvement on his previous season's figure, which had been well short of Henderson's haul. That reflected the extent to which Nicholls was able to capitalise on the absentees in the Henderson

team, with key injuries to Sprinter Sacre and Simonsig, but regaining the title was still a remarkable achievement amid the upheaval at Manor Farm Stables.

The big earners of the Nicholls golden years are gone, with Big Buck's now having joined Kauto Star, Denman, Master Minded and Neptune Collonges in retirement, and the next generation did not follow smoothly after them. In the past two seasons Nicholls has

had only two Cheltenham Festival winners and his last Grade 1 victory there was the 2012 World Hurdle with Big Buck's.

On the human side, too, there have been big changes. Clifford

▸▸ *Continues page 132*

From old to new: (clockwise from far left) Silviniaco Conti wins the King George VI Chase, exciting novice chase prospect Calipto and highly promising French recruit Le Mercurey

STRENGTH IN DEPTH

From established stars to new recruits, Paul Nicholls gives his view of ten horses who could carry the flag this season

Alcala We like him a lot – he's a real beauty. He ran with a lot of promise in the Adonis and it's good he's a novice for the whole season

All Set To Go He's built to go jumping, has done lots of schooling and is an exciting prospect as a juvenile hurdler

Calipto He was so unlucky in the Triumph when a broken stirrup leather cost him all chance. I'm really looking forward to when he goes chasing

Emerging Talent He's a big, gorgeous chasing type who has schooled well

Irish Saint He ran two really good races over hurdles last season but to my eyes he's always been a chaser in the making

Le Mercurey He's one of those unexposed young horses in the 'could be anything' category. He looked good when landing two of his three starts over hurdles at Auteuil and would have won but for falling on his other outing

Rocky Creek He's a true staying chaser we hold in the highest regard. The National is our number-one goal

Silviniaco Conti I hope there's still a lot of improvement to come and I'm really looking forward to having another crack at the Gold Cup

Southfield Theatre He started last season winning a small novice hurdle and ended it going down by a very small nose in the Pertemps Final and winning a Listed race. He's a really exciting prospect

Wonderful Charm He was troubled by a foot problem after Christmas and wasn't quite at his best in the spring. He's shaping into a top-class chaser

Baker, head man since 1996, still provides the backbone of the team but Ruby Walsh and assistant trainer Dan Skelton, both key players during the glory days, left before the start of the 2013-14 season. As inevitable as those moves were – Walsh opting for a more settled family life in Ireland, Skelton making an impressive start as a trainer in his own right – they left big shoes to fill. Tom Jonason, after three years with the yard, took over from Skelton, but another change long regarded as inevitable – the appointment of Sam Twiston-Davies as stable jockey – did not happen until May this year.

"I always said that once Ruby and Dan had gone it was going to take a lot of restructuring and I keep saying Rome wasn't built in a day," Nicholls says. "To get back to the top so quickly reflects well on everybody. It was good for Tom and the new team and it probably meant a lot more to us – me and Clifford and probably some of the owners and the people close to me – than ever before."

Despite his recent battles with Henderson, Nicholls, 52, insists the championship is not the same driving force it was a decade ago when he was determined to take the

No.1 spot from Martin Pipe. "When you're younger and keener, you want to win it because you're competitive," he says. "We don't set out to win it now because we buy nice horses with the aim of producing them to win nice races. Hopefully the two go together and if the championship comes along it's fantastic.

"I see it as much as anything not for me but as being great for the team and everyone who's involved. Sometimes too much can be made of it, it's almost as if some people are trying to make out you focus your life on it, which is completely not the case. Champion trainer is a fantastic and privileged position to be in, but it's awfully hard to do and it's not the be-all and end-all."

Silviniaco Conti is the new stable star and he stepped up again in a carefully planned campaign that brought victory in the King George, another Grade 1 win at Aintree and a hefty £250,000 in prize-money.

Whereas the previous season he had won the Betfair Chase after starting out in the Charlie Hall Chase, this time Silviniaco Conti's reappearance was delayed until Haydock and he lost to a match-fit Cue Card. A month later, however, he was in peak condition and he

turned the tables in the King George when he outstayed Cue Card to score by three and a half lengths.

If that was a triumph of planning, fourth place in the Betfred Cheltenham Gold Cup was a head-scratcher – "I still can't quite work out what happened that day," Nicholls says – but the re-crowned champion trainer is looking forward, not back.

"We've got some exciting young horses," he says. "I've got an incredibly strong team of novice chasers and Saphir Du Rheu is going to be very exciting over fences. The hardest thing for me is there are fewer opportunities for novice chasers because they're turning so many races into handicaps. The number of winners we train will probably go down because we've always excelled in novice chases and those opportunities are getting fewer. It's a little bit tougher but we have exciting horses to go chasing with and that's what I look forward to most every year."

With Twiston-Davies on board, everything is set for another successful season. The championship might not matter to Nicholls as much as it once did, but the fire burns as brightly as ever.

Have you ever considered racing thoroughbreds in South Africa – the Land of Opportunity?

With the highly favourable exchange rate, you can have a horse trained for less than 400 Pounds a month in the country which has given the world such star racehorses as outstanding miler Variety Club, Dubai Carnival winners too many to mention, International Gr 1 winners like the outstanding fillies Irridesence, Crimson Palace, Perfect Promise and Dane Julia, genuine Gr 1 sprinters J J The Jet Plane, Shea Shea and National Currency, and the disqualified Arlington Million winner The Apache. And the list doesn't stop there.

So, why wait for your opportunity to join in this booming market? The best value-for-money thoroughbreds in the world are awaiting you, and Paul Lafferty Racing Stables is waiting to train them for you! Paul runs a Gr 1 – winning yard at the magnificent Summerveld training centre in Kwazulu-Natal and in the 2013/2014 racing season he trained HARRY'S SON to Gr 1 success and earned the official Equus Award for South Africa's Champion Two-Year-Old Male in the process.

A regular traveller to racing jurisdictions worldwide, Paul is au fait with the latest international trends in racing. He travels horses all around South Africa having won graded races in all the four major provinces. He is also the South African representative for Magic Millions and annually attends all of the sales company's principal auctions in Australia. It goes without saying that he is in attendance at all important horse sales in South Africa, and his consistent success during a training career which spans a quarter of a century is testament to both his eye for a horse and everything thereafter. Not afraid to travel horses around South Africa in search of the best opportunities, he strongly believes that placing horses in the right races is a key component of running a successful yard.

So, once again, what are you waiting for? Invest in South African racing, join a vibrant winning stable at a price that would be the envy of every other country on earth, and during the long and dreary European winter head out to our spectacular sunny climes to watch your dream horse in action! Interested?

Paul Lafferty
RACING STABLE

BALANCING ACT

Ruby Walsh's decision to base himself in Ireland brought him a happy blend of top-level success and family contentment

ONLY the most successful sports stars earn the luxury of being able to plot their own career path, rather than having to react to events or have decisions forced on them. Ruby Walsh is one of that rare breed, a man so good at his job and so much in demand that he was able to give up a plum job with Paul Nicholls and still remain at the top.

To be precise, Walsh's decision to part company with Nicholls in May 2013 and base himself with Willie Mullins was instrumental in putting him back on top in Ireland. Twelve months later, at the end of his first full season since ending his regular commute to Britain, Walsh was Irish champion jump jockey for the first time in four years.

Not only that, he was still the top rider at the Cheltenham Festival – for the eighth time in 11 years – and he had an enviable amount of talent at his disposal. As well as old favourites such as Hurricane Fly and Quevega, who continued their record-breaking ways, he had exciting new stars such as Faugheen,

Vautour and Annie Power. With 13 Grade 1 winners in Britain and Ireland, he still had the edge on big rivals Tony McCoy and Barry Geraghty in that department.

Being at the top of your profession does not always bring the ideal work-life balance but Walsh, 35, has been able to engineer that for himself too. The driving force behind his decision to base himself in Ireland was being able to spend more time with wife Gillian and their growing family. In

April they had their third daughter, Gemma, who joined Isabelle, 5, and Elsa, 2, and to be at home with them he had to leave behind those winter-morning flights out of Dublin at 6.30am, which for more than a decade had taken him on his way to the Nicholls yard in Somerset to ride work and often to spend a couple of days racing in Britain.

Reflecting on his move shortly before the 2014 Cheltenham Festival, Walsh told Alastair Down in

the Racing Post: "It's been great. All right, you might be at Navan instead of the Paddy Power meeting and a bit of you misses big occasions like that and the crowds. But there is a world to be said for not rushing to airports for the first plane out and the last one back.

"There were times when I'd be looking ahead through the calendar, finding a Plumpton meeting and thinking: 'Great. Paul won't have anything there, I can have a day off.'

▶▶ All-round winner: (from left) Ruby Walsh with his family at Tipperary in October after winning on his comeback ride from a shoulder operation; Boston Bob lands the Punchestown Gold Cup; Walsh celebrates on Vautour after their victory in the Supreme Novices' Hurdle at Cheltenham; Abbyssial wins the Champion Four Year Old Hurdle at Punchestown; Faugheen (below) takes the Champion Novice Hurdle at Punchestown

"When I was away Gillian was here on her own with two small kids, and that's tiring. It was not going home that tipped it for me. Before we had kids Gillian could come over with me, which was great. And when I was riding at Fairyhouse or Leopardstown I could be home in time to give the girls their tea and be part of their lives. But leaving early and getting back late was very different. I was away a lot."

Settled back home in Kilcullen, County Kildare, Walsh won the 2013-14 Irish title with 122 winners, the third-biggest total of his career and the best since 2007-08. If he had not missed six weeks after breaking his arm at the Cheltenham Festival, he would almost certainly have set a personal best. But the risk of injury is the one thing no jump jockey can control – and Walsh is as vulnerable as anyone else.

Cheltenham week had started with Jason Maguire's horror fall at Stratford that almost cost him his life and the festival brought constant reminders of the dangers faced by jump jockeys. Bryan Cooper suffered

a badly broken right leg, Daryl Jacob fractured his left leg, knee and elbow and Walsh sustained a compound fracture of his right humerus – the bone in the upper arm – and dislocated his right shoulder when he came down on Abbyssial in the Triumph Hurdle, the first race on the final day. In a sense Walsh was the lucky one. While he missed Aintree and the Irish Grand National, he was back before the end of April in time for a grand finale at the Punchestown festival. Jacob did not return until August, Maguire came back a month after that and Cooper was absent until October.

The highs and lows were summed up by Walsh after collecting his prize as champion jockey. His first thought was that the season had been "wonderful" but then he added: "It wasn't easy. The family were great for me and they were a big help."

Family: the most important word in the Walsh lexicon, giving him a sense of perspective that had been evident again after he opened the Cheltenham Festival with victory on Vautour in the Supreme Novices'

Hurdle. With Maguire in a coma after his fall the previous day and McCoy's seven-month-old son Archie having just undergone heart surgery, Walsh said. "You can make too much of winning here. This morning was a cold and timely reminder with Jason Maguire. There's a lot more to life than riding winners at Cheltenham. AP showed a picture of Archie before racing and you think 'Jesus, thank God my kids are all right at home'. It's a big week but there's more to life than Cheltenham."

Yet, in the heat of battle out on the racecourse, Walsh is as competitive as they come. When he returned from his broken arm, he was straight back with a winner in a Grade 2 hurdle at Auteuil on Un De Sceaux. The following week, he was leading jockey at Punchestown with six winners. Five of those were Grade 1 scorers, emphasising again that nobody can rival Walsh for range of weaponry in the big races.

Walsh later revealed his desire to be back for those big winners, who included his Cheltenham faller

Abbyssial in the Grade 1 Champion Four Year Old Hurdle, had led him to postpone surgery on the shoulder he damaged in that fall. He waited until the summer to have the operation, missing another four months but ensuring he was fully fit for the more important winter campaign.

"I realised I was running the risk of dislocating my shoulder again and so had to have the operation to repair the ligaments," he said. "I wanted to come back for Punchestown, and then to ride in some big races in France and have no regrets. That was the chance I took." Once he had the operation, however, he did not rush back – "probably the first time I've given an injury sufficient time to heal fully," he said.

Typically, Walsh was back with a winner on his first ride at Tipperary in October and now another exciting winter stretches out ahead of him. Whether he is at home with Gillian and the girls, or at the Mullins yard with all the firepower stockpiled there, the champion can see he's in the right place.

IN THE PICTURE

Summer days for Henderson warriors before return to fray

One of the most welcome sights of late summer – though perhaps not for their rivals – had the imagination whirring forward to crisp winter days and the thrill of the chase. Sprinter Sacre (right, ridden by Nico de Boinville) and Simonsig (Peter Carberry) were freshly back at Nicky Henderson's Seven Barrows yard in Lambourn after major health issues and hopes were high that they would be able to make up for lost time.

Still by far the top-rated jumps horse in training after capping a brilliant 2012-13 season with victory in the Queen Mother Champion Chase, Sprinter Sacre was pulled up on his only start last winter having suffered an irregular heartbeat, while 2013 Arkle Chase winner Simonsig missed the whole campaign after developing a splint on his near-fore.

On Sprinter Sacre's return from his summer break at Juliet and David Minton's Mill House Stud in Much Wenlock, Shropshire, Henderson was in positive mood. "He looks magnificent and everything is A1 with him," he said. "We've tweaked a couple of minor things and he's fine. I imagine he'll start off in the Tingle Creek and then I would think it'll be a similar programme to the winter before last leading up to Cheltenham."

Simonsig spent the summer at Charlie and Tracy Vigors' Hillwood Stud, the Wiltshire holiday home for many of Henderson's horses, and was reported to be at his most alert and particularly close to Hennessy winner Triolo D'Alene. "Some get on well as part of a group, others form bonds with a specific fieldmate," said Charlie Vigors during the grey's time there. "Simonsig and Triolo D'Alene are practically joined at the hip, they're obsessed with each other, it's almost unhealthy."

Henderson said he could have got Simonsig back for the second half of the 2013-14 season but decided to take no chances, instead looking to the long term and longer distances.

"His splint has been repaired and there's no reason why he shouldn't be every bit as good," he said. "There's no doubt we'll be trying Simonsig over further. He won a Neptune, so he's proved two miles and five furlongs at Cheltenham is no problem. We might be looking at the King George. He's seriously good, the only horse we had two years ago capable of going with Sprinter Sacre and very capable of doing so."

The absence of Sprinter Sacre and Simonsig was a major factor in Henderson losing the 2013-14 trainers' title to Paul Nicholls, but here was fresh hope to stoke all the old dreams of what could be achieved with them on top form.

Picture: EDWARD WHITAKER (RACINGPOST.COM/PHOTOS)

RISING FORCE

World Hurdle winner
More Of That and a talented
team of staying chasers give
Jonjo O'Neill a strong hand

By Nick Pulford

C AN Jonjo O'Neill win the British jumps trainers'
title this season? Yes, says Paul Nicholls, who reckons
the master of Jackdaws Castle could pose the biggest
threat to his crown. "I have a feeling he might be
the one we have to beat," the reigning champion
told the assembled throng on his annual owners' day in the
autumn, repeating a view he had aired on the final day of
last season. "His team have been buying stacks of new horses
and nowadays Jonjo has the quality and quantity to mount a
serious challenge for the championship."

Ask O'Neill, however, and he prefers to play down his title
chances. "There's no point talking silly about that," he says.
"Paul is only trying to pile the pressure on somebody else; he's
got all the good horses, we haven't. I'd love to have a go if I had
as many good ones as he has, but we don't have enough good
Saturday horses. You've got to have runners every Saturday in
the good races, that's the only way you can win the prize-
money, and we don't have that."

What is beyond dispute is that O'Neill is a serious player
throughout the entire season nowadays, not just peaking
for the big meetings but competing hard at every level from
summer jumping onwards. In the 2013-14 season he recorded
his highest number of winners (134) and his prize-money haul
(£1,570,452) was not far shy of his best mark in 2009-10,
which was boosted considerably by Don't Push It's Grand
National winnings. His big-race winners stretched from
Johns Spirit in the Paddy Power Gold Cup – widely seen
as the start of the 'proper' jumps season in November – to
Shutthefrontdoor in the Boylesports Irish Grand National in
late April.

Most significantly of all, he assembled perhaps his strongest
battalion of young warriors for the Cheltenham Festival
and left with three successes, two of them at Grade 1 level.
After Holywell had taken the Grade 3 handicap chase on the
opening day, More Of That revived memories of Iris's Gift with
victory over the much-touted Annie Power in the Ladbrokes
World Hurdle and Taquin Du Seuil landed the JLT Novices'

▸ *Continues page 140*

Chase. At Aintree the following month, Holywell joined them as a Grade 1 winner by taking the Betfred Mobile Mildmay Novices' Chase.

More Of That will be aged seven at the next Cheltenham Festival, with Taquin Du Seuil and Holywell just a year older, and that raises hope of further big-race success with all three. In particular, More Of That has immense promise in a staying hurdlers' division he could dominate now that Big Buck's is out of the picture. He returned a Racing Post Rating of 172 in the World Hurdle, higher than the mark achieved by Big Buck's in his third and fourth wins in the race, despite being described by O'Neill at the time as "still a big frame of a horse, coming to himself".

More Of That has some way to go on the figures in order to match Iris's Gift, who had an RPR of 176 in winning the same race for O'Neill ten years earlier, but the potential is there. Asked if More Of That could be as good, O'Neill replies: "Oh God, yeah. He's a similar type to Iris's Gift, good stayer, same level of class and ability. It's lovely to have him, he's a brilliant horse."

Holywell is a different type, a pocket battleship, but he is a firm favourite at Jackdaws Castle after winning at consecutive Cheltenham Festivals. Both victories – first in the Pertemps Final over hurdles and then as a novice chaser in a handicap – were under Richie McLernon, who describes him as "the horse of a lifetime". Tony McCoy took over at Aintree, where Holywell's jumping was considerably less sketchy than in his early chase runs and his ten-length victory over Don Cossack bettered the Cheltenham figure posted by fellow novice Taquin Du Seuil.

"Holywell was disappointing early in the season with his jumping," says O'Neill, "then he got the hang of things and really came good at the end. He's only little but he's amazing." In a staying-chase division with room at the top after last season's scrappy events, Holywell was disputing Cheltenham Gold Cup favouritism with 2013 winner Bobs Worth as winter approached.

O'Neill's three Cheltenham Festival winners of 2014 demonstrated the wider diversity of owners that underpins his improving numbers. While More Of That carries the famous green and gold of landlord JP McManus, who will always be central to the stable's success, Taquin Du Seuil is owned by a partnership headed by Martin Broughton, deputy chairman of British Airways' parent company, and Holywell

▶▶Stable stars: (clockwise from left) Jonjo O'Neill and Taquin Du Seuil after morning exercise at Jackdaws Castle; Holywell and Tony McCoy clear the last in the Mildmay Novices' Chase at Aintree; Shutthefrontdoor and Barry Geraghty win the Irish Grand National at Fairyhouse; (previous page) More Of That after his victory in the World Hurdle at Cheltenham

runs in the colours of Gay Smith. Johns Spirit, meanwhile, races for Christopher Johnston, who has been with O'Neill for more than a decade.

McCoy, one of the linchpins of Jackdaws Castle's success, emphasised that factor last season, saying: "Jonjo can train anything but people still think it is something of a closed shop [at Jackdaws] when it is anything but. There is nothing JP likes more than for Jonjo to train a winner for someone else."

O'Neill, 62, has a tremendously loyal and talented team around him – including assistant trainer Guy Upton and senior staff Johnny Kavanagh and Adelle O'Brien, who run the two yards – and he was delighted that last season's haul repaid their efforts. "Certainly it's the best season we've had and the horses held their form, which was great. It's always important that you don't get a cough or a cold that knocks you out for a month or two, but they stayed good and healthy all season.

"It was brilliant for the yard, for everyone, and we were thrilled to bits. You get up every morning hoping everything goes well and sometimes it doesn't, but we love the job. It's a magical job. You need to love the job to

put the effort in and it's nice when you get paid back now and then. It's what everybody works for."

The final big victory of 2013-14 was for McManus, as Shutthefrontdoor became another of O'Neill's novices to shine in a big handicap with his Irish National triumph. Barry Geraghty was on board, as he had been on More Of That at Cheltenham, and he drove Shutthefrontdoor to victory by three-quarters of a length. The Grand National at Aintree seems a natural target but O'Neill may have other plans – "he has a bit of class and could be a Gold Cup horse," he said at Fairyhouse.

Only a couple of weeks later, the slate was wiped clean as a new season opened. In this age of virtually continuous jump racing, there is no time for resting on laurels and certainly not at Jackdaws Castle. At the end of the first third of the jumps calendar – the summer season – O'Neill had posted the best figures among British trainers in terms of both winners and prize-money.

Where he ends up in the final standings may be a matter of opinion but, with three Gold Cup possibles in the yard and the World Hurdle winner to boot, this promises to be another exciting winter.

MARKET AVENUE
RACING CLUB

Over the past 12 years Market Avenue Racing Club has established itself as one of the most prolific and prestigious racehorse ownership syndicates in the country.

With well over 100 winners to its name and appearances at some of the biggest race meetings including Royal Ascot, Irish Champions Weekend and the 1,000 Guineas in both the UK and Dubai.

The Club has just enjoyed its most successful Turf Flat Season ever with over 20 winners and some very lucrative trips to the sales ring. (Truancy brought in £140,000 in the September 2014 Doncaster Horses in Training Sales).

Market Avenue Racing Club prides itself on purchasing young racehorses with real potential and good quality racing bloodlines and placing them with top quality trainers. With a few established proven performers, this is the recipe for continued success.

Being part of a horse racing syndicate can be as rewarding and exciting as buying one outright, without the risk, responsibility or substantial financial outlay.

With Market Avenue Racing Club a 10% share in a quality racehorse can cost as little as £2,000, with very reasonable monthly training fees of around £250 per calendar month.

If racehorse ownership and membership of an exclusive successful Club has always appealed to you, why not contact us for a friendly discussion and become part of a winning team.

SPONSORED BY

LENAT

Tel: Matthew Hilton (Racing Manager) on 07792 384 420
or email: info@marketavenueracingclub.co.uk
www.marketavenueracingclub.co.uk

HAPPY TUMMY®
Charcoal
From Fine Fettle® Products
The worlds best gastric conditioner

> **Works quickly and effectively**
> **Removes acidic toxins.**
> **Re-establishes the correct gut PH.**
> **Enables a stronger immune system.**
> **Improves digestion.**
> **Improves condition.**
> **Improves circulation**
> **Improves perfomance.**
> **Improves behaviour.**
> **Reduces stress.**
> **Very economic to use.**
> **Can be used when racing.**
> **BHRA & FEI compliant.**

For expert advice and more information, or to order:

01600 712496
www.finefettlefeed.com

1 Never Never and Tony McCoy win the opener for trainer Donald McCain and owners Paul and Clare Rooney on their first visit to Cartmel

2 Trainer Ben Haslam with a different kind of winner after landing the camel race final on Sahara at Catterick in August

3 A wet and cold start to ladies' day at York's Ebor meeting

4 Pale Mimosa and Pat Smullen after winning the Lonsdale Cup at York in August

5 A racegoer poses with Johnny King after his win on Flight Plan in the Pat O'Sullivan Catering Equipment Pro/Am Flat Race at Killarney in August

6 Supermodel Edie Campbell wins the Magnolia Cup charity ladies' race on See The Storm at Glorious Goodwood

7 Richard Hannon (second right) on the stands rail at York on the final day of the Ebor meeting

8 The fourth day of the Galway festival draws to a close

9 Danny Tudhope celebrates his first Group 1 win aboard the David O'Meara-trained G Force in the Haydock Sprint Cup

10 Tony McCoy after winning the Galway Hurdle on Thomas Edison – the first victory in the race for owner JP McManus after decades of trying

11 Ladies' day on the champagne lawn at Glorious Goodwood

12 Runners in the Goodwood Stakes walk around the paddock at the Glorious meeting

A LESSON TO US ALL

Sharron Murgatroyd, paralysed by a fall in 1991, died in March aged 54. Her unquenchable spirit made her an inspiration and won admirers throughout racing

By Lee Mottershead

RACING lost one of its most genuinely inspirational figures in March when former jockey Sharron Murgatroyd, adored and admired by those who witnessed her courageous readjustment to life with major disability, died aged 54.

Murgatroyd, left severely paralysed by a fall at Bangor in August 1991, was spoken of in the most glowing terms by close friends, including Injured Jockeys Fund president John Francome and former weighing-room colleague turned broadcaster Clare Balding, who said the author, poet and charity fundraiser had been "a lesson to us all in terms of loving something that has hurt you".

Despite having been in even more pain than usual in the weeks before her death, Murgatroyd, who as a respected amateur rode winners on the Flat and over jumps, had planned to attend an Injured Jockeys Fund event at Aintree's Grand National meeting. However, she suffered a heart attack and became increasingly ill with a chest infection and pneumonia. She died on March 28 at West Suffolk Hospital in Bury St Edmunds.

Flat fans at Doncaster the following day took part in a minute's applause in honour of a great child of Yorkshire, while jockeys and racegoers at Uttoxeter and Stratford paid their respects to Murgatroyd,

whose first of four books was entitled Jump Jockeys Don't Cry. In a poignant message on Twitter after her death was announced, close friend Michael Caulfield noted: "They will today."

While Murgatroyd lived not far from Newmarket, mother Thelma continued to be based in Yorkshire, from where she travelled to see a daughter who had received 24-hour assistance from carers Anne Frost, Esther Wainwright, Debbie-Jane Challenger, Kelby Frost and Pam Fitsall. Murgatroyd herself referred to them not as her carers, but her "ladies".

"We got to her after she died but I asked them to keep her on the ward," said Murgatroyd's mother. "We arrived at the hospital at about 9.30pm and saw her on the bed. She looked so peaceful. All the pain had gone from her face. She looked absolutely beautiful. She was at peace."

Although not from a racing background, Murgatroyd became "hooked on horses" at the age of three. At 16 she began to work for trainer Bob Ward and was put in touch with Michael Dickinson, for whom she rode work on triple Champion Chase winner Badsworth Boy. She later moved to Newmarket, where Alan Bailey became a keen supporter, and at the time of the Bangor accident her profile as an amateur was rising.

A final-flight fall in a claiming hurdle ended her career and monumentally changed the life of

a jockey who had been booked to take a mount for Henry Cecil the following day.

"She has been an inspiration to an awful lot of people, particularly me," said Francome. "I never once heard her moan. Instead she always saw the funny side of her predicament. She had been in quite a bit of pain recently, not that she would ever have mentioned it. She lived a lot longer than people expected but that's because she was so tough.

"A lot of people thought an awful lot about her and, very sadly for her mother and all those who looked after her, this will be very hard."

Among those who rode against Murgatroyd on the ladies' amateur circuit were Balding and Gee Bradburne, both of whom paid tributes.

Balding revealed Murgatroyd had contacted her earlier that week, asking if she would play Wind Beneath My Wings on her Radio 2 show on Mother's Day. She had selected the song as a way of thanking her mother, who had recently turned 80. Balding did play the song that day, March 30, two days after Murgatroyd died.

"Her lack of resentment and bitterness towards racing was astonishing," said Balding. "She is a lesson to us all in terms of loving something that has hurt you. She made the weighing room a place of love and laughter, and in the ancient tradition of the amateur sport she

▶▶ *Continues page 146*

'She inspired people and you never came away from seeing her without having your outlook on life changed. She was amazing'

did it because she loved it. That was her ethos. I admired her hugely."

As did Bradburne, who along with Francome, Caulfield, Richard Phillips, Neale Doughty, Steve Smith Eccles, Graham Bradley and others, annually enjoyed a Christmas lunch with Murgatroyd on the second Tuesday of December.

"She was amazing and made the rest of us realise how lucky we are," said Bradburne. "At the lunch she would hold court around the table and had something to say about everything and everyone. She also made up a quiz every year, which showed her knowledge of racing was extraordinary. She loved the sport and was never bitter about what happened."

Caulfield, former chief executive of the Professional Jockeys Association, was another to become a good friend of Murgatroyd. "When the book of lady jockeys is written she'll be up there towards the top," he said.

"I'm not sure we ever appreciated how much pain she was in or how hard it was for her to function. What she did to come back from what happened to her was truly remarkable.

"She had two passions in life – riding horses and David Bowie. The safest ante-post bet is that something by Bowie will be played at the funeral."

Doughty, who regularly rode with Murgatroyd in the north of England, added: "She inspired people and you never came away from seeing her without having your outlook on life changed. She was amazing.

"I've met a few brave people, but I've never met one braver than Sharron."

This is an edited version of an article that appeared in the Racing Post on March 30

▸▸Truly remarkable: Sharron Murgatroyd, author, poet and charity fundraiser, at home near Newmarket

'SHE STRESSED HOW LUCKY SHE WAS'

Brough Scott pays tribute to a dear friend lost

The text had John Francome's name on it. That usually guarantees a decent joke but not this time. It was to tell of Sharron's passing. You could feel the hurt.

He was in the Bahamas, I was on the beach in Dubai. You could hear her laughing at us for being a pair of softies. She liked to take the mickey, not deal in heavy sympathy, although heaven knows she deserved it more than most. We had first met when I interviewed her on the July course in Newmarket after she had won a race in Jack Ramsden's colours. She would love to remind me of it and add: "All those stupid questions."

It was the final hurdle at Bangor that changed everything, changed it utterly. She was at the back of the field, went to pop over and got buried for her pains. It was never

possible to see her afterwards without thinking what a price to pay for being one jump too brave. But she would stress how lucky she was to have had the thrill of riding winners, to have lived her dream. She wrote beautifully about it in her poems and in books like Jump Jockeys Don't Cry.

True, there were a few lines that hinted at some pretty dark nights of the soul, but she always wanted to celebrate what she could do, not lament what she could not.

She would pace herself. On our Injured Jockeys Fund holidays to Tenerife she would soak up the sun and revel in the warmth and freedom of the swimming pool before hours later appearing elegant and lovely to make sure she graced the evening occasion.

Despite her hard-working, stable-door background there had become

something slightly regal about her, as befits a woman who has learned to play so impossible a hand.

One splendid summons came a couple of summers ago. It was either her 50th birthday or the anniversary of the Bangor disaster, quite possibly both. It was a lovely August evening, all the usual suspects were gathered for drinks and a sumptuous barbecue next to her specially equipped bungalow in Herringswell. She kept us waiting a wee while but when she wheeled in, she did not disappoint. Not one of us left there without a lift in the heart.

Nelson Mandela, in explaining how he survived his years on Robben Island, wrote: "The strength of the human spirit is a flame with a light all of its own."

That applied to Sharron Murgatroyd's imprisonment too.

Kudo Rock

Performance Horse Syndications

Kudo Rock is designed to bring people together to support, learn and enjoy the equestrian world like never before.

We want to make a difference by allowing dreams and genuine talent to fly.

Join us in our quest and become part of something extraordinary.

SEE the Power

FEEL the Passion

LOVE the Performance

We take care of the rest.

CAYLINN - COURTESY OF ULTIMATE

- Performance horse syndicates
- Lease shares available
- Quality sport horse advertisements
- Rider profiles
- Clinic's, yard visits and much more

 WINNER – 2014 Venus Awards
For Cobweb Solutions
'New Media and Online Award'

BENJAMIN CLARK PHOTOGRAPHY

www.kudorock.co.uk

Call 07815 669 482 *Email* info@krphs.co.uk

 Find us on Facebook Kudo Rock Ltd for exciting updates, days out, gift ideas and much more!

THE
BIGGER
PICTURE

Gold at the end of the rainbow as the Richard
Lee-trained Grey Gold (Jamie Moore) lands a
2m handicap chase at Sandown in February
**EDWARD WHITAKER
(RACINGPOST.COM/PHOTOS)**

By Scott Burton

FULL HOUSE

Andre Fabre joined the select few to have won all five British Classics when he took the 1,000 Guineas with Miss France

IN the aftermath of Miss France's neck victory in the Qipco 1,000 Guineas, the media encircled winning trainer Andre Fabre. The French master had just achieved something rare and remarkable – his last missing piece in the jigsaw of British Classics – but he claimed it did not mean anything to him. "It is just another racing day," he said.

Of course, it was much more than that. Most trainers never win a Classic, many have to be content with just one special occasion, and only the few become serial winners. It is rarer still to complete the full set of Classics, even for a trainer based in Britain. Fabre, 68, is now one of only four current trainers with that distinction, the others being Sir Michael Stoute, Saeed Bin Suroor and Aidan O'Brien.

O'Brien's feat from his base in Ireland is phenomenal – the only other Irishman to claim the full set was his predecessor at Ballydoyle, Vincent O'Brien – but for him the British Classics are a top priority. It is a different matter for Fabre, as he indicated with a seemingly throwaway line in the media scrum at Newmarket. "I was waiting for the right horse, and for a sunny day, which is rare in Newmarket," said Fabre, referring to Miss France's win with what seemed a hint of mischief.

Fabre has 207 horses registered in training with France Galop and should therefore have enough talent at his disposal to target the Classics systematically in both Britain and France. Yet for him talent is not enough and, while he is a regular visitor to the top British races, he is by no means a habitual traveller across the English Channel. In that context, becoming the first French trainer to complete the full house of British Classics is an incredible achievement.

On top of that, Fabre has the full set in France – with a total of 22 Classic victories – as well as three Irish Classics, a record seven Prix de l'Arc de Triomphes, four successes at the Breeders' Cup and 25 French trainers' titles.

At one stage in the spring it seemed Miss France might not be ready for the 1,000 Guineas, even though the race had been in Fabre's mind since the previous autumn when he sent her from Chantilly to test the waters on the Rowley Mile and she won the Group 3 Oh So Sharp Stakes.

When Miss France reappeared in the traditional Guineas trial for French fillies, the Prix Imprudence, things did not go well. A funereal pace gave

SMART SET

FABRE'S BRITISH CLASSICS

2,000 Guineas Zafonic (1993), Pennekamp (1995)

1,000 Guineas Miss France (2014)

Derby Pour Moi (2011)

Oaks Intrepidity (1993)

St Leger Toulon (1991)

Maxime Guyon no chance of settling her and she tanked through the first half-mile before trailing home sixth behind Xcellence.

It would have been a brave observer who viewed that Maisons-Laffitte outing as having in any way enhanced her 1,000 Guineas prospects and it can only have been her trainer's matchless reputation that halted her retreat in the bookmakers' lists at 7-1 behind new favourite Tapestry.

But Fabre was seeing a different filly in the mornings in Chantilly. Miss France's long stride and searing acceleration were more than intact and, in the week before the Guineas, rumours circulated of a scintillating piece of work.

Among the happy band in the winner's enclosure at Newmarket, owner Diane Wildenstein confirmed what very few had been on hand to witness. "It was quite a gallop," said Wildenstein, granddaughter of the bloodstock empire's founding father Daniel. "She showed exactly what we wanted to see."

Fabre added: "The Imprudence was not a race, it was anything but a race. I was waiting for her morning work and I got very confident when she worked so well in the morning."

The performance of Guyon at Newmarket on that first Sunday in May pointed to Fabre's skill as a trainer of men as well as of racehorses. Fabre was happy to praise Guyon for "not listening to me" after the rider sat on the heels of the leaders with Miss France when the expected fast pace failed to materialise. As well as myriad opportunities to win big races, Fabre gives his jockeys the confidence to make big decisions. That was also evident in 2011 when Mickael Barzalona, then just 19, belied his lack of international experience to give Fabre his only Derby triumph with Pour Moi.

The latest graduates of the 'Fabre academy' are Guyon, Barzalona and Pierre-Charles Boudot, who progressed as apprentices under the master's eye in three consecutive years of intake from the AFASEC jockeys' school. Boudot, who flourished during Barzalona's time in Newmarket with Godolphin, scored his first two Group 1 successes this year with Gallante in the Grand Prix de Paris and Esoterique in the Prix Rothschild.

Miss France's success at Newmarket did not, as it turned out, herald a great season for Fabre. He failed to win a home Classic and Arc weekend came and went without any addition to his disappointing tally of just three domestic Group 1 victories in a difficult year when a virus sidelined many potential stable stars. Even so, he almost pulled another Arc out of the bag when Flintshire was beaten only by the resurgent Treve.

Fabre's handling of the volatile Miss France and his perceptive eye during those early mornings on the gallops are evidence enough that he retains the full range of his powers. He said it best himself shortly before Pour Moi's Derby: "We don't have many occasions on which to judge these horses, so it is a matter of feeling."

Pride and joy

Gordon Lord Byron wrote another chapter in his incredible story with a historic Group 1 win in Sydney

By Nick Pulford

TAKE a good look at the picture. Something extraordinary has just happened, something unique, but you wouldn't necessarily know it. And that man leading the horse, you wouldn't realise that just last year he was told he had little chance of walking again. Now he is taking the proudest walk of his life.

The date is 29 March 2014, the place is Rosehill Gardens racecourse and the horse is Gordon Lord Byron, and what just happened is that he became the first horse from the northern hemisphere to win a Group 1 in Sydney. There had been successful Group 1 raids on Melbourne, but not on Australia's other great racing centre. In the ever shrinking racing world, Gordon Lord Byron's connections had found an unconquered corner and planted an Irish flag there. This was a moment of history.

The man at Gordon Lord Byron's side is Eddie Power, travelling head man for trainer Tom Hogan. He had been there every step of the way, from quarantine in Newmarket before the flight to Australia to another spell in isolation in Melbourne and then finally to Sydney for Group 1 glory on the other side of the world. Yet, in truth, Power's journey was longer and more remarkable than that, as was Gordon

Lord Byron's, and Hogan's.

Let's go back first to 3 May 2013. This time the place is Kilbeggan racecourse and the horse is Ballinahow Oscar, who has just unseated Power at the second flight in a maiden hurdle. Power, just starting his 12th season as a jump jockey, will not be walking away from this one. His race-riding career, highlighted three years earlier by a Grade 2 victory on former Queen Mother Champion Chase winner Newmill, is over.

"I shattered my T5 vertebra and cracked the T7, T6, T4, T3 and dislocated my spine as well," says Power, now 29. "I had to get two rods and 14 screws in my back. It was quite a delicate operation and before the surgery I was given a low percentage of ever walking again. The top part of my back is solid now with all the rods and screws and the bottom part is high-risk. It's too risky to give me back my licence and for me to ride again."

Power's rehabilitation took more than six months but, with determination and a lot of help and support, he got back on his feet. "Getting through it and getting mobile again was the number one aim. I'm quite lucky to be as good as I am. I'm very good, to be honest, you wouldn't know I'd had any fall."

Then came the question of what he was going to do with the rest of his life. It is difficult enough when
▸▸ *Continues page 154*

there has been time to plan for a post-riding career, but even more so when the end comes so abruptly and a long period of rehabilitation takes you out of sight and out of mind. "You're very soon forgotten in this game," Power says, but fortunately he wasn't by Hogan.

The two of them go back a long way, to Power's late teens when he started out as an amateur rider. Hogan gave him his first winner, Premier Rebel at Ballinrobe in 2004, and nine years later the one that turned out to be his last, Coolnagorna Giggs at the same track. Three days later, on his very next ride, came the fateful fall. At that time, Power had been combining race-riding with an assistant/head man role at Hogan's yard in County Tipperary and, by happy coincidence, he was back on his feet after his long rehabilitation at just the moment Hogan needed a travelling assistant to take Gordon Lord Byron to Hong Kong's big December meeting.

Not for the first time, Gordon Lord Byron was about to rescue someone from dark despair and send them on an unimaginable journey to the glittering hotspots of the racing world. Hogan knew the feeling, because it had happened to him.

LET'S go back in time again, to June 2012, and a knife-edge decision that every trainer dreads. Hogan had almost been dragged under by the recession and nearly lost Gordon Lord Byron, the one horse who might save him, to a pelvic injury. Now, having nursed him back, he faced the possibility that owner Morgan Cahalan would sell the then four-year-old just when he was ready to break through into top handicap and black-type races. Cahalan could have done with the money – close to €200,000 – but in the end he reasoned that he would never have the opportunity to own another like Gordon Lord Byron.

No wonder Hogan did not hesitate when asked this summer if this was a career-saving horse. "Oh yeah," he said. "If I didn't have Gordon I wouldn't still be in the game, I wouldn't still be going."

More brave decisions followed, and many of them were rewarded, as Gordon Lord Byron travelled around winning fans and big prizes. In his last four races of 2012, he won a Listed race at York, finished

TWISTS IN THE TALE

Gordon Lord Byron is the success story that almost never was

When the credit crunch hit and the Celtic Tiger stopped roaring, Tom Hogan was badly affected. He had to sell horses – his string went to barely 20 per cent of its former strength – and dispose of land to keep the banks at bay. And when Gordon Lord Byron fell into his lap almost by chance, Hogan's financial desperation almost drove him to throw away a golden opportunity.

"You have to have patience with these horses and we were a bit impatient with him because we needed to earn some prize-money," he admitted this year. "He fractured his pelvis the first day he ran at Roscommon as a two-year-old and they wanted to know if I wanted to put him down. It was that close to being over."

Gordon Lord Byron (above with Hogan) had come to the trainer only because he had proved difficult to get rid of. Jessica Cahalan, who worked at the yard as a secretary, had pinhooked him as a foal for €2,000 but did not get a bid when she sent him back to the sales as a yearling and then could not get him into the breeze-up sales. Only then did Morgan Cahalan, Jessica's father, ask Hogan to train Gordon Lord Byron.

The twists did not stop with the story of how the sales reject wound up with Hogan, nor even with the pelvic injury that almost ended his life, let alone his racing career. When Hogan nursed him back to health, the latent talent poured out to such an extent that Cahalan was offered almost €200,000 for the then four-year-old after he had finished second in a Listed race at Naas in June 2012. He asked Hogan's view and the trainer, while advising him to take the money if he needed it, said he would be disappointed if Gordon Lord Byron could not win that much in prize-money by the end of September.

"He drove away out of the yard, I didn't know which way it would go," Hogan recalled, "and he drove in again the following morning and said: 'I have no money but I have no mortgage. No-one else is going to own this horse because I'll never have another horse like him.'"

Cahalan's hunch was right. Gordon Lord Byron now has career earnings of £1,262,975 (more than €1.6m) but has given his connections so much more than money. "This is the thing we dream about, it just doesn't happen," Cahalan said after the historic win in Sydney. "I have only one other horse in training, a National Hunt horse. We took him [back from the sales] and he has taken care of us since."

'If I didn't have Gordon I wouldn't still be in the game. I wouldn't still be going'

second in the Haydock Sprint Cup, won the Prix de la Foret on Arc day at Longchamp and finished fourth in the Hong Kong Mile at Sha Tin. Hogan had won that €200,000, and more, for Cahalan.

As he was a gelding who loved travelling, there was no reason to stop with Gordon Lord Byron. In 2013 he made the first four in Group 1 races in four different countries, the highlight being his Haydock Sprint Cup triumph over Slade Power, and ended up in Hong Kong with Power alongside him. Then came the invitation from Racing New South Wales, principally for The Championships at Randwick in early April that had been created to encourage international competition. The connections of Gordon Lord Byron, globetrotter par excellence, were hardly likely to turn down that opportunity.

SO HERE they all were, together in Sydney: the horse who was once a cripple, the former jockey who might never have walked again, the trainer who had been on the brink of going under and the owner who had almost sold the horse of a lifetime. United in a quest for a slice of racing history.

Things did not start well. Hogan had been promised a work horse while Gordon Lord Byron was in quarantine in Melbourne but that horse bled on the first morning they went out. "It was a little bit tricky," recalls Hogan, with masterly understatement. "But full marks to my team out there, they did a great job."

The team was Power and work rider Kate O'Brien, for whom this was a last great adventure with her beloved Gordon Lord Byron before she headed off to London to study physiotherapy. O'Brien knew the horse inside out and Power, having been involved with the Hogan

▶▶ *Continues page 156*

Irish rover: Gordon Lord Byron (far left) makes history with his Group 1 victory in the George Ryder Stakes at Rosehill in Sydney; (below left) he scores his first win since the Australian trip in the Group 2 British Champions Sprint, following a pair of Group 1 seconds at Haydock and Longchamp; (below right) trainer Tom Hogan with Gordon Lord Byron in the Ascot winner's enclosure

yard for so long, knew the training programme to follow.

"At this stage I'm like one of his sons," he says. "I know exactly how Tom likes everything done and how he trains the horses, so I carry on Tom's routine and make sure it's done to his standards. Kate was riding, she knows him better than I do. She's in love with him. When we got to Sydney they gave us a second work horse and he was a lot better."

The TJ Smith Stakes at Randwick was the main aim, but first there was a Group 1 opportunity in the George Ryder Stakes at Rosehill, way out in Sydney's western suburbs. Gordon Lord Byron had been out of quarantine for only ten days and this was viewed as more of a prep race but conditions were right for him: seven and a half furlongs, a right-handed track and ground with just a bit of cut. "They called it soft," Hogan says, "but in Ireland we would say it was good to yielding, where they just put a print in the ground." All in all, conditions were

similar to the day he had won the Prix de la Foret at Longchamp.

Gordon Lord Byron's performance was similar too. He travelled well in midfield under Australian jockey Craig Williams, was ridden well over a furlong out to chase the leaders, ran on strongly in the final furlong and got up in the final 100 yards. He won by a short neck – a remarkable performance so soon after arriving.

For Power, leading in the horse, it was an unforgettable moment. "Everything clicked that day," he says. "One day like that makes it all worthwhile for 100 hard days. What he did was exceptional."

Gordon Lord Byron was the first northern-hemisphere horse to win at the top level in Sydney and, while it may not rank as highly as Dermot Weld's Melbourne Cups with Vintage Crop and Media Puzzle, the many British and Irish raiders who have failed in that race put into perspective the difficulty of winning on the other side of the globe.

"After the George Ryder, Chris

Waller – he's the champion trainer there at the moment – asked me if I realised what I'd just done," Hogan recalled. "He said they bring out horses from Europe and they can't get them to show form for months and they were amazed that I could do it straight out of quarantine."

Power was surprised there was not the same reaction in Ireland. "We got a great reception in Australia, especially from the Irish community," he says. "He had a good following in Australia but not back home. I was expecting to come back and find people thought something amazing had happened but I don't think people realised what he had accomplished."

That could not take the gloss off the trip for Power, nor the fact that Gordon Lord Byron was well beaten in the TJ Smith at Randwick a fortnight later. This time the ground was heavy, properly gluey, and that scuppered his chance. "When the ground becomes heavy in Australia, it becomes unstable, and he hated

it," Hogan says. "He just couldn't get traction on it. He's a good-actioned horse who has had pelvic problems and he needs to get traction."

For a while, after returning home, it seemed the rigours of the journey had taken their toll but the moral of Gordon Lord Byron's tale is never to write him off. In the autumn he bounced back to form with second places in the Haydock Sprint Cup and Prix de la Foret, giving him the proud record of having finished in the first four in 11 of his 16 Group 1 starts. His next run was in a Group 2, the British Champions Sprint at Ascot, and this time he won, for the first time since Rosehill.

It was a fitting finale to another incredible year for Gordon Lord Byron and his connections. His is an uplifting story of triumphing against the odds, of coming back from the brink, and the people around him have their own remarkable tales to tell. On 29 March 2014 they all wrote a unique chapter together and the story is far from over.

HOME OF THE IRISH GRAND NATIONAL
Experience the electrifying atmosphere

TOP QUALITY HOSPITALITY PACKAGES
FANTASTIC GROUP DISCOUNTS

FAIRYHOUSE FIXTURES FOR THE REMAINDER OF

2014

PREMIER JUMP RACING WEEKEND
29 NOV SATURDAY NH | 30 NOV SUNDAY NH
20 DEC SATURDAY NH (CHRISTMAS PARTY RACE DAY)

FAIRYHOUSE FIXTURES FOR

2015

01 JAN	THURS		NH	07 APR	TUES		NH	10 OCT	SAT	NH
11 JAN	SUN		NH	22 APR	WED	(EVE)	NH	04 NOV	WED	NH
21 JAN	WED		NH	28 MAY	THUR	(EVE)	F	18 NOV	WED	NH
31 JAN	SAT		NH	10 JUN	WED	(EVE)	F	28 NOV	SAT	NH
21 FEB	SAT		NH	01 JUL	WED	(EVE)	F	29 NOV	SUN	NH
05 APR	SUN		NH	05 JUL	SUN		F	19 DEC	SAT	NH
06 APR	MON		NH	29 SEPT	TUES		F			

Tel: +353 1 825 6167 | www.fairyhouse.ie | info@fairyhouse.ie

THE
BIGGER
PICTURE

Joseph O'Brien takes part in the Paddy Power Zorb Derby in aid of the Jack & Jill Children's Foundation on the first day of the Irish Derby festival at the Curragh in June. When it came to the serious business of horseracing, O'Brien was successful on Australia in the following day's Dubai Duty Free Irish Derby

PATRICK McCANN
(RACINGPOST.COM/PHOTOS)

The incredible story of California Chrome captured the imagination of an American public more used to negative headlines about racing. But there was no fairytale ending as another Triple Crown bid came unstuck at Belmont Park

By Nicholas Godfrey

California Dreamin'

I F YOU think British racing is struggling with the wider public, then perhaps you ought to take a look at North America, where a beleaguered industry has spent the last couple of decades hanging on by its fingertips to an audience that seems to be dwindling by the day.

Receded into history are the sepia-tinted glory years of Citation and Kelso, of Secretariat, Seattle Slew and Spectacular Bid. Lack of interest is one thing, but often the US racing community now faces outright antipathy, alleviated only rarely by glimpses of something rather more welcome – a Zenyatta perhaps, or a Rachel Alexandra. Otherwise, the sport is in real danger of being submerged beneath a mass of negative headlines focusing on equine fatalities and illegal drugs. And legal drugs, for that matter.

Fortunately in 2014 there was an equine hero on the horizon in the shape of California Chrome, the unlikely colt from the wrong side of the tracks who won the first two legs of the Triple Crown. Forget the Breeders' Cup, barely a ripple in the wider domestic waters, it is the Kentucky Derby that really commands the attention of the general public. Apart from when there's a Triple Crown on the line at Belmont Park, that is.

Sadly, Big Brown (2008) and I'll Have Another (2012), the two most recent Triple Crown chasers, had been hellish difficult to love, representing a pair of trainers in Rick Dutrow and Doug O'Neill who came with unwanted baggage. Then, like manna from the gods, came California Chrome, a blue-collar colt representing humble connections and a veteran trainer in Art Sherman

whose record bears the closest scrutiny. Sherman, 77, handles a string of about 20 at Los Alamitos in southern California, hitherto better known as a quarterhorse venue. Sherman had to move his horses there when Hollywood Park closed in December 2013.

California Chrome had already earned superstar status by the time he reached New York for his date with destiny as he attempted to become the first Triple Crown winner for 36 years in the Belmont Stakes. That he was unable to win may have been an anticlimax given the pre-race hoopla, but in reality there was no shame in such a heroic

failure as he exited the track with blood seeping from a nasty gash in his off-fore hoof, having been asked to race over a distance well beyond his optimum.

The Hollywood screenwriters based just down the freeway from California Chrome's Los Angeles base would have struggled to come up with a story to match the cheap colt's extraordinary rise to fame. Carrying distinct echoes of the Depression-era celebrity Seabiscuit, California Chrome was a latterday rags-to-riches hero taken to the hearts of the public.

Part-owner Steve Coburn, who works for a company that makes

magnetic strips for credit cards and hotel keys, was asked to explain the horse's appeal. "I think it's the story behind the horse – it shows a dream can come true," he said. "For working-class people, they need a hero, and if it's a horse, let it be."

Much of the initial popularity of the California Chrome story derived from his small-time owner-breeders, Coburn and his racing partner Perry Martin, who owns a product-testing company in Sacramento. More comfortable in Levi's, stetsons and boots than any more fancy get-ups, the pair raced as part of the modest Blinkers On

▸▸ *Continues page 162*

Partnership before that fell apart and they struck out on their own to buy California Chrome's dam Love The Chase for just $8,000, using the name 'DAP'. The initials stand for 'Dumb Ass Partners': at the sale, someone was heard to remark that only a dumbass would buy the Maryland-bred mare, who won just one of her six career starts. For her first mating, they bred her to cheap stallion Lucky Pulpit, who won only three of his 22 races. The offspring was California Chrome and he carries signature silks: purple with a green donkey – a bucktoothed jackass, to be precise – on the back. On the front of the silks and on his blinkers are the letters DAP.

California Chrome was beaten on four of his first six career starts before a spree during which he developed the habit of scoring by 'daylight' margins. His last four wins before Churchill Downs were achieved by a cumulative 24 lengths, climaxing in a breathtaking runaway victory in the $1 million Santa Anita Derby, the foremost trial on the west coast. Soon after that five-length romp, his owners were able to turn down a $6m offer for a controlling interest in California Chrome, reasoning that any new owner would remove the horse from Sherman's barn. Who were the dumbasses now?

Much of the preamble to the 140th running of the Kentucky Derby was overwhelmed by a series of negative headlines in the wake of a Peta (People for the Ethical Treatment of Animals) exposé of alleged malpractice at the operation of leading trainer Steve Asmussen. The dual Eclipse Award-winning trainer was the target of a four-month hidden-camera operation, details of which were revealed in a sensational New York Times feature where Peta accused Asmussen and his top assistant Scott Blasi of subjecting their horses to cruel treatment, administering drugs for non-therapeutic reasons and – potentially most damagingly in terms of reputation – knowingly employing one of their jockeys to use a banned electrical device known as a 'buzzer' or a 'machine'. Asmussen's name was removed from the Hall of Fame ballot; Blasi was fired, although the trainer reinstated him in late July.

Against this benighted backdrop came the latest rendition of America's greatest race. Not for nothing, though, is the Kentucky Derby billed as the greatest two minutes in sport and California Chrome did much to banish the demons – for a while, at least – as he justified strong favouritism in the $2m

event with a resounding victory that took his winning streak to five under jockey Victor Espinoza.

Kentucky bluegrass bloodstock dominates American breeding to such an extent that California Chrome was the first Californian-bred to win the nation's most celebrated race since Decidedly in 1962. He was Californian through and through; the 'chrome' refers to the chestnut's distinctive white markings, four socks and a blaze. Such paint is referred to as 'chrome' in US racing parlance.

Espinoza had won the race before, in 2002 on War Emblem, but the other members of the California Chrome team were novices. Well, sort of. Sherman had never before saddled a

▸ Blue-collar colt: California Chrome, the product of an unlikely mating far from the bluegrass of Kentucky, was the first Californian-bred to win the Kentucky Derby since 1962 and made 77-year-old Art Sherman, who had never before had a Derby runner, the oldest winning trainer in the race's history

Derby runner, but he had been to the Derby – as a teenage work rider for the great Swaps in 1955. "To be my age and have something like this happen, what can you say?" said Sherman, who became the oldest trainer ever to win the race, surpassing Charlie Whittingham, who was 76 when Sunday Silence won in 1989.

"You know, I never really thought this would happen to me. I mean, we've had some nice stakes horses in our barn but never a Derby horse," he said a couple of days before the Preakness Stakes as he stood outside Barn 40 at Pimlico, the stable traditionally reserved for Derby winners at the venue known colloquially as Old Hilltop. "When I went back

▸ *Continues page 164*

The Hotel Royal Barrière in Deauville, the place to be in France!

© Patrick McCann

'It's a dream come true. You can't believe the fanfare – he's a rock star'

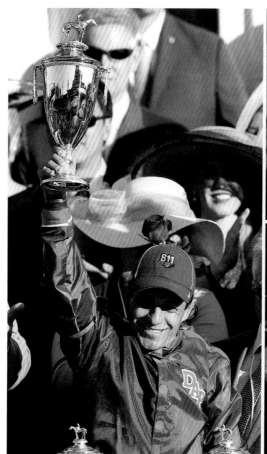

to Los Alamitos, on the marquee it said: 'California Chrome, Home of the Kentucky Derby Winner'. It was really cool – and I hear they went bananas when he won.

"You wake up in the morning and say, 'Hey, wait a minute, I just won the Kentucky Derby.' It's a dream come true for me. You can't believe the fanfare – he's a rock star. It's a different ball game for me. I've been in the game for so long and I never had the big stable or the money people behind me, just mom-and-pop operations and people that were always good friends."

Coburn, who lives with wife Carolyn at Topaz Lake, Nevada, turned 61 on Kentucky Derby day. "I said a long time ago that he'd win the Kentucky Derby," said the owner, who added another folksy aspect to an incredible story when he related an anecdote in which he claimed he told his wife he saw the colt in a dream three weeks before he was foaled.

"I said, I believe it's going to be a big chestnut colt," said Coburn. "We drove over, saw him the day after he was born. She walked up to that birthing stall and said, 'Come here, this is your dream.' We held on to that dream. I've said it a hundred times or a thousand times, if you're willing to ride a dream out, they will come true for you. We're living proof of it. I believe this horse will win the Triple Crown."

California Chrome duly took the Preakness in a decisive if unspectacular display to set up his Triple Crown bid three weeks later at Belmont, where America's new hero would face a tough field running a mile and a half – a marathon in US dirt terms – around the wide, open spaces of the New York racetrack known colloquially as the Big Sandy.

"We've got 'Chromies' on our side," suggested Coburn ahead of his horse's attempt to become America's 12th Triple Crown winner, the first since Affirmed in 1978, a notorious drought during which 12 horses had won both the Kentucky Derby and the Preakness before coming unstuck in the Belmont.

Sherman, for his part, was well aware of the significance. "There's a lot of cameras and stuff around in the mornings now, that's for sure," he said. "There's a lot of pressure on us. It means a lot to the whole industry and to racing, which we needed – we need stars right now and I think we've got a chance.

"I have a good feeling about it," he added. "I'm really confident going into this race. I don't care how many fresh shooters they've got there – he's the real McCoy. He's been a super horse for us. He's one of those horses that you're going to have to outrun to beat him. Maybe they won't be able to beat him. I'm looking forward to that race – they better have their running shoes on."

Unfortunately, they did. Although California Chrome was riding on a tide of goodwill, America's Triple Crown dreams were dashed when the hugely popular favourite was outrun in the final furlong and could only dead-heat for fourth place behind 9-1 shot Tonalist. The winner had not run in either of the previous legs of the Triple Crown – much to the chagrin of Coburn, who launched an extraordinary post-race outburst live on NBC Sports.

"You know what, he's run three very big races," said a visibly upset Coburn, whose churlish comments could easily

▶▶One heck of a ride: (clockwise from left) jockey Victor Espinoza celebrates with the trophy after winning the Kentucky Derby on California Chrome; trainer Art Sherman after the Preakness; Steve Coburn, the colt's part-owner, salutes the crowd before the Belmont, which was to end in disappointment as the Triple Crown dream was dashed

have taken some of the gloss off the California Chrome fairytale. "These other horses – they always set them out and try to upset the applecart. I'm 61 years old and in my lifetime I'll never see another Triple Crown winner because of the way they do this.

"It's not fair to these horses that have been in the game since day one," added Coburn, whose wife attempted to shut him up. "I look at it this way: if you can't make enough points to get in the Kentucky Derby, you can't run in the other two races. It's all or nothing. Because this is not fair to these horses who have been running their guts out and for the people who believe in them. To have someone come up like this – this is the coward's way out in my opinion. Our horse had a target on his back."

Coburn later apologised for his emotional tirade; it also emerged his colt had injured his off-fore during the race. California Chrome returned, battered and bruised, to his Los Alamitos base for a well-earned rest.

While the unlikely hero may not have won the Triple Crown, he had achieved the near-impossible in putting a smile back on the faces of the US racing community. How long it lasts is anybody's guess.

مهرجان سُمُّو الشيخ
منصور بن زايد آل نهيان
العالمي للخيول العربية
الأصيلة

HH Sheikh Mansoor
Bin Zayed Al Nahyan
Global Arabian Horse
Flat Racing Festival

جائزة دارلي
Darley Award

سمو الشيخة فاطمة بنت مبارك
HH Sheikha Fatima Bint Mubarak
Darley Award

HOLLYWOOD 2015

April 3, 2015
HH Sheikha Fatima Bint Mubarak Darley Awards

◻◻ DOLBY THEATRE
at hollywood & highland center

April 4, 2015
HH Shk Mansoor Bin Zayed Al Nahyan Festival World
Gala Dinner

Organised by:	Coordinated by:	In association:	Supported by:	Official Partner	Official Carrier:

Sponsored by:

▸▸Centre stage: The action unfolds in the Group 1 Jebel Ali Racecourse Zaabeel International Stakes, won by Al Mouhannad and jockey Jean-Baptiste Hamel, on Dubai International Arabian Raceday at Newbury (main picture); (below, clockwise) the jockeys line up for the Newbury leg of the HH Sheikha Fatima Bint Mubarak Apprentice World Championship; the HH Sheikha Fatima Bint Mubarak Darley Awards in Hollywood; the World Arabian Horse Racing Conference in London; Loraa (green and yellow) wins the Qatar Total Arabian Trophy at Longchamp on Arc weekend; happy connections in the winner's enclosure after Loraa's victory
Pictures: DAVID DEW (RACINGPOST.COM/PHOTOS) & MORHAF AL ASSAF

IN THE
PICTURE

Arabian racing takes growing role on major racedays

From Hollywood to Hereford, and all the way to Abu Dhabi via Newbury, Arabian racing has an increasing presence on the equestrian sporting scene and in 2014 Britain took a central role in its growth.

As the host of Dubai International Arabian Raceday, the biggest fixture in Britain, Newbury racecourse has long been a supporter of the sport and in August there was a new event at the Berkshire track with a leg of the HH Sheikha Fatima Bint Mubarak Apprentice World Championship, held as the curtain-raiser to a Sunday thoroughbred card.

The mile-and-a-quarter race was won by the French-trained Karar, with British apprentice Jack Gilligan in third place on Noble Athlete for Welsh trainer Delyth Thomas.

Gilligan, 18, who has ambitions to become a professional jockey under thoroughbred rules, says: "That was my first Arab race and it was a great experience. It was something different and it was great to share my experiences with all the other apprentice jockeys from around the world."

The apprentice races are a key component of the Sheikh Mansoor Global Arabian Festival, which comprises four different race series and travels the world throughout the year before culminating in a finals day in Abu Dhabi in November. The importance of developing the next generation of jockeys was emphasised when Lara Sawaya, executive director of the Global Arabian Festival and a driving force in the sport, was promoted recently to Chairman of Apprentice Jockeys and Racing in the International Federation of Arabian Horse Racing Authorities.

The festival also visited Britain when Newbury hosted a race in the Sheikha Fatima Ladies World Championship and Hereford – which closed for jump racing in 2012 but has been revived by Arabian racing – held three racedays, featuring

six legs of the Wathba Stud Farm Cup at each meeting.

Britain was also chosen as the venue for the 2014 World Arabian Horseracing Conference, held in London for the first time. Run as part of the Sheikh Mansoor Festival, this five-day event culminated in two Arabian races at Newbury, including the £70,000 Zayed Cup, and an endurance event in Thetford.

Another glittering event took place at the Dolby Theatre in Hollywood – the iconic venue used for the Oscars – and British rider Rachel King was among the winners. The 23-year-old amateur, who has won under rules and in point-to-points as well as Arabian races, beat off worldwide competition to pick up the trophy as top lady jockey at the Sheikha Fatima Bint Mubarak Darley Awards, which honoured the best in the sport. "My trip to Hollywood was amazing, made even better by winning the award," King said.

This different branch of racing is becoming more visible as part of thoroughbred racedays – and often for better prize-money. Both factors help to attract the top professional riders and increase the profile of the sport.

The most valuable Arabian race held in Britain is the Qatar Racing and Equestrian Club Harwood International Stakes, worth £150,000 and now part of the St Leger card at Doncaster. Among the leading Flat jockeys who took part this year were Andrea Atzeni, fresh from his victory in the St Leger, although victory went to the amateur Simon Walker on the Julian Smart-trained Al Atique.

Walker, who has ridden around 600 winners in Arabian racing, says: "It was smashing to win that race, especially back in Yorkshire, which is my home county. It's great to have an Arab race on Leger day."

Arabian horses, which have shorter necks,

dished faces and high tail carriages, are generally seen as slower than thoroughbreds but Walker counters that view. "Real good Arab horses ride like thoroughbreds, there's not a lot of difference at all," he says. "They put their head down, lengthen and quicken up."

To reiterate the point, the winning time of the Smart-trained Djainka Des Forges in the Qatar Arabian World Cup on Arc day compared favourably with thoroughbred handicappers at Longchamp that weekend. Djainka Des Forges was ridden by Christophe Lemaire and the previous day's big Arabian winner at Longchamp, Loraa in the Qatar Total Arabian Trophy, was partnered by Christophe Soumillon – another sign of the growing prestige attached to this branch of the sport.

Racegoers can expect to see a lot more of Arabian racing on the biggest days in the thoroughbred calendar.

CROWD PLEASER

At the age of 12 Sizing Europe brought the house down at the Punchestown festival with a remarkable return to the Grade 1 honours board

By Nick Pulford

FOR sheer emotion, Sizing Europe's victory in the Boylesports.com Champion Chase at Punchestown was hard to beat. Just when it seemed his racing days, let alone his best days, would be a thing of the past, he conjured another spellbinding moment of magic. At the age of 12, he was a Grade 1 winner again.

Watching on the big screen in the parade ring, Henry de Bromhead screamed for his life as Sizing Europe and Andrew Lynch landed over the final fence with a clear lead. The trainer was so wrapped up in the moment he "felt like the only fella roaring" but he was far from alone. All around him, tumultuous scenes unfolded as a record first-day festival crowd of 19,459 cheered Sizing Europe to the line and all the way to the winner's enclosure.

"Oh man," De Bromhead said as he greeted his old warrior, breathless and overwhelmed by the moment. He wiped away lipstick, unsure whose lips had delivered it amid the heady throng of well-wishers, and tried to make sense of it all. Then he summed it up in one word: "Unbelievable."

This was a turning back of the clock to a time that had seemed long gone. Sizing Europe had won Punchestown's Champion Chase as a ten-year-old in 2012 – his record in the race also includes two seconds and a third – but the light had faded gradually since then and retirement appeared to be looming. Perhaps the end would have come that very day if Sizing Europe had been among the also-rans but instead he was the star of the show with the eighth Grade 1 success of his glittering career.

One of jump racing's enduring attractions is the longevity of its stars and the cementing of bonds between

▶▶ Day to remember: (clockwise from main picture) Sizing Europe and jockey Andrew Lynch are greeted by owner Ann Potts after winning the Champion Chase at Punchestown; lining up at the start; trainer Henry de Bromhead welcomes back his stable star; Ann and Alan Potts with the trophy; Sizing Europe clears the final fence

horses and people – owners, trainers, jockeys and fans alike - over many years. Even so, Sizing Europe's feat was a rare achievement. He was the first 12-year-old Grade 1 winner in Ireland since Florida Pearl landed his fourth Hennessy Gold Cup a decade earlier, while the most recent in Britain was Monet's Garden – not by coincidence another great public favourite – in the 2010 Ascot Chase.

It seemed churlish to observe that the Champion Chase field was the weakest in years. Sprinter Sacre, who had wowed Punchestown in a different way the previous year, was sidelined and Queen Mother Champion Chase winner Sire De Grugy had concluded his season at Sandown three days earlier. In their absence the favourite was Hidden Cyclone, who had never won above Grade 3 level over fences.

Sizing Europe needed only a Racing Post Rating of 163 to claim victory, 10lb below the level of his

second place to Sprinter Sacre 12 months earlier. That measured the standard of the performance but could not reflect the emotional impact.

Reflecting in the autumn on that heady day at Punchestown, De Bromhead said: "I wanted it to happen so much and it was pretty emotional for him to come back like that. Everything fell right. The ground was super for him, he got a dream run through the race and Andrew gave him a great ride. The crowd was amazing. It was a great atmosphere and everyone was so complimentary about him. It was a brilliant day for everyone involved."

Before his Punchestown heroics, Sizing Europe had seemed to be heading towards retirement, albeit with gallantry by continuing to operate almost exclusively in Grade 1 races. De Bromhead said the 'R' word had not been discussed directly with Ann and Alan Potts, Sizing

Europe's owners, but the subject was a natural line of inquiry after the race.

Alan Potts said "yes" at one point in answer to the retirement question, then stepped back to "possibly". By late summer, after more dispassionate consideration, it was a "no". In October, Sizing Europe started another season, eight years after his first, with victory in Gowran Park's PWC Champion Chase.

De Bromhead admitted his nerves were as bad as they have ever been before a race, but Sizing Europe was magnificent again and so was the deafening roar that greeted him on his return to the winner's enclosure.

"He deserves that reception," said De Bromhead. "We just didn't feel he was ready to be retired and fair play to Alan and Ann for allowing him to keep going. As Alan said, he will tell us when he is ready."

What Sizing Europe achieved in 2014 spoke volumes.

PUNCHESTOWN
in pictures

1 All the fun of the fair on the festival's family day

2 Rozanna Purcell, former Miss Universe Ireland, visits the festival

3 Robbie McNamara performs a miracle to keep his partnership intact with Vital Plot at the final fence of the Donohue Marquees Champion Hunters Chase. Despite the jockey's efforts, Vital Plot was a well-beaten second behind On The Fringe

4 Be Positive (right) and Nina Carberry race up with the pace on their way to victory in the Kildare Hunt Club Fr Sean Breen Memorial Cross Country Chase

5 Sizing Australia (nearside) and Andrew Lynch narrowly get the better of Be Positive and Nina Carberry in a close finish to the Irish Field Cross Country Chase

6 Forgotten Rules (Robbie McNamara) bolts up by 13 lengths in the Finlay Motor Group INH Flat Race

7 The runners at the start of the Three.ie Handicap Chase won by the Tim Doyle-trained Mallowney (third left), the mount of Davy Russell

8 Horses studying the form

9 A fashionable racegoer

10 The crowd watches the action unfold on the final day

THE ANNUAL 20

Our selection of the horses and people – some established, some up-and-coming – who are likely to be making headlines in 2015

SIMONSIG

This is the season that will reveal whether Simonsig can take the final step into the superstar bracket that he has long seemed destined to join. Having missed the whole of last season – which would have been his first in the senior chasing ranks – the talented grey will attempt a second coming after being given plenty of time to recover from a splint problem.

Simonsig's last appearance before injury brought victory in the 2013 Arkle Chase – his second consecutive win at the Cheltenham Festival after his Neptune Novices' Hurdle triumph – and his rare blend of speed and stamina gives trainer Nicky Henderson plenty of options.

Connections have long had the King George VI Chase in mind for him, but it is not inconceivable that he could line up in the Queen Mother Champion Chase later in the season if Sprinter Sacre, his fellow returning stablemate, is ruled out again. The Ryanair Chase, over the intermediate distance of two miles and five furlongs, is another possible target at Cheltenham.

To some extent, Simonsig has been overshadowed throughout his career by Sprinter Sacre – who preceded him as Arkle winner before joining the ranks of the greats – but he has a first-class record. He won eight of his nine starts under rules before his injury, with the sole defeat blamed on tacky ground, and had a Racing Post Rating of 162 as a novice hurdler and 167 as a novice chaser.

The potential is there to reach an RPR of 180 or more as a senior chaser and, all being well after injury, Simonsig should make up for lost time.

JOHN F KENNEDY

"We've had a lot of bad American presidents." Keen observers of the political scene across the Atlantic might agree with that comment, but of course John Magnier was not making a serious point.

The Coolmore supremo was light-heartedly referring to the names of some of the flops to have emerged from Ballydoyle over the years – like Abraham Lincoln, who won only two minor races for Aidan O'Brien and ended up running in a claimer on the all-weather at Wolverhampton on his final start as a six-year-old.

Magnier can afford to laugh, as there have been successes too. George Washington's four Group 1 wins included the 2,000 Guineas and Queen Elizabeth II Stakes and Coolmore will be hoping their latest American president is more Washington than Lincoln.

The early signs were good for

John F Kennedy, a full-brother to 2014 Yorkshire Oaks winner Tapestry. With his pedigree, the thinking was clearly towards the Derby from an early stage and he started in a mile maiden at Leopardstown in July, finishing a rather green second.

O'Brien felt he was still babyish next time at the Curragh, although this time he broke his maiden by four and three-quarter lengths, and then it was up to Group 3 company, back at Leopardstown.

John F Kennedy revealed much more this time, showing plenty of pace to win by three and a quarter lengths. By now he was favourite for next year's Derby and his likely destination is Epsom rather than Newmarket, even though O'Brien pointed to the colt's turn of foot and even contemplated dropping him back to seven furlongs to contest the Dewhurst.

At this stage John F Kennedy gets our vote.

MILSEAN

Milsean was so impressive in his only point-to-point – winning by five lengths in a fast time even though he did not look fully wound up and his rider lost his irons after the second last – that he was bought soon after for £115,000 to run in the colours of Gigginstown House Stud.

Having been put away for seven months, he won by eight lengths at Navan on his bumper debut for Willie Mullins in January 2014,

with the trainer commenting: "He's a huge staying chaser in the making but he's not slow either."

Disappointment followed on Milsean's next start at Naas when he was beaten by No More Heroes (another highly promising Gigginstown youngster, trained by Gordon Elliott) but that defeat also brought a handy lesson about the best way to ride him.

On Milsean's third and final start of his bumper season, Patrick Mullins made all on him for the first time and they powered to a 25-length victory. "The change in tactics brought about the improvement in him," said the rider. "We let him go on as he's a relentless galloper. We weren't making use of his cruising speed before."

The quality of that performance at Limerick is evident in a Racing Post Rating of 145 – a mark bettered in bumpers only three times since 2007 – and Milsean looks set to climb even higher this season.

JONATHAN BURKE

Three months. That's all it took for Jonathan Burke to go from amateur rider to 5lb claimer and then to first jockey for the powerful string of Alan and Ann Potts, who last season ranked sixth in the Irish jump owners' standings. Few jump jockeys have had such a meteoric rise but the 18-year-old looks well equipped to handle the pressure of his new job.

Twenty-four hours after his appointment was announced in September, Burke won on his first ride in the Potts colours when Loosen My Load struck at Galway. Just for good measure, he had another winner that day for their main trainer Henry de Bromhead, while the following week he had four successes at the Listowel festival.

Even then, his career total was less than 40 winners but there is little doubt in Irish jump racing that he is heading for the top. As the son of County Cork trainer Liam Burke, the young rider has been around horses all his life and his calm, composed style has earned many admirers.

Trainer Mick Winters says Burke is "very talented, very intelligent with a grand, quiet manner. He has a very quiet style on a horse. Horses jump and travel for him." De Bromhead has also been impressed, saying: "He seems very good over a fence, which is great, and he's a good judge of pace. He's still a 5lb claimer, but he's really clued in."

Burke himself views his elevation in simple terms. "I've been picked because of the way I've been riding. I don't see why I should change anything. If I keep doing what I've been doing, hopefully things will fall into place."

ANDREA ATZENI

Half of the top ten Flat jockeys in the 2014 British championship are twentysomethings and the latest sign of change in the weighing room is the elevation of Andrea Atzeni to first jockey for Qatar Racing next season.

Atzeni, 23, is the youngest rider in the top ten and he announced himself on the big stage with Classic victory on Kingston Hill in the St Leger, followed within 24 hours by another Group 1 success on Cursory Glance in the Moyglare Stud Stakes.

Both winners were for Roger Varian, the Sardinian-born rider's chief supporter during his rapid rise through the ranks, but already by then the contract had been signed for Qatar Racing. Atzeni replaces dual British champion Jamie Spencer, who has retired at the age of 34 to take up a management role with the burgeoning operation owned by Sheikh Fahad Al Thani and his brothers.

Another fast-climbing rider, 19-year-old Oisin Murphy, will be Qatar's second jockey.

Amid the tall jockeys who populate the weighing room, such as Richard Hughes, Atzeni is a throwback to the old days of the 'pocket rocket'. His busy, elbow-pumping style is reminiscent of five-times British champion Willie Carson and has taken him to consecutive centuries.

Qatar Racing had a largely disappointing 2014 but, with more than 150 horses and 26 trainers in Britain and Ireland alone, the job holds plenty of promise for Atzeni.

"I look at this as the future," he told Brough Scott in a Racing Post interview shortly after his appointment. "Not next year, or maybe not even the year after, it could be the best job in racing. Sheikh Fahad is very ambitious. He wants to be a champion. And so do I. I want to ride good horses in big races and travel the world."

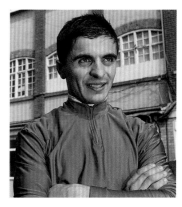

FOUND

The temperature of two-year-old maiden races in Ireland is usually set by whatever Aidan O'Brien chooses to run and one of the hottest contests in 2014 was at the Curragh on August 23.

O'Brien, as so often, had a multiple entry in the Irish Stallion Farms EBF Fillies' Maiden over a mile and one of them was the 11-10 favourite, Together Forever, who had the benefit of a previous run.

She finished second, however, to a debutante from Ballydoyle in Found, who went off at 14-1 and beat her better-fancied stablemate by three-quarters of a length.

The form would work out very well indeed and O'Brien hinted as much in his post-race comments on Found: "She shouldn't have been able to come from where she was off such a slow pace unless she was smart. She had been working well."

That was the start of an impressive few weeks for Found. The daughter of Galileo went straight up to Group 1 company, finishing third behind Cursory Glance and Lucida in the Moyglare Stud Stakes, and then won the Prix Marcel Boussac.

Together Forever boosted the form further by winning the Group 1 Dubai Fillies' Mile at Newmarket. O'Brien said they were "both exciting, high-class fillies" but the betting on next year's Classics suggested Found is superior.

"She's a very good filly and is one to follow because she still has a lot of scope to improve," said jockey Ryan Moore after her Longchamp victory.

From a man of few words, those look worth heeding.

JOE DOYLE

"The next Oisin Murphy" is a difficult tag to live up to, but Joe Doyle looks ready to be one of the top Flat apprentices in 2015 after making impressive progress throughout his first full year in Britain.

The comparison with the champion apprentice came from Newmarket trainer Phil McEntee and he is not the only one impressed by Doyle, who has ridden winners for 16 different trainers in 2014.

At 18, Doyle is a year younger than Murphy but they know each other well from their successful days on the Irish pony racing circuit. Doyle, from Tipperary, won the coveted Dingle Derby in 2011 and had two weeks' work experience at Ballydoyle that year before he began working for Charlie Swan.

Having ridden four winners on the Flat in Ireland, he joined John Quinn's North Yorkshire yard in June 2013 and rode three more winners in Britain that year. From the start of 2014, however, he made great strides and quickly pushed his career total towards the half-century.

Doyle has a strong family background in racing. Father Jim rode over jumps for Roger Fisher and cousins Jack Doyle and Michael Byrne are forging careers in that branch of the sport, while his uncle Pat Doyle (Jack's father) is a leading Irish point-to-point trainer.

Doyle has a long way to go if he is to match Murphy, who has already been signed as Qatar Racing's second jockey for 2015, but he is heading the right way.

JACK GARRITTY

Andrew Balding's Kingsclere establishment is renowned as a jockeys' academy – a tradition the trainer inherited from his father Ian – and Jack Garritty is one of the latest to show the benefits of a first-rate education.

As a son of former jump jockey Russ Garritty, he had a head start with riding horses before his youthful talent was polished at Kingsclere. In the summer of 2014, his apprenticeship was transferred to Richard Fahey – another trainer with the willingness and ammunition to help young riders – and his impressive progress accelerated.

Garritty, 18, spent two years at Kingsclere and, after five winners from 76 rides in 2013, he really kicked on this year with more than 30 winners. He finished the season strongly under Fahey's wing, describing the move as "the best decision I've ever made".

Even during his time with Balding, Garritty forged strong contacts in the north. He would often stay overnight with his parents in Middleham, where his father is assistant trainer to Patrick Holmes, and the move back to his roots made sense for the Malton-born rider.

Fahey was pleased to secure his services. "Jack rides well, conducts himself well and is keen and light," he said.

At 5ft 10in, Garritty is on the tall side for the Flat but amazingly can ride at 7st 7lb. "It's not a struggle," he said, "though I appreciate things may change. If I get heavier I doubt I'd switch to jumping. I'd rather go overseas to be a work rider."

Whatever the long term brings, right now Garritty is well worth his 5lb claim and looks set for a bright 2015.

CURSORY GLANCE

Twenty-four hours after his first Classic success with Kingston Hill in the St Leger, trainer Roger Varian raised hopes of more to come next season when he sent out Cursory Glance to land the Group 1 Moyglare Stud Stakes at the Curragh.

"Hopefully she has a massive year in front of her next year," said Varian, leaving no doubt about his regard for the filly. "She has tremendous natural speed, is very talented and gets this trip well."

As he had with Kingston Hill, winner of the Racing Post Trophy at two, Varian was prepared to test this Classic prospect from an early stage. After a maiden victory on the all-weather, she won the Group 3 Albany Stakes at Royal Ascot before succumbing to the superior speed of Tiggy Wiggy in a high-calibre Group 2 Lowther Stakes at York.

Stepped up to seven furlongs for the Moyglare, she justified favouritism despite not impressing everyone with a neck victory over Lucida, subsequent winner of the Group 2 Rockfel Stakes. Found, who was third, went on to land the Group 1 Prix Marcel Boussac.

Varian had an explanation for the seemingly prosaic performance: "It was the strangest race I've watched. Andrea [Atzeni] said she felt a bit lazy in the middle of the race and he gave her a squeeze and she took off. Then he felt he was in front too soon and she was pulling up in front."

Varian has treated Cursory Glance like a top filly all the way and "she's definitely a Guineas filly" was Atzeni's verdict after the Moyglare. With her preference for fast ground, Cursory Glance could be a force throughout next summer in the top mile races for fillies.

DARYL JACOB & BRENDAN POWELL

Changing times on the riding front at the Tizzard stable, with Joe having hung up his boots to become assistant trainer to father Colin, and that has opened the door for others to make their mark with a string that has increased in size and significance in recent seasons.

Daryl Jacob (above left) takes the reins on stable star Cue Card, along with the other jumpers owned by Bob and Jean Bishop. Having seen the No.1 position with champion jumps trainer Paul Nicholls slip from his grasp, the 31-year-old is trying to rebuild his reputation to some extent, albeit with three consecutive top-12 finishes behind him in the jockeys' standings, and Cue Card is likely to keep him in the spotlight all winter.

Jacob is riding as a freelance but the Bishop horses give him a solid foundation and Colin Tizzard is delighted to have him on board. "Daryl did not become number one jockey with Nicholls for nothing. He is used to riding in the biggest races and dealing with pressure. It's an ideal appointment."

Powell (above right), already a trusted member of the team, is likely to see his opportunities increase. It can be difficult to remember he is only 19, such is his composure in the saddle and his level of achievement. He has had a winner at each of the past two Cheltenham Festivals – first with the Tizzard-trained Golden Chieftain and then with Present View for Jamie Snowden, whose rising stable is another source of good rides for Powell.

As one of the major up-and-coming talents in the weighing room, Powell looks set for more big-race success.

SAPHIR DU RHEU

Big Buck's may be gone but owner Andy Stewart and trainer Paul Nicholls are sure to enjoy more big days together and hopes are high that Saphir Du Rheu will be capable of taking them to the major novice chases.

Nicholls has always viewed the grey as a chaser in the making but there was a bonus last season with an impressive hat-trick in handicap hurdles, rounded off by victory over subsequent Coral Cup and Liverpool Hurdle winner Whisper in the Welsh Champion Hurdle. In just three months Saphir Du Rheu took his official hurdles rating from 130 to 165.

The five-year-old was lined up as a potential substitute if Big Buck's was unable to run in the World Hurdle but Nicholls never intended to take him to Cheltenham and in any case his winning run came to an end with a disappointing fourth in the Grade 2 National Spirit Hurdle at Fontwell in late February. That was ascribed to the effects of a busy winter and he was promptly put away until this season.

Nicholls has his usual strong team of novice chase prospects but Saphir Du Rheu is often the first name that comes to his lips. Last season he said: "I told Andy we must look after him as he could be the best horse he has ever had with me over fences."

At his owners' day in September, however, Nicholls raised the possibility of a hurdles outing in top company "to see where we stand with him".

That is understandable in view of Saphir Du Rheu's elevated rating in that sphere, where he would need little improvement to be competitive in the major staying hurdles, but chasing is his future.

Wwingate
signs & graphics

Your message on the inside track of racing

As a family run business we understand the importance of brand and how it translates on and off the UK's racecourses.

Maximising your brand exposure: creatively, professionally and ensuring value for money.

- Signs and banners
- Event activation
- Promotions
- Vehicle wrapping
- Bespoke branding campaigns
- Services for sponsors, venues and business requirements
- Supporting your own racing requirements: branded colours, rugs and clothing

Contact us for advice and to discuss your requirements.

Wingate Signs are proud of their association with The Jockey Club and its sponsors.

JOSSES HILL

Recent Arkle Chase winners Sprinter Sacre and Simonsig are a hard act to follow at Nicky Henderson's yard but Josses Hill could emerge as the trainer's top two-mile novice chaser and possibly also the best in Britain.

Even as a novice hurdler last season, he tended to jump more like a chaser and Henderson has always believed he will come into his own over fences. Even so, he reached a high level over hurdles in finishing second in the Supreme Novices' Hurdle (albeit well beaten by the hugely promising Vautour) and then winning a Grade 2 at Aintree on his final start.

The six-year-old was game rather than impressive at Aintree, despite scoring by six lengths, but that was put down to the effects of his previous efforts and there is no disguising the high regard in which he is held.

"He's a gorgeous, big horse with bags of scope for two-mile chases," Henderson said in the autumn. It would be difficult to argue with that assessment.

HIGHLAND REEL

Goodwood's Vintage Stakes has a rich history of producing top-class three-year-olds and all the signs are that Highland Reel could be another for Aidan O'Brien.

The 460,000gns yearling purchase arrived for the Group 2 contest with a big reputation after winning a mile maiden at Gowran Park by 12 lengths and he was sent off odds-on, with O'Brien having no qualms about dropping back to seven furlongs.

The confidence was justified as Highland Reel travelled well, quickened smoothly and finished strongly to score by two and a quarter lengths.

The Vintage has produced both Guineas and Derby winners over the years – Sir Percy ran in both Classics in 2006, finishing second at Newmarket before winning at Epsom – and Highland Reel appears to have a potent mix of speed and stamina.

The Derby distance certainly looks within the Galileo colt's compass, as he is a half-brother to Australian Group 1 middle-distance performer Valdemoro and his dam was third in a Group 1 Oaks in Australia.

O'Brien was keen to stress Highland Reel's speed, saying he would have been happy to run him over six furlongs, and he is likely to have plenty of options with this highly promising colt.

TIGGY WIGGY

In seasons gone by, the calculation with two-year-olds as high-class and devastatingly fast as Tiggy Wiggy (above) was whether they would be able to stretch as far as the Guineas mile the following spring.

If that proved beyond them, as it often did, life could become extremely difficult as the sprinting option against older rivals is notoriously difficult for three-year-olds.

Now, as part of what has been called a sprint revolution in European racing, there is a new avenue for the speedballs and the Richard Hannon-trained Tiggy Wiggy could be one of the first beneficiaries.

In an effort to provide more opportunities for sprinters, Royal Ascot will hold a new six-furlong Group 1 race in 2015, open only to three-year-olds and worth £375,000.

Although the Guineas option can still be explored, Tiggy Wiggy looks made for the Royal Ascot race. She is seriously fast, with her victories over five furlongs including a six-length demolition job off top weight in the Super Sprint at Newbury, and as a Group 1 winner in the Cheveley Park Stakes there is no doubt about her quality either.

As usual, jockey Richard Hughes seemed spot on in his assessment. "She's probably a sprinter through and through, but we might as well contemplate a crack at the Guineas – if she stays I can't envisage anything beating her. If she doesn't stay she can have the new Group 1 sprint at Royal Ascot as her aim."

At least now there is another option for Tiggy Wiggy.

DON POLI

"He has staying chaser written all over him," said Willie Mullins last season when summing up Don Poli in his simple, straightforward way. This could be the season the five-year-old adds more substance to that statement with a first campaign over fences that will have the RSA Chase as the ultimate goal.

Don Poli was far from quiet over hurdles last season. He won a Grade 3 novice hurdle on heavy ground over three miles at Clonmel in February, followed up three weeks later in the Martin Pipe Conditional

Jockeys' Handicap Hurdle at the Cheltenham Festival and ended his campaign in Grade 1 novice company with a close second to Beat That – a potential RSA Chase opponent – at the Punchestown festival.

Mullins' previous Martin Pipe winner was Sir Des Champs, at the same age as Don Poli, and he went on to novice-chase success at the Cheltenham and Punchestown festivals the following season before taking high rank among the seniors.

Similar hopes are entertained for Don Poli in the same Gigginstown House Stud colours.

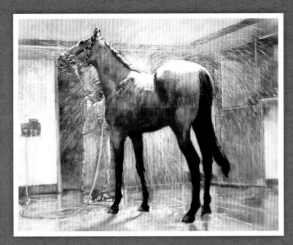

ALI STRONGE

In little more than 18 months since taking out a trainer's licence, Ali Stronge has caught the eye with her impressive strike-rate and ability to improve moderate horses.

Having started under her maiden name of Brewer, the 31-year-old married jockeys' agent Sam Stronge this year and they make a formidable team – her patience and expertise with her string combining with his knowledge of the form book.

The Stronges are based just outside Lambourn at Castle Piece Stables, which was rebuilt virtually from scratch after they moved there in 2009. Having come from a hunting and eventing background, Ali initially ran a pre-training yard before taking the plunge into training in May 2013.

In her first jumps season, 2013-14, she had 11 winners from 72 runners at a strike-rate of 15 per cent and did even better in the 2014 Flat season with a strike-rate of 30 per cent.

Meetings Man is a prime example of Stronge's talent. Claimed for £7,000 in May 2013, he won a selling hurdle less than a fortnight later before adding two low-grade handicaps on the Flat. For a while it seemed as if he might have reached his limit, but in 2014 he won four more Flat handicaps – the last of them off a 13lb higher mark than when Stronge acquired him.

As her string increases in size and class, which seems assured, Stronge is a trainer to watch.

CAM HARDIE

It was a particularly good Friday for Cam Hardie when he rode his first winner for boss Richard Hannon.

Every apprentice needs that opportunity to get noticed, and for the then 17-year-old it came on the Hannon-trained Viewpoint in the apprentice race that opened Lingfield's all-weather championships day in April.

More significantly, this was the first race ever run on a Good Friday in Britain and that put Hardie in the media spotlight after his victory.

At the time he was starting to feel under pressure to make his mark at the Hannon yard, but soon everything fell into place for the Yorkshireman. "It was a great confidence boost and hopefully an eye-opener for the boss," he says. "I got a lot of publicity and a lot of other trainers started to use me."

Six months later Hardie had ridden nearly 60 winners for the year and his mounts had earned almost £600,000 in prize-money.

The son of a jump jockey, Hardie was born to ride and raised at Tim Easterby's Habton Grange stable in North Yorkshire. The only question growing up was whether he would follow in father Willie's footsteps and ride over jumps or go for the Flat.

Now 18, and down to a 3lb claim, Hardie looks well placed to shine again in 2015.

JAMES BEST

Channel 4 viewers were left in no doubt how much race-riding, and winning, means to James Best when he burst into tears following his first Cheltenham success on Paddy Power Gold Cup day last season.

But it was the manner of the 3lb claimer's victory on Return Spring that marked him out for special attention. Five lengths behind a Paul Nicholls-trained pair at the last, and with his mount bumped by a rival on landing, Best conjured an incredible run to snatch victory by a short head and a nose.

Best, 24, went on to a seasonal-best 25 winners and this tactically astute horseman is held in high regard by his boss Philip Hobbs, who trains Return Spring. He has the talent to thrive even when he rides out his claim.

FINIAN MAGUIRE

Coming from a famous racing family tends to get a rider noticed but it is not just his surname that makes Finny Maguire a rider to watch.

At the age of 16, Maguire had his first winner in June when Mm Dazzler scored on the Flat at Listowel. That winner was provided by his father Adrian Maguire, the former top jump jockey, but just as significantly his next success came at the Galway festival for Dermot Weld. As the top trainer at the meeting, Weld chooses his jockeys on merit and he described Maguire as "very promising" after his victory on Whitey O' Gwaun.

With cousin Jason Maguire among the top jump jockeys in Britain, young Finny has a lot to live up to but appears to have what it takes to make a name for himself.

CONVEY

"I'm loving all of it absolutely as much as I ever have," Sir Michael Stoute said this summer, shortly after continuing his journey out of the doldrums by finishing Royal Ascot as top trainer.

With exciting prospects like Convey to dream about over the winter, the 69-year-old trainer can look forward to an even more enjoyable 2015.

Convey – a Khalid Abdullah homebred by Dansili out of Prix du Moulin winner All At Sea – made his debut on the Kempton all-weather in October. He was well supported at 4-6 in a seven-furlong maiden and sped clear to win by five lengths.

Race watchers were impressed and so was jockey James Doyle. "He's a big, raw baby but had done some nice work," he said. "He's got natural speed, he travelled easily and he picked up well."

Stoute says his favourite time of the training year is February and March – "I think they're *our* horses then and connections haven't really tuned in" – and Convey looks likely to be one of those receiving special attention.

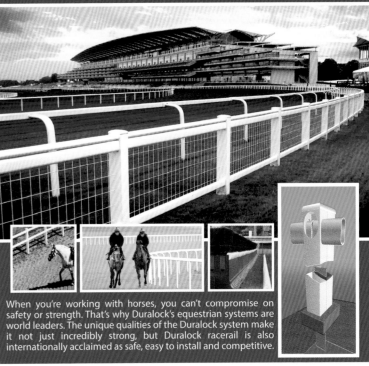

IN THE PICTURE

Ice cold in York for Dettori and Balding as charities benefit by the bucketload

The Ice Bucket Challenge became a global summer phenomenon and racing got in on the act, with many of its leading names being drenched in freezing cold water to raise money for charity.

The format was simple: somebody had water, usually full of ice cubes, dumped over their head. They then nominated three more people to do the same. Participants were typically invited to donate to charity after completing the challenge, or a larger sum if they declined to take part.

Everyone seemed to be doing it, from celebrities such as David Beckham and Justin Bieber to politicians (former US president George W Bush) and even fictional characters (Kermit the Frog and Homer Simpson). Among those to turn down the challenge were incumbent US president Barack Obama and British Prime Minister David Cameron.

At the height of the craze Frankie Dettori and Clare Balding took the challenge on the Friday of York's Ebor meeting (right). They had been nominated, along with Richard Hughes (who took his soaking at Goodwood's Friday evening meeting), by Tony McCoy after he had completed the challenge at Newton Abbot the previous evening. McCoy, in turn, had been nominated by Ruby Walsh, his great friend and rival.

And on it went. Among those nominated next was Balding's Channel 4 Racing colleague Nick Luck, who in turn challenged the winning trainer and jockey of the Ebor Handicap on the final day of York. The unfortunate pair turned out to be Johnny Murtagh and Louis Steward, following their victory with Mutual Regard, and they were soaked in the York winner's enclosure.

Other racing figures to take part in the challenge included trainer Richard Fahey, who had a dunking with a difference when water was poured from a JCB digger at the Malton open day, Gigginstown House Stud owner Michael O'Leary and jockeys Paul Townend and Barry Geraghty.

The challenge started in the United States as a means of raising money and awareness for the Amyotrophic Lateral Sclerosis (ALS) Association. When it spread across the Atlantic, the British equivalent of the ALS, the Motor Neurone Disease Association, was one of the chief beneficiaries. Before the phenomenon took hold, the MND Association received an average of £200,000 a week in donations. In the final week of August alone, it received £2.7m. Many participants chose instead to donate to charities such as Macmillan Cancer Support or in racing's case to organisations like the Injured Jockeys Fund and the Irish Jockeys Accident Fund.

Picture: EDWARD WHITAKER (RACINGPOST.COM/PHOTOS)

final furlong

stories of the year – from the serious to the quirky

Different paths to same goal

Sheehan and Sexton impress with title successes

BOTH were champion pony riders in Ireland and this year, having pursued their careers on different sides of the Irish Sea, both graduated to title successes as conditional jockeys. For Gavin Sheehan and Kevin Sexton, the future looks bright.

Sheehan, 21, from Dunmanway, County Cork, won the British conditionals' title with 50 winners in 2013-14, which showed how far he had come since his wild days back home in Ireland, when by his own admission he was "mad as a brush".

Like so many before him, Sheehan was advised to seek an escape and fresh focus by moving to Britain. In 2011 he joined Charlie Mann in Lambourn before moving across the village to current boss Warren Greatrex in the summer of 2013. Twenty-two of last season's haul came for Greatrex, who said: "He still has quite a lot to work on but he's very professional for one so young. If he continues to progress in the way he did

last season I believe he'll be one of the best jockeys around in a year or two."

Sheehan also linked up successfully with Emma Lavelle, with his new-found maturity shining through as much as his talent. "He has a racing brain," she said. "He tends to be in the right place at the right time, he's very straightforward to deal with and he's good at talking to owners afterwards."

Aware that high-flying conditionals can crash and burn, Sheehan worked hard over the summer and was already halfway to

last season's total by early September at a strike-rate of 29 per cent. "I'm going flat out to try to ensure I don't follow what is a bit of a well-trodden road," he said. "I'm well aware I have a lot to live up to after winning the conditionals' title as it always gets harder taking on the more experienced jockeys at levels. However, I've put a marker down early and I'll go anywhere to try to ride a winner."

While Sheehan finished 16 winners ahead of Michael Byrne, the Irish conditionals' title race was much closer

▶▶ The right stuff: Gavin Sheehan (left) and Kevin Sexton have both been hailed as future stars of the senior ranks

as Sexton edged out Jody McGarvey by two. Sexton, 19, from Nurney, County Kildare, started with Jessica Harrington before moving to Henry de Bromhead early last season, which gave him the push he needed to go for the championship.

Sizing Australia was among his winners for his new yard, but it was hard graft and long hours on the road that earned him the title. His 22 winners came for 16 different trainers and he showed rare ability, with one pressroom veteran hailing him as a future senior champion after an impressive double at Thurles.

Sexton, like Sheehan, was down to a 3lb claim for the new season but still reached double figures by mid-August. "If things keep going the way they are for me, I won't have to follow a lot of good lads who have moved," he said last season. "The best racing in the world is in Ireland and I don't want to be riding anywhere else."

Inevitably, though, big opportunities will come Sexton's way if he continues his impressive progress.

Dream double for McNamara

Cheltenham joy for amateur who almost gave up

By Nick Pulford

IN the summer of 2013 Robbie McNamara almost admitted defeat in the constant battle with his weight but one thing kept him from retiring: the dream of a Cheltenham Festival winner. Little more than six months later, amid high emotion, the dream came true not once but twice.

McNamara, 26, is one of Ireland's most gifted amateur riders, with the trust and backing of trainer Dermot Weld and leading owner Ronan Lambe, but at 6ft 3in he has the frame of a goalkeeper more than a jump jockey. That makes weight a big issue and he was close to calling it a day after a difficult 2013 Galway festival.

"I'd given up in my own head, I'd retired," he says. "But I knew I'd look back at 40, 50 or 60 and, although I've ridden a lot of winners and some big winners, I wouldn't be able to say I'd ridden a Cheltenham winner. That would have hurt."

McNamara soldiered on and, with Weld having two live contenders for the Weatherbys Champion Bumper in Vigil and Silver Concorde, it was clear he would be booked for one good ride. "I knew three weeks in advance there was a fair chance I'd be riding in the Bumper and I'd have to do 11st 5lb," he says.

▶▶ Jump jockey: Robbie McNamara makes a flying dismount from Spring Heeled

"There's no point leaving it until the last minute, so I worked hard at the weight for a month. I was running eight miles a day and cycling 12 miles and really watching what I ate."

With Weld's Flat stable jockey Pat Smullen on the better-fancied Vigil, McNamara's Bumper ride was Silver Concorde and that suited him. "I couldn't understand how Vigil was 5-1 and mine was 16-1. If I'd had the choice before the race, I'd have picked Silver Concorde," he says.

McNamara was proved right with a convincing victory that made all the hard work worthwhile and, as he came back in, Weld said: "I'm delighted for Robbie. Seeing him do 11st 5lb today said something." Meanwhile, the jockey was approached by Pat Healy, the Irish racing photographer and a good friend, and asked to do a flying dismount for the cameras. "I was afraid

to do it on Silver Concorde because he's a nervous horse, so I said to Pat: 'No, no, I'll do it on my next winner.'"

Little did McNamara know the next one would come less than 24 hours later when he partnered the Jim Culloty-trained Spring Heeled – owned, like Silver Concorde, by Lambe – in the Fulke Walwyn Kim Muir Handicap Chase. He was up with the pace all the way and won by a length and three-quarters.

This was the race in which John Thomas McNamara, Robbie's cousin, had suffered his life-changing fall 12 months earlier and emotions flooded to the surface. As he pulled up, McNamara raised both hands to the heavens and he recalls: "When I came in, somebody handed me an Irish flag and it said 'Thinking of you JT'. It was a lovely moment. A sad moment, but a lovely moment."

Another thought came to McNamara's mind: his promise to Healy. "I'd never done a flying dismount before – I'm 6ft 3in!" he says. "I was afraid in case my foot got stuck in the irons and I ended up making a fool of myself or breaking my wrist or something." McNamara fulfilled his promise, however, with a leap straight out of the Frankie Dettori textbook.

Having weighed out at 11st 6lb on Spring Heeled, McNamara was 11st 8lb when he got back on the scales after the race.

How had that happened? "It was very warm and at the start I had a drink of water, that's why," he explains. It was a mistake that cost him a three-day suspension, along with two more for breaching the whip rules.

But the only days that really mattered to McNamara were the glorious Wednesday and Thursday of the 2014 Cheltenham Festival. The days that fulfilled his dream twice over.

JP MEETS YOUNG FAN

JP McManus was happy to be left holding the baby after ending his long wait for a first Galway Hurdle success.

After the Tony Martin-trained

Thomas Edison had won under Tony McCoy, McManus posed for pictures with six-month-old Conor Jordan, from Navan, who was handed out of the crowd bedecked in the owner's famous green and gold.

McManus has won the Galway Plate

five times but the festival's hurdling feature had been one of the few races missing from his long roll of honour. "It was on my to-do list," he said. "It's fantastic to win the race at last and it hasn't been for the want of trying over the years."

The Annual Awards 2014
Our pick of the best of the year

Horse of the Year (Flat)
Kingman

Khalid Abdullah and his team don't just know how to breed and campaign champions, they are also pretty good when it comes to choosing names. Having waited for the right horse to call Frankel – in honour of Abdullah's late, great American trainer Bobby Frankel – they alerted everyone to the potential of Kingman from the very start, and in 2014 he did indeed rule supreme. Frankel was sent from the gods, but in the mortal world Kingman had regal bearing and achievements to go with his name.

Horse of the Year (jumps)
Sire De Grugy

Some of the best performers (Sprinter Sacre, Cue Card) fell by the wayside in a somewhat unsatisfactory 2013-14 season but Sire De Grugy was there all the way from late October to the final day in April, winning hearts and big prizes. Tough and classy, he took his popular connections on the journey of a lifetime – captured in a sea of red and blue after his Queen Mother Champion Chase triumph.

Ride of the year (Flat)
Richard Hughes on Sole Power

Patience, skill, confidence and, above all, ice-cold veins are needed to ride Sole Power – step forward, Richard Hughes. With a furlong to run in the Group 1 Nunthorpe at York in August, Hughes had enormous horsepower ready to be unleashed but eight rivals still in front of him and no clear gap to go for. So he waited, and waited some more. Finally the gap opened and Hughes eased through for a half-length win. Spellbinding.

Ride of the year (jumps)
Barry Geraghty on Jezki

Tony McCoy could have won this award for any number of brilliant rides but on this occasion he had to give best to Barry Geraghty, on a ride that could have been his. McCoy instead plumped for My Tent Or Yours and, in a battle of the JP McManus pair, Geraghty held him off by a neck. But it was not just in the finish where Geraghty got it right – his brave decision to strike for home off the bend, burning off Hurricane Fly and ensuring The New One had no chance to get involved, gave him a crucial advantage.

Race of the year (Flat)
2,000 Guineas

It was messy and the result might have been different in other circumstances, but as a scene-setter for the Flat season it was perfect – leaving everyone wanting more and eager to see what the rest of the campaign had in store for the principals. Often the Guineas turns out to have featured only one or two top-class horses at most, but this had Kingman, Australia, Charm Spirit, Kingston Hill and The Grey Gatsby. Oh, and Night Of Thunder, the winner, let's not forget him.

Race of the year (jumps)
Cheltenham Gold Cup

Even if Lord Windermere ranked at the lower end of Gold Cup winners, the race lacked nothing in drama on the famous hill. Jumping the final fence, the fight was on between Silviniaco Conti and Bobs Worth – the first two in the betting – but then a trio of horses drove up the hill in unison to turn the race on its head. In a breathless finish, Lord Windermere held on by a short head from On His Own with The Giant Bolster close behind and Silviniaco Conti wondering what had hit him in fourth.

Comeback of the year
Treve

Troubled by brittle feet and a bad back, Treve hobbled from one disaster to the next for most of the year. All seemed lost after another limp display in the Prix Vermeille, but Criquette Head-Maarek simply would not give up and just four weeks later she produced Treve to win the Arc for the second year running. A stunning performance by both the filly and her trainer.

Most improved horse
G Force

Three-year-old sprinters are supposed to find things tough against their elders, especially at the top level – tell that to G Force. Raced once as a juvenile by Richard Hannon snr, he was then sold for 25,000gns and started this year in a class five maiden at Newcastle for new trainer David O'Meara. Having won, he was given a handicap mark of 87 but just over four months later he was 31lb higher after a decisive victory over Gordon Lord Byron in the Group 1 Sprint Cup at Haydock.

Disappointment of the year
Godolphin

A disappointing year for Sheikh Mohammed's flagship operation for sure, although admittedly nowhere near as bad as the annus horribilis of 2013 brought on by the Mahmood Al Zarooni steroids scandal. There was to be no quick recovery as the team had to wait until Future Champions Day in October for their first Group 1 winner in Europe. At least in Middle Park winner Charming Thought there is hope for next year.

Unluckiest horse Cotai Glory

Here was the archetypal snatching of defeat from the jaws of victory. The Charlie Hills-trained two-year-old was three lengths clear and 50 yards from victory in the Group 2 Flying Childers at Doncaster when he suddenly swerved right, seemingly distracted by the gate where he had come out on to the track, and unseated George Baker. "As he was hanging right my saddle moved slightly round and that was it, I came off," said the rueful jockey. The spoils went instead to Richard Hannon's Beacon, whose jockey William Buick admitted: "We were lucky to win, no doubt about it."

THE ALTERNATIVE AWARDS

The We'll Never Have Paris Award
Frankie Dettori

Having missed the 2013 Arc-winning ride on Treve through injury, he was denied the chance to partner her this year after being jocked off in favour of Thierry Jarnet.

The How To Lose Friends And Alienate People Award
The Daily Mirror

The newspaper caused outrage with its front-page 'expose' featuring a photograph of a vet pointing a gun at the head of the injured Wigmore Hall beside the headline: 'Shot in the head . . . a tragic end for a £1.3m champion'.

The Idiot Of The Year Award
The bloke who threw a beer can at Tony McCoy

The champion jockey rode a four-timer at Worcester in September, only to be greeted by a hail of abuse and then a beer can from one errant racegoer. Well done to Arena Racing Company for banning the culprit and two of his mates from all of their courses.

The It's Good To Talk Award
Martin Lane and Matt Chapman

The Flat jockey used his Twitter

account to thank the broadcaster for clearing up why he had been beaten on a Godolphin odds-on favourite at Wolverhampton. The bit slipped – as Lane detailed on Twitter, and Chapman explained on TV.

The 'Can Someone Please Return My Toys To The Pram?' Award
Steve Coburn, part-owner of California Chrome

After the colt blew the US Triple Crown, Coburn lambasted rivals who turned up only for the final leg of the series.

The 'Which Way Did They Go?' Award
Tom Scudamore

The experienced jump jockey set off on the wrong track at Cartmel in July and jumped the first fence on the chase course, while the other ten riders managed to remember it was a hurdle race. "It was very unprofessional of me," admitted Scudamore, who was banned for 12 days.

The Can't Keep A Good Man Down Award
Davy Russell

He lost his job with Gigginstown House Stud in December, then won the Cheltenham Gold Cup in March on Lord Windermere – for a different owner.

The Keep Calm And Carry On Award
Scotland's five racecourses

Having worried about being separated from the rest of British racing, they welcomed the 'no' vote in the Scottish referendum.

The 'I'll Just Try To Blend Into The Crowd' Award
Tom Cruise

Of course, the Hollywood superstar found that was mission impossible on his first visit to Glorious Goodwood.

The Great British Turn-Off Award
Channel 4 Racing

Racing's audience on Channel 4 continued on an alarming downward trend, with the Derby peaking at 1.55m viewers – less than half the 3.3m that watched the BBC's last broadcast of the race in 2012.

The Never Ending Story Award
The Emirates Racing Authority and Pat Cosgrave

The ERA's pursuit of Cosgrave for his alleged riding offence on Anaerobio at Meydan in March dragged on for months. The ERA banned him and put him on the forfeit list but all to no avail as Cosgrave fought them at every turn and found support from the BHA.

The Cliff Richard 'We Don't Talk Anymore' Award
Kieren Fallon and Matt Chapman

The former champion jockey lambasted the broadcaster for alleged comments on At The Races, saying: "When you are slagged off by individuals who have no experience of what they are talking about – and Chapman has to be in that category – then it really angers me."

The Coulda Woulda Shoulda Award
The New One

He might well have won the Champion Hurdle for Nigel Twiston-Davies had he not been badly hampered in the early stages; fortunately, a degree of compensation awaited at Aintree (above).

Drama all the way

Happy ending after owner's Cheltenham heart attack

By Nick Pulford

Winning with a homebred at the Cheltenham Festival is a dream come true for any owner-breeder and for 84-year-old John Reynolds victory for Midnight Prayer was the highlight of his life. The only problem was he wasn't there to see it.

Reynolds had been at the racecourse until an hour before the race but by the time his Alan King-trained homebred won the marathon National Hunt Chase he was in Cheltenham hospital, having suffered a heart attack. Thankfully he lived to tell the tale – and quite a tale it is.

"I was walking to the gents' loo with my partner's grandson, Jason, when it happened," Reynolds says. "I was totally out of it, I can't remember anything, but luckily Jason's a fireman and he's done all his resuscitation training. I was taken to Cheltenham hospital and they stabilised everything."

The sight that greeted him later that evening might have brought on more palpitations, especially if he had known the circumstances of Midnight Prayer's victory.

"When I woke up in hospital my partner, Janet, was there at the bedside holding the cup, but I couldn't make out what it was at first." Then he was told the story of how Midnight Prayer had held on by a fast-diminishing neck in what might have been described as a heart-stopping finish.

Finally, having been discharged from hospital

▶▶ Perfect tonic: Midnight Prayer wins the National Hunt Chase

more than a week later, Reynolds got to see for himself. "It was thrilling to watch the replay," he says. "He jumped beautifully, he never touched a twig. He's always been a good jumper.

"To be quite honest, I wasn't sure he'd get the four miles. He'd only won over three and a quarter miles up to then but Alan King felt very confident he'd get the distance and of course he did. Winning at Cheltenham was the highlight of my life, I suppose. It was wonderful."

Reynolds, who lives in Cirencester, has spent his whole life around horses but fell into the breeding side almost by chance. He bought Midnight Prayer's

dam, Onawing Andaprayer, to ride himself but found she was "an absolute lunatic" and it was suggested he might breed from her as she was well conformed and had a good pedigree.

He sent Onawing Andaprayer to Midnight Legend and when the resultant offspring won a bumper first time out he decided to return her to the same stallion – those were the only two thoroughbred coverings she had. The second produced Midnight Prayer.

The first foal, Itsa Legend, finished third at the festival in the 2007 Brit Insurance Novices' Hurdle (now the Albert Bartlett) but

Midnight Prayer bettered that and now Reynolds is hoping he will be good enough for the Welsh National.

Will his heart stand the excitement? "I've been fitted with a defibrillator in my chest, so I'm okay," he says. "Touch wood, it's been fine since. I feel better than I did before. It's nice to know we've got the horse and we're looking forward to the season."

STEWARD IN DREAMLAND

Johnny Murtagh had never heard of him until August, but Louis Steward (above) managed to make quite a name for himself in the 2014 Flat season. As if winning the Ebor for Murtagh on Mutual Regard was not enough, the 19-year-old apprentice promptly followed up with two more big handicap victories on Bronze Angel.

Murtagh booked Steward for Mutual Regard on owner Andrew Tinkler's advice – "I didn't know who he was until Andrew suggested him" – but was impressed when he spoke to him before the Ebor and even more so by his ride on the 20-1 winner.

Steward, who is apprenticed to Michael Bell, said: "I have run the race through my mind 1,000 times in recent days and, of course, you begin to dream of what might happen – and it has."

A month later, Steward was in dreamland again with Cambridgeshire victory on Bronze Angel. Trainer Marcus Tregoning praised his "ice-cool" ride at Newmarket and booked him again for the even more valuable Balmoral Handicap at Ascot on British Champions Day.

Steward won again on Bronze Angel, completing an incredible two months in which his mounts in those three handicaps earned £400,000.

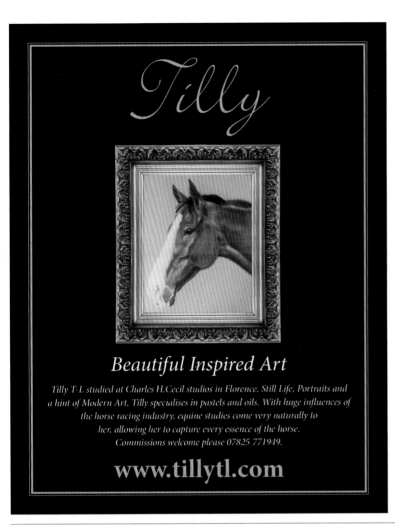

Champagne moment

£2 punter Craig Brazier shares in record Scoop6

By Tom Bull

CRAIG BRAZIER used to be a wheelie bin cleaner. That was until one day in May changed his life. One day, one decision, one bet and six horses. By the end, he had achieved the dream of every small-staking punter by turning £2 into a whopping £1,342,599.

Brazier, 39, was one of eight winners of the Scoop6 on May 24, sharing a pot that had swelled to a record £10,740,797, but it was his story that captured the imagination and the headlines. A keen fisherman, he had been shopping that Saturday morning for new angling gear and was about to spend the last £2 in his pocket on a jar of maggots. Instead, he crossed the road to a Betfred shop and put it on the Scoop6.

A few hours later he was rich and now he has all the time in the world to indulge his passion. "I've given up cleaning wheelie bins and I'm doing a lot of fishing," he says. "I'm trying to get better at it."

Brazier, who lives in Mansfield Woodhouse, Nottinghamshire, with his partner Tracy and their daughters Jessica, 14, and Casey, 8, adds: "I've put most of the money I won into savings. I've bought two houses and a caravan and we've been on a couple of holidays, but I've put the rest of the money away."

GOLIATH PAYOUT

SMALL-STAKING punter Clive Wallace picked up nearly £100,000 in July for a bet costing less than a tenner – and was only one winner away from scooping close to £1m.

The self-employed roof tiler from Carlton, near Newmarket, struck it rich with a 2p each-way Goliath on races at Ayr and Market Rasen, after seven of his eight selections won.

He also placed a 10p each-way accumulator on the same horses and if favourite Lilac Tree had been successful in the opening leg at Ayr it would have taken his combined winnings close to seven figures.

Wallace, 49, collected £95,496, having invested £9.88. The Goliath, which consists of 247 bets, is his regular weekend wager with William Hill, who, unlike some other operators, accept 1p and 2p each-way multiples.

"The most I've won before was around £4,500, so this is fantastic," Wallace said. "I listened to the live running of the races on the radio at home and thought I had around £5,000 going on to the final leg, but I'm not very good at working out these things and when I found out how much I'd won it was quite overwhelming.

"It would have been a lot more if the accumulator had come in, but I'm not complaining."

The Scoop6 win fund shared by Brazier was a record in the 15-year history of the bet. By late May the competition, which involves picking the winners of six specified races on a Saturday, had not been won for three months and consequently the prize fund had snowballed.

Although some had got close, including two desperately unlucky punters whose final-leg selections came within one place of landing a huge payout, none had managed to land the elusive six out of six until Brazier and his fellow winners came up trumps.

After his life-changing bet, Brazier said: "I started panicking after I got three out of three. I couldn't see the telly for the last leg because I was running up and down the room."

Chatez, saddled by Brazier's favourite trainer Alan King, won the final leg by half a length at 7-1. The other winners in Brazier's bet were Bear Behind (16-1), Conry (17-2), Wee Jean (8-1), Joyeuse (3-1) and Johnny Cavagin (9-2).

"I went absolutely berserk when Chatez won and I was still up at 4am wondering if it had really happened," Brazier said. "On the Sunday I went fishing to let it all sink in, but all I caught was some sleep on the bank."

The bet did not end there, however, because Brazier had a shot at the bonus fund the following Saturday along with the other seven winners. They included another £2 punter, who opted to remain anonymous, and one who staked £6, as well as big staker Bernard Marantelli, chief executive and founder of Colossus Bets. Marantelli managed to put together a syndicate with two other ticket-holders, but Brazier was among those who opted to go it alone.

The bonus fund, which had not been won since the previous August, had also

reached record proportions – £5,481,763 – and the chance to add to the previous week's gains rested on picking the winner of an 18-runner five-furlong handicap at York.

Brazier chose Tumblewind but the 16-1 shot finished a disappointing 11th. It was all the harder to take as he watched 12-1 chance Top Boy, one of the horses picked by the Marantelli syndicate, finish with a rattle and got up to win in the shadow of the post. Marantelli and his two partners had each taken their total winnings to £3,169,853.

The ticket-holders who joined forces with Marantelli were big stakers who wished to remain anonymous and it was Brazier, happy to be in the public spotlight, who symbolised the dreams of ordinary punters. He was

▶ Differing fortunes: Craig Brazier and partner Tracy celebrate his Scoop6 win (opposite page); Brazier and family cheer on his selection in the bonus race but to no avail (top); Brazier with Bernard Marantelli (right), one of the three punters who formed a syndicate to land the £5,481,763 bonus

a good loser, too, and later shared a glass of champagne with Marantelli. "I've enjoyed every minute of it," he said. "I take my hat off to them who found the winner."

Reflecting a few months on, Brazier remains philosophical. "I don't regret the decision to go it alone. I've never even thought about it."

▶ Rarity value: the pure-white foal with her dam

White magic
Unusual foal creates a stir

PURE-WHITE horses are a rare sight, making this family scene of mare and foal a double vision of curiosity.

The mare, The Opera House, was the first pure-white horse sold at public auction in Australia when she went through the ring as a yearling in 2008, and in September she produced a carbon-copy pure-white filly foal by High Chaparral – a completely unexpected arrival despite the mare's colour.

The Opera House's previous two foals were bay and chestnut, while High Chaparral had only ever produced bay or grey offspring.

Michael Kirwan, general manager at Coolmore

Australia, which stands dual Derby winner High Chaparral, said: "It's a first for High Chaparral to the best of our knowledge and obviously an extremely rare occurrence to have a foal of that colour."

The white thoroughbred foal was also a first for Windsor Park Stud in New Zealand in its 40-year history and stud manager Steve Till said: "High Chaparral is a pure-breeding bay, so we didn't expect a white foal. It's a rarity. It's a bit early to say whether we'll sell her or keep her to race."

Wherever she turns up, in the sale ring or on the racecourse, the filly will be hard to miss.

Star line-up at Cheltenham

Statues removed for safe keeping during redevelopment

CHELTENHAM embarked on a £45m redevelopment of its main grandstand in March, soon after the conclusion of the festival meeting, with the aim of being ready for the 2016 festival.

The normal race programme will go ahead with minimal disruption to racegoers during the 22-month redevelopment but the statues of four Cheltenham Gold Cup-winning icons were removed for safe keeping as the building work commenced. During their absence from the track, the statues of Golden Miller, Arkle, Dawn Run and Best Mate were cleaned and polished so that they could return as good as new.

Two of the statues – Arkle and Best Mate – were back in place at Cheltenham in October, but the other two will not return until later in the redevelopment as their usual positions are too close to the building work.

The signs of Cheltenham's rebuilding were evident last season when a three-tier temporary stand replaced the 1920s A&R blocks which had housed the royal box but were demolished in the first phase. With the redevelopment now in full swing, racegoers will be greeted by a rapidly changing landscape in the new season but updated facilities, such as the refurbished weighing room and new bars, will be opened.

Once all the work is complete, the new grandstand – which will be five and a half storeys high – will include new annual members' facilities, general public viewing areas, private boxes and royal box facilities.

The scheme is Jockey Club Racecourses' largest single investment in facilities. Nearly £25m was raised through a retail bond, the first of its kind in British sport. The remainder of the capital came from cashflow, commercial agreements and bank financing.

In total 2,100 people invested in the retail bond, which is over a five-year fixed term and offers a mix of 4.75 per cent gross returns in cash and a further

▸▸ Legendary figures: (left to right) Golden Miller, Arkle, Dawn Run and Best Mate

three per cent in interest in Rewards4Racing points, the Jockey Club's loyalty scheme. Such bonds have become a popular way to raise funds due to the squeeze on bank lending.

NATIONAL INSTITUTION MEETS THE QUEEN

BY ROYAL appointment: smart staying chaser Teaforthree met the Queen at the Cotts Farm Equine Hospital in Pembrokeshire in April.

The Cheltenham Festival winner, also runner-up in a Welsh Grand National and third in a Grand National, is trained by Rebecca Curtis, who said: "The Queen was visiting Cotts Farm, our local veterinary clinic, and we were asked to bring Teaforthree as she likes the horse."

Curtis was unable to go and Teaforthree was accompanied by stable employee Rebecca Morris, who knows the horse well having ridden him in much of his slower, dressage-type work.

Morris, 29, recalls: "I came to work that morning and Rebecca asked whether I'd like to go and meet the Queen. That was the first I knew of it and I wasn't exactly dressed for it. I had to borrow Rebecca's make-up as well as some trousers and a jacket to smarten myself up."

Morris, whose role now is to help with the recuperation and treatment of the Curtis string having qualified as an equine sports massage therapist,

will never forget the day.

"It's not every day you get to meet the Queen and it was amazing. It was in all the papers and on the national news and now there are pictures in my mother's house and my grandmother's house. It was such an exciting day."

A-Z of 2014

The year digested into 26 bite-size chunks

A is for Australia. The son of Derby winner Galileo and Oaks heroine Ouija Board fulfilled his destiny to give Coolmore a fourth consecutive Derby.

B is for Bittar end. Paul Bittar, the Australian who has been BHA chief executive since 2011, announced he is to step down early in 2015.

C is for Chelmsford City. The Essex racecourse, rising from the ashes of Great Leighs, will start racing in January after fixtures were granted for 2015.

D is for double handful. Eddie Lynam had not one but two star sprinters and dominated the scene as Sole Power and Slade Power each bagged a pair of Group 1 wins.

E is for Estimate. Having been a star of 2013, the Queen's mare was in the headlines in unfortunate circumstances when she was disqualified from second place in the Gold Cup at Royal Ascot after testing positive for morphine. No wrongdoing was involved, as she was one of several horses affected by a batch of contaminated feed.

F is for false start (at the Grand National – again). Thirty-nine jockeys were found in breach of the rules for attempting to line up early but were only cautioned after a BHA hearing found other failings in the starting procedure were also to blame. For different reasons, Epsom and Ludlow also had false-start embarrassments. Not a good year all round.

G is for Good Friday. No longer a day of rest for British racing after this year's ground-breaking fixtures at Lingfield and Musselburgh.

H is for Hurricane Fly. The Willie Mullins-trained star was denied a third Champion Hurdle as the younger generation led by Jezki came of age in a vintage renewal, but let's not forget he extended his jumps prize-money record to £1,670,963 and his record Grade 1 wins to 19.

I is for Injured Jockeys Fund. The charitable organisation celebrated its 50th anniversary in 2014, having paid out more than £18m in aid and helped more than 1,000 people in half a century of magnificent service.

J is for jumps-only. That is the situation at Warwick after Jockey Club Racecourses called a halt to more than 300 years of Flat racing at the track.

K is for Kingman. Defeat in the 2,000 Guineas proved a temporary setback as the star miler blazed a trail through the summer with four Group 1 wins.

L is for lights out. The BHA put the kibosh on Newcastle's controversial plans to convert its turf Flat track to all-weather, with floodlit meetings, although the issue is likely to be revisited in 2015.

M is for Manton. The historic Wiltshire training centre was put on the market for a reputed £26m by the Sangster family and bought by Paul Clarke, 65, who made his fortune in the bulb-growing business.

N is for Noble Mission, who was the star of British Champions Day with a thrilling and poignant victory for Lady Cecil.

O is for offshore drift. Bet365 became the last major online bookmaker to move its remote gambling business from Britain to Gibraltar, adding urgency to racing's calls for changes to the levy system – not least extending it to offshore operators.

P is for persistence. Davy Russell got his head down and worked hard after losing his job with Gigginstown and, in doing the

T

S

▶▶ Star appeal: Tom Cruise presents Edie Campbell with her prize and is the centre of attention in Lord March's box

same on Lord Windermere in the Cheltenham Gold Cup, achieved his biggest success.

Q is for Quevega. The Willie Mullins-trained mare made history with her sixth Cheltenham Festival success and then headed off to make baby Quevegas.

R is for retirements. British Champions Day lost much of its lustre when top three-year-olds Australia, Kingman and Taghrooda were sent to stud before what is supposed to be the flagship end-of-season meeting.

S is for Stand Guard. The ten-year-old became Britain's record all-weather winner with his 26th victory in March. He was retired in June after finishing last on his 76th and final run.

T is for Towcester. The jumps venue sold seven of its 17 racing fixtures to Arena Racing Company and announced plans to stage 156 greyhound meetings on a track in the centre of the course.

U is for unquenchable. Records continued to tumble for Tony McCoy as he roared towards his 20th consecutive jump jockeys' title.

V is for Victor. Still part of the name of the company but no longer the boss after leading racehorse owner Michael Tabor acquired ownership of BetVictor from Victor Chandler.

W is for Wigmore Hall. The Daily Mirror caused outrage in

September with its front-page photo of the Michael Bell-trained stalwart being put down at Doncaster.

X is for excessive use. Of the whip, that is, as an emotive subject reared its ugly head again on British Champions Day with a spate of bans.

Y is for you can't win 'em all. Tony McCoy chose wrong with My Tent Or Yours in the Champion Hurdle and again two days later with At Fishers Cross in the World Hurdle. Barry Geraghty was the grateful beneficiary who picked up the winning rides on Jezki and More Of That.

Z is for zero to hero(ine). After a blank summer, Treve rediscovered her form to win a second Arc.

Glorious day

Cruise enjoys Goodwood visit

TOM CRUISE stole the show on ladies' day at Glorious Goodwood when he made a surprise appearance during a break from shooting his new Mission: Impossible film in London.

The Hollywood heart-throb was spirited into the racecourse as a guest of Goodwood owner Lord March but word quickly spread and he posed for an endless stream of selfies with fans, while the on-course military band greeted him with the theme tune from Mission: Impossible.

Cruise presented the trophy for the Magnolia Cup charity race to

supermodel Edie Campbell, who was as surprised as everyone else to find him there after her tiring effort on See The Storm. "I didn't know he was presenting until after the race – about three minutes before it happened," she said. "My legs still felt so weak I was worried I might fall on top of him."

Harry Herbert, who chaperoned Cruise, said: "Tom had great fun and backed the winner of the maiden, Shagah, because he loved the name. He's a good friend of Lord March and he's done motor racing here with him. But I'm pretty sure this is his first time horseracing in Britain."

IN THE PICTURE

And they're off! Pedal power takes over as Le Tour wows Yorkshire

The Tour de France made a celebrated visit to Yorkshire in July and racing joined in the festivities as the world's biggest cycle race made its way through the county.

Following the Grand Depart from Leeds on July 5, the first stage passed through the training centre of Middleham on its way to the finish in Harrogate. The next day, stage two started from York racecourse in front of packed grandstands before finishing in Sheffield.

Five million spectators lined the roadsides over the two days and Middleham, like every other Yorkshire village and town on the route, was *en fête* as the race passed through.

Mark Johnston's string came down the main street early that morning with the work riders all in yellow and the outside of the trainer's Kingsley House yard was decorated with yellow bikes. Just down the road at Micky Hammond's Oakwood Stables, the gateway was festooned with bunting in all the important Tour colours – yellow (the colour of the jersey denoting the overall race leader), green (points leader), white (best young rider) and red polka dots (King of the Mountains).

Hammond, who gave up his usual trip to Eclipse day at Sandown to stay at home and watch the Tour instead, invited family, friends and owners to an all-day celebration at the yard, with a bar and a barbecue. "The cyclists rode right past the front of the yard," he said. "It had glitz, glamour and colour and everyone was there to enjoy the spectacle of it all. It was exceptionally good for Yorkshire and it brought good publicity to Middleham as well."

With Middleham in virtual lockdown after the roads were closed at 9am, many waited seven hours to see the cyclists pass through in early afternoon. In a matter of 90 seconds and a blur of colour they were gone again, but everyone agreed it was worth the long wait. "There's a lovely spirit here, an exciting atmosphere, a special day," said Jane Baker, who arrived just before 8am with husband Mike and their friends Dee and Jeremy Wickins.

York racecourse had free entry for the start of stage two and, such was the interest, 20,000 tickets were snapped up within four hours of their release in January. The infield was packed too, as the racecourse hosted live music and a big screen to watch the cycling action all the way to Sheffield.

Among those enjoying a different kind of raceday were David and Mandy Curzon, who had travelled from Gloucester. "We just wanted to be part of the atmosphere, part of the whole unique experience. We love the way the city has taken the race to its heart. It's a great feeling."

JUMPS CHAMPIONS 2013-14

Two-mile chaser

SIRE DE GRUGY

Trainer **Gary Moore**
Owner **The Preston Family and Friends**

RACING POST RATINGS

Sire De Grugy	174
Cue Card	172
Somersby	167
Arvika Ligeonniere	166
Benefficient	166
Module	166

Sire De Grugy improved his RPR from 162 to 174 in the course of a tremendously successful and popular campaign, yet he still lagged far behind the 190 achieved by Sprinter Sacre in 2012-13. With the reigning champion pulled up in his only race of the season, the

way was clear for Sire De Grugy to take control of the division and he was superb in landing four Grade 1 races. The crowning glory was his Queen Mother Champion Chase triumph, although his Clarence House Chase victory at Ascot in January was rated the better performance by 1lb.

Two-and-a-half-mile chaser

MENORAH

Trainer **Philip Hobbs**
Owner **Diana Whateley**

RACING POST RATINGS

Menorah	172
Al Ferof	168
Dynaste	168
Hidden Cyclone	166
Arvika Ligeonniere	165

Menorah, well behind Sprinter Sacre and Cue Card in this category the previous season, did not need to improve his RPR to take the honours in a weakened division. Having disappointed for most of the season, beating only two horses in three Grade 1 runs, he finally returned to his best mark with a Listed victory at Sandown on the final day of the season. That snatched the

honours from Dynaste, who had Menorah 71 lengths behind in winning the Grade 1 Ryanair Chase at the Cheltenham Festival, and Amlin Chase winner Al Ferof (fifth in the Ryanair)

Three-mile-plus chaser

CUE CARD

Trainer **Colin Tizzard**
Owner **Jean Bishop**

RACING POST RATINGS

Cue Card	180
Silviniaco Conti	179
Captain Chris	176
Dynaste	175
Tidal Bay	172

A confirmed and consistent performer in the 170s (with six consecutive runs rated at least 170), Cue Card reached 180 with a Betfair Chase victory that marked his breakthrough as a three-mile chaser. Although he was outfought by Silviniaco Conti next time in the King George VI Chase and did not appear again due to a pelvic injury, none of his rivals could reach the same standard.

The first three in a below-par Cheltenham Gold Cup – Lord Windermere, On His Own and The Giant Bolster – did not even make the top five after all recording 170.

Novice chaser

HOLYWELL

Trainer **Jonjo O'Neill**
Owner **Gay Smith**

RACING POST RATINGS

Holywell	165
Taquin Du Seuil	164
O'Faolains Boy	163
Smad Place	163
Balder Succes	162
Oscar Whisky	162
Uxizandre	162

Jonjo O'Neill had the best two novice chasers, with Holywell just edging the division after his Grade 1 Mildmay Novices' Chase victory at Aintree (rated 3lb better than his

handicap-chase win at the Cheltenham Festival). Until then the ratings were led by stablemate Taquin Du Seuil, who was also a Grade 1 winner in the JLT Novices' Chase at Cheltenham. RSA Chase one-two O'Faolains Boy and Smad Place were close behind in a tightly packed group who were already within touching distance of the seniors.

Two-mile hurdler

JEZKI

Trainer **Jessica Harrington**
Owner **JP McManus**

MY TENT OR YOURS

Trainer **Nicky Henderson**
Owner **JP McManus**

THE NEW ONE

Trainer **Nigel Twiston-Davies**
Owner **Sarah Such**

RACING POST RATINGS

Jezki	173
My Tent Or Yours	173
The New One	173
Hurricane Fly	170
Captain Cee Bee	161
Our Conor	161

The Champion Hurdle, as it should be, was the crucial race in this division. Although the spoils went to Jezki, he could not be separated on ratings from neck runner-up My Tent Or Yours or The New One, who was two and a half lengths back in third but most unlucky to have been held up by the fatal fall of Our Conor. With Jezki and The New One both going on to subsequent Grade 1 wins (albeit with lesser performances on RPR), a new order has taken shape.

Two-and-a-half mile-plus hurdler

MORE OF THAT

Trainer **Jonjo O'Neill**
Owner **JP McManus**

RACING POST RATINGS

More Of That	172
At Fishers Cross	166
The New One	166
Celestial Halo	165
Diakali	165
Rock On Ruby	165
Zarkandar	165

As Big Buck's departed the stage he had illuminated so gloriously, a new player emerged as the six-year-old More Of That landed an impressive World Hurdle triumph. Having won his only start in a maiden hurdle prior to the 2013-14 season, More Of That remained unbeaten as he made great strides from winning off an official mark of 130 in a Wetherby handicap hurdle in

November to Cheltenham Festival glory just four months later. His winning RPR was the best in the World Hurdle since the second victory of Big Buck's in 2010.

Novice hurdler

BEAT THAT

Trainer **Nicky Henderson**
Owner **Michael Buckley**

FAUGHEEN

Trainer **Willie Mullins**
Owner **Susannah Ricci**

RACING POST RATINGS

Beat That	159
Faugheen	159
Vautour	158
Kings Palace	154
See You At Midnight	154

Faugheen has raised his RPR with every start, culminating in a mark of 159 for his 12-length Grade 1 success at Punchestown. That eclipsed even his dominant display at Cheltenham in the Neptune Novices' Hurdle (RPR 155). Beat That, having missed Cheltenham, came back from four months off to record 159 with a Grade 1 victory over three miles at Aintree and rounded off the season with another top-level victory at Punchestown (though down to 152 on RPR). The equally promising Vautour was close behind on 158.

JUMPS SEASON 2013-14

Top 10 Jump Jockeys in Britain in 2013-14

	Wins-rides	Strike rate	Win and place prize-money £
1 Tony McCoy	218-903	24%	2,250,140
2 Richard Johnson	155-831	19%	1,880,985
3 Jason Maguire	130-662	20%	899,185
4 Noel Fehily	127-596	21%	1,315,413
5 Sam Twiston-Davies	115-774	15%	1,550,268
6 Tom Scudamore	100-629	16%	1,587,003
7 Aidan Coleman	97-647	15%	1,113,027
8 Brian Hughes	86-617	14%	678,359
9 Paddy Brennan	77-527	15%	636,526
10 Tom O'Brien	74-528	14%	723,083

Top 10 Jump Jockeys in Ireland in 2013-14

	Wins-rides	Strike rate	Win and place prize-money €
1 Ruby Walsh	122-403	30%	2,556,562
2 Davy Russell	75-418	18%	1,360,095
3 Paul Townend	55-381	14%	984,560
4 Andrew Lynch	53-587	9%	1,031,849
5 Barry Geraghty	50-275	18%	1,294,093
6 Bryan Cooper	48-344	14%	1,069,645
7 Mr Patrick Mullins	40-143	28%	375,167
8 Mark Walsh	39-410	10%	736,569
9 Davy Condon	37-330	11%	541,992
10 Andrew McNamara	36-390	9%	443,209

Top 10 Jumps Trainers in Britain in 2013-14

	Wins-runs	Strike rate	Win and place prize-money £
1 Paul Nicholls	118-587	20%	2,469,892
2 Nicky Henderson	124-514	24%	2,019,935
3 Philip Hobbs	106-542	20%	1,583,307
4 Jonjo O'Neill	135-810	17%	1,572,505
5 David Pipe	90-591	15%	1,433,118
6 Nigel Twiston-Davies	77-559	14%	1,166,344
7 Alan King	75-444	17%	1,112,822
8 Venetia Williams	86-574	15%	1,110,493
9 Donald McCain	142-775	18%	964,606
10 Dr Richard Newland	38-167	23%	929,129

Top 10 Jumps Trainers in Ireland in 2013-14

	Wins-runs	Strike rate	Win and place prize-money €
1 Willie Mullins	185-665	28%	3,817,778
2 Gordon Elliott	56-436	13%	1,133,837
3 Dessie Hughes	57-439	13%	1,102,221
4 Jessica Harrington	35-233	15%	851,380
5 Henry de Bromhead	48-315	15%	791,442
6 Noel Meade	45-367	12%	685,230
7 Tony Martin	31-272	11%	584,272
8 Philip Fenton	19-117	16%	438,980
9 Michael Winters	16-91	18%	378,220
10 Mouse Morris	16-158	10%	366,995

Top 10 Jumps Owners in Britain in 2013-14

	Wins-runs	Strike rate	Win and place prize-money £
1 John P McManus	121-610	20%	2,052,076
2 Dr R Lambe	3-7	43%	401,840
3 Andrea & Graham Wylie	8-54	15%	397,015
4 RS Brookhouse	29-93	31%	377,261
5 The Preston Family & Friends	6-7	86%	362,679
6 Bloomfields	49-213	23%	360,141
7 Gigginstown House Stud	4-31	13%	330,360
8 Mrs Diana Whateley	25-68	37%	328,615
9 Mrs S Ricci	5-14	36%	326,001
10 Potensis Limited	10-25	40%	306,155

Top 10 Jumps Owners in Ireland in 2013-14

	Wins-runs	Strike rate	Win and place prize-money €
1 John P McManus	98-875	11%	2,337,137
2 Gigginstown House Stud	109-608	18%	2,311,545
3 Mrs S Ricci	43-117	37%	1,094,447
4 Andrea & Graham Wylie	23-46	50%	621,455
5 Barry Connell	20-149	13%	457,030
6 Ann & Alan Potts Partnership	17-88	19%	416,492
7 Mrs P Sloan	11-44	25%	294,532
8 George Creighton & Mrs Rose Boyd	3-4	75%	222,400
9 Supreme Horse Racing Club	13-58	22%	191,405
10 Mrs Vanessa Hutch	1-1	100%	158,600

JUMPS WINNERS 2013-14

 ## British Grade 1 Winners 2013-14

Winner	Race	Course (Distance, Month)
Cue Card	Betfair Chase	Haydock (3m1f, Nov)
My Tent Or Yours	Fighting Fifth Hurdle	Newcastle (2m, Nov)
Sire De Grugy	Tingle Creek Chase	Sandown (2m, Dec)
Hinterland	Henry VIII Novices' Chase	Sandown (2m, Dec)
Reve De Sivola	Long Walk Hurdle	Ascot (3m1f, Dec)
My Tent Or Yours	Christmas Hurdle	Kempton (2m, Dec)
Silviniaco Conti	King George VI Chase	Kempton (3m, Dec)
Annacotty	Kauto Star Novices' Chase	Kempton (3m, Dec)
Le Rocher	Finale Juvenile Hurdle	Chepstow (2m1f, Dec)
Captain Cutter	Challow Novices' Hurdle	Newbury (2m5f, Dec)
Royal Boy	Tolworth Novices' Hurdle	Kempton (2m, Jan)
Sire De Grugy	Clarence House Chase	Ascot (2m1f, Jan)
Oscar Whisky	Scilly Isles Novices' Chase	Sandown (2m5f, Feb)
Captain Chris	Ascot Chase	Ascot (2m6f, Feb)
Jezki	Champion Hurdle	Cheltenham (2m1f, Mar)
Vautour	Supreme Novices' Hurdle	Cheltenham (2m1f, Mar)
Western Warhorse	Arkle Chase	Cheltenham (2m, Mar)
Sire De Grugy	Queen Mother Champion Ch	Cheltenham (2m, Mar)
O'Faolains Boy	RSA Chase	Cheltenham (3m1f, Mar)
Silver Concorde	Champion Bumper	Cheltenham (2m1f, Mar)
Faugheen	Neptune Novices' Hurdle	Cheltenham (2m5f, Mar)
More Of That	World Hurdle	Cheltenham (3m, Mar)
Dynaste	Ryanair Chase	Cheltenham (2m5f, Mar)
Taquin Du Seuil	JLT Novices' Chasee	Cheltenham (2m4f, Mar)
Lord Windermere	Cheltenham Gold Cup	Cheltenham (3m3f, Mar)
Tiger Roll	Triumph Hurdle	Cheltenham (2m1f, Mar)
Very Wood	Albert Bartlett Nov Hurdle	Cheltenham (3m, Mar)
Silviniaco Conti	Betfred Bowl Chase	Aintree (3m1f, Apr)
Guitar Pete	IJF 4yo Juvenile Hurdle	Aintree (2m1f, Apr)
The New One	Aintree Hurdle	Aintree (2m4f, Apr)
Uxizandre	Manifesto Novices' Chase	Aintree (2m4f, Apr)
Boston Bob	Melling Chase	Aintree (2m4f, Apr)
Holywell	Mildmay Novices' Chase	Aintree (3m1f, Apr)
Beat That	Sefton Novices' Hurdle	Aintree (3m1f, Apr)
Whisper	(Liverpool) Stayers' Hurdle	Aintree (3m1f, Apr)
Balder Succes	Maghull Novices' Chase	Aintree (2m, Apr)
Lac Fontana	Mersey Novices' Hurdle	Aintree (2m4f, Apr)
Sire De Grugy	Celebration Chase	Sandown (2m, Apr)

 ## Irish Grade 1 Winners 2013-14

Winner	Race	Course (Distance, Month)
Roi Du Mee	JNwine.com Champion Chase	Down Royal (3m, Nov)
Hurricane Fly	Morgiana Hurdle	Punchestown (2m, Nov)
Don Cossack	Drinmore Novice Chase	Fairyhouse (2m4f, Dec)
Jezki	Hatton's Grace Hurdle	Fairyhouse (2m, Dec)
The Tullow Tank	Royal Bond Novice Hurdle	Fairyhouse (2m, Dec)
Arvika Ligeonniere	John Durkan Memorial Chase	Punchestown (2m4f, Dec)
Briar Hill	Navan Novice Hurdle	Navan (2m4f, Dec)
Defy Logic	Racing Post Novice Chase	Leopardstown (2m1f, Dec)
Benefficient	Dial-A-Bet Chase	Leopardstown (2m1f, Dec)
The Tullow Tank	Future Champions Nov Hurdle	Leopardstown (2m, Dec)
Zaidpour	Christmas Hurdle	Leopardstown (3m, Dec)
Bobs Worth	Lexus Chase	Leopardstown (3m, Dec)
Carlingford Lough	Topaz Novice Chase	Leopardstown (3m, Dec)
Hurricane Fly	Ryanair Hurdle	Leopardstown (2m, Dec)
Hurricane Fly	Irish Champion Hurdle	Leopardstown (2m, Jan)
Trifolium	Arkle Novice Chase	Leopardstown (2m1f, Jan)
Last Instalment	Hennessy Gold Cup	Leopardstown (3m, Feb)
Vautour	Deloitte Novice Hurdle	Leopardstown (2m2f, Feb)
Guitar Pete	Spring Juvenile Hurdle	Leopardstown (2m, Feb)
Ballycasey	Dr PJ Moriarty Novice Chase	Leopardstown (2m5f, Feb)
Adriana Des Mottes	Mares Novice Hurdle Final	Fairyhouse (2m4f, Apr)
Rebel Fitz	Powers Gold Cup	Fairyhouse (2m4f, Apr)
Carlingford Lough	Champion Novice Chase	Punchestown (3m1f, Apr)
Sizing Europe	Champion Chase	Punchestown (2m, Apr)
Faugheen	Champion Novice Hurdle	Punchestown (2m, Apr)
Shaneshill	Champion INH Flat Race	Punchestown (2m, Apr)
Boston Bob	Punchestown Gold Cup	Punchestown (3m1f, Apr)
Beat That	Irish Daily Mirror Nov Hurdle	Punchestown (3m, Apr)
God's Own	Ryanair Novice Chase	Punchestown (2m, May)
Jetson	World Series Hurdle	Punchestown (3m, May)
Jezki	Racing Post Champion Hurdle	Punchestown (2m, May)
Vautour	Champion Novice Hurdle	Punchestown (2m4f, May)
Annie Power	Mares Champion Hurdle	Punchestown (2m2f, May)
Abbyssial	AES Champion 4yo Hurdle	Punchestown (2m, May)

THE
BIGGER
PICTURE

Sandown is in full bloom in early July as the large crowd on Eclipse day soaks up the warm weather and the atmosphere around the paddock

**EDWARD WHITAKER
(RACINGPOST.COM/PHOTOS)**

Older horse

TREVE

Trainer **Criquette Head-Maarek**
Owner **Al Shaqab Racing**

RACING POST RATINGS

Treve	127
Cirrus Des Aigles	126
The Fugue	126
Flintshire	125
Magician	125
Olympic Glory	125
Telescope	125

When Treve was edged out by a short neck against Cirrus Des Aigles in the Prix Ganay in April and then The Fugue beat her at Royal Ascot, top spot in this category started to

look unlikely for the 2013 Arc winner. But the summer passed without a performance to match either of those two and everything was up for grabs on Arc weekend in October. Treve had sunk to an RPR of 113 in her trial, the Prix Vermeille, but incredibly she improved a stone as she skimmed round the rail to score by two lengths from Flintshire, although her winning mark of 127 was down from 131 in 2013.

Three-year-old colt

AUSTRALIA

Trainer **Aidan O'Brien**
Owner **Derrick Smith, Sue Magnier, Michael Tabor and Teo Ah Khing**

RACING POST RATINGS

Australia	129
Kingman	128
The Grey Gatsby	126
Charm Spirit	124
Night Of Thunder	124

The top five in this division took it in turns to beat each other and, despite some excellent individual performances, none established absolute superiority. Having ruled the mile-and-a-half Classics with wins in the Derby and Irish Derby, Australia dropped back to a mile and a quarter to record his best figure with victory over The Grey Gatsby in the Juddmonte International at York but

then his level dipped as the tables were turned in the Irish Champion. Kingman, meanwhile, was the top miler with four consecutive Group 1 wins before he, like Australia, was retired to stud without the chance of a grand finale on British Champions Day.

Three-year-old filly

TAGHROODA

Trainer **John Gosden**
Owner **Sheikh Hamdan Al Maktoum**

RACING POST RATINGS

Taghrooda	126
Tapestry	121
Avenir Certain	118
Dolniya	117
Marvellous	117
Miss France	117

Having recorded an RPR of 118 for her Oaks success at Epsom, Taghrooda reached her peak figure with a clear-cut victory over mainly older rivals – and all colts – in the King

George at Ascot in July. She was below par next time (RPR 120) when beaten half a length by Tapestry in the Yorkshire Oaks and, although third in the Arc on what turned out to be her final career start, she recorded an RPR of 119. It was an admirable record and none of her divisional rivals came close, even though Avenir Certain was a dual Classic winner in France.

Sprinter

SLADE POWER

Trainer **Eddie Lynam**
Owner **Sabena Power**

RACING POST RATINGS

Slade Power	123
G Force	121
Gordon Lord Byron	121
Sole Power	120
Maarek	118
Rangali	118

The summer sprints were dominated by the Eddie Lynam-trained pair Slade Power and Sole Power, with two Group 1 victories apiece. The admirably consistent Slade Power had the edge on his stablemate, recording an RPR of 123 in the Diamond Jubilee at

Royal Ascot (as well as 122 on two more occasions, including the July Cup). In the autumn the three-year-old G Force burst on the Group 1 scene with victory in the Sprint Cup at Haydock but then he finished last as Haydock runner-up Gordon Lord Byron won the British Champions Sprint (currently Group 2 but Group 1 from next year) on Ascot's Champions Day.

Stayer

LEADING LIGHT

Trainer **Aidan O'Brien**
Owner **Derrick Smith, Sue Magnier and Michael Tabor**

RACING POST RATINGS

Leading Light	121
Brown Panther	119
Kingston Hill	119
Tac De Boistron	119
Cavalryman	118

Leading Light took the most important staying contest of the year, the Gold Cup at Royal Ascot, but it was not that performance which brought him the honours in this division. His best display was at Navan in his Group 3 prep for Ascot when he beat former Irish St Leger winner Royal Diamond by three lengths. At the royal meeting it was a much closer affair, as he narrowly edged out (subsequently disqualified) Estimate and Missunited. Next in the list came Leger winners Kingston Hill and Brown Panther (who outmanoeuvred Leading Light in the Irish version), along with Sagaro winner Tac De Boistron.

Two-year-old colt

BELARDO

Trainer **Roger Varian**
Owner **Prince A A Faisal**

RACING POST RATINGS

Belardo	119
The Wow Signal	118
Charming Thought	117
Ivawood	117
Estidhkaar	116
Gleneagles	116
Hootenanny	116
Limato	116
Toocoolforschool	116

This was a division in desperate need of a leader and Belardo did his best to fill the gap with his two-length victory in the Dewhurst, which was the best performance on Future Champions Day at Newmarket. The Roger Varian-trained colt, previously beaten in Group races by Ivawood and Estidhkaar, was helped by soft ground at Newmarket and a first-time hood. The other big winner on the day was Charming Thought in the Middle Park. Prix Morny winner The Wow Signal led the division for much of the summer but then finished last in the Prix Jean-Luc Lagardere.

Two-year-old filly

TIGGY WIGGY

Trainer **Richard Hannon**
Owner **Potensis Ltd, Chris Giles and Merriebelle Stables**

RACING POST RATINGS

Tiggy Wiggy	117
Anthem Alexander	115
Found	115
Cursory Glance	113
High Celebrity	111
Lucida	111
Together Forever	111

Speed was of the essence in the juvenile filly division and nothing was faster than Tiggy Wiggy, who won the Super Sprint at Newbury, a strong-looking Lowther at York and the Cheveley Park at Newmarket – recording an RPR of 117 each time. At York she reversed Royal Ascot form with Anthem

Alexander, as well as beating subsequent Moyglare winner Cursory Glance, and she held Anthem Alexander again at Newmarket. The best Aidan O'Brien-trained filly to appear in a Group 1 was Found, who won the Prix Marcel Boussac in decisive style.

FLAT SEASON 2014

Top 10 Flat Jockeys in Britain in 2014

	Wins-rides	Strike rate	Win and place prize-money £
1 Richard Hughes	151-855	18%	3,365,264
Ryan Moore	151-734	21%	4,275,719
3 Graham Lee	115-777	15%	1,255,934
4 James Doyle	112-635	18%	2,374,390
William Buick	112-612	18%	2,539,430
6 Joe Fanning	107-723	15%	1,769,616
7 Adam Kirby	105-637	16%	1,309,035
8 Andrea Atzeni	100-571	18%	2,737,659
9 George Baker	99-480	21%	968,710
10 Daniel Tudhope	90-534	17%	1,221,417

Covers period from March 29, 2014 to October 12, 2014

Top 10 Flat Trainers in Britain in 2014

	Wins-runs	Strike rate	Win and place prize-money £
1 Richard Hannon	191-1234	15%	4,152,417
2 John Gosden	114-535	21%	4,027,105
3 Mark Johnston	215-1318	16%	3,031,889
4 Richard Fahey	171-1381	12%	2,759,855
5 Aidan O'Brien	10-72	14%	2,559,042
6 William Haggas	114-474	24%	2,208,416
7 Sir Michael Stoute	75-425	18%	2,181,270
8 Roger Varian	78-434	18%	1,963,824
9 David O'Meara	112-793	14%	1,667,244
10 Andrew Balding	95-575	17%	1,596,658

Covers period from November 10, 2013 to October 12, 2014

Top 10 Flat Owners in Britain in 2014

	Wins-runs	Strike rate	Win and place prize-money £
1 Hamdan Al Maktoum	125-613	20%	3,495,392
2 Godolphin	148-793	19%	2,585,094
3 Sheikh Hamdan Bin Mohammed Al Maktoum	121-651	19%	1,849,972
4 K Abdullah	66-297	22%	1,469,543
5 Cheveley Park Stud	43-339	13%	1,126,649
6 Al Shaqab Racing	24-112	21%	1,078,839
7 Qatar Racing Limited	42-298	14%	982,417
8 Dr Marwan Koukash	49-397	12%	837,283
9 Mrs John Magnier	13-111	12%	826,804
10 M Tabor	17-109	16%	820,587

Covers period from November 10, 2013 to October 12, 2014

Top 10 Flat Jockeys in Ireland in 2014

	Wins-rides	Strike rate	Win and place prize-money €
1 Pat Smullen	104-501	21%	2,351,553
2 Joseph O'Brien	83-359	23%	3,369,653
3 Fran Berry	56-410	14%	1,075,355
4 Colin Keane	53-319	17%	857,570
5 Kevin Manning	50-400	13%	1,359,898
6 Wayne Lordan	48-419	11%	936,500
7 Chris Hayes	36-480	8%	741,343
8 Declan McDonogh	34-295	12%	654,923
9 Shane Foley	33-445	7%	764,190
10 Leigh Roche	30-263	11%	516,093

Covers period from March 23, 2014 to October 12, 2014

Top 10 Flat Trainers in Ireland in 2014

	Wins-runs	Strike rate	Win and place prize-money €
1 Aidan O'Brien	100-478	21%	4,789,588
2 Dermot Weld	90-388	23%	2,180,915
3 Jim Bolger	57-449	13%	1,382,488
4 Ger Lyons	46-229	20%	899,185
5 Michael Halford	29-328	9%	698,900
6 Kevin Ryan	1-5	20%	602,000
7 John Oxx	27-177	15%	527,025
8 Willie McCreery	19-193	10%	461,120
9 David Wachman	27-238	11%	431,665
10 Edward Lynam	19-167	11%	416,545

Covers period from March 23, 2014 to October 12, 2014

Top 10 Flat Owners in Ireland in 2014

	Wins-runs	Strike rate	Win and place prize-money €
1 Derrick Smith & Mrs John Magnier & Michael Tabor	27-108	25%	1,094,785
2 Michael Tabor & Derrick Smith & Mrs John Magnier	26-116	22%	1,065,800
3 D Smith & Mrs John Magnier & M Tabor & T Ah Khing	2-4	50%	952,055
4 Mrs J S Bolger	40-404	10%	950,278
5 K Abdullah	17-56	30%	790,695
6 Mrs John Magnier & Michael Tabor & Derrick Smith	23-117	20%	776,588
7 H H Aga Khan	30-154	19%	603,560
8 F Gillespie	1-1	100%	590,000
9 Hamdan Al Maktoum	14-86	16%	550,980
10 Moyglare Stud Farm	23-53	43%	494,360

Covers period from January 1, 2014 to October 12, 2014

IN THE PICTURE

Former champion Spencer announces shock retirement from the saddle

Jamie Spencer stunned the racing world in August when he announced he would retire from the saddle at the end of the 2014 Flat season to take up a role with Qatar Racing's management team.

The shock news came on the second day of York's Ebor meeting and put Spencer in the spotlight as he went out to take his first ride that afternoon in Qatar Racing's maroon and gold colours aboard the Kevin Ryan-trained Gaudy. The pairing finished fourth in the DBS Premier Yearling Stakes.

In a year when the 49-year-old Kieren Fallon returned to the Classic winner's enclosure aboard 2,000 Guineas victor Night Of Thunder, Spencer's decision to bow out at the age of 34 seemed premature to many. But he felt that starting a new chapter with Qatar Racing, for whom he has been retained jockey for two years, was the right move.

"This is a fantastic opportunity and if I've learned anything in my riding career it is that you should take such opportunities when they come along," Spencer said. "As much as I love race-riding, it is not something I want to do for the rest of my life and, while I am not necessarily ready to retire now, I feel at a stage when I'm ready for a change.

"This has been a big decision and not one I have taken lightly. My priority is my family, and thinking of them and their future has played a key part in my decision. I feel I still have a lot to give to racing, and not just as a jockey."

Spencer, originally from County Tipperary, burst to prominence aged just 17 when he became the youngest jockey to win a major European Classic, aboard Tarascon in the Irish 1,000 Guineas in 1998. He landed three more Irish Classics in his career (the Irish 1,000 with Gossamer in 2002 and Just The Judge in 2013 and the 2009 Irish Oaks on Sariska) and two in Britain (the 2003 St Leger on Brian Boru and the 2009 Oaks with Sariska). His prodigious talent also brought him, unusually for a Flat jockey, a Cheltenham Festival victory in the 2002 Champion Bumper on Pizarro.

Having been Ireland's champion apprentice in 1999, Spencer moved to Britain and was mentored by Barney Curley. He became Irish champion in 2004 during an ill-starred year back home as stable jockey for Aidan O'Brien and was twice champion in Britain, winning outright in 2005 and sharing the title with Seb Sanders two years later.

Qatar Racing was quick to announce that Spencer's place as retained rider would be taken in 2015 by the fast-rising Andrea Atzeni, 23, with 19-year-old Oisin Murphy as second jockey.

Picture: EDWARD WHITAKER (RACINGPOST.COM/PHOTOS)

FLAT WINNERS 2014

British Group I Winners in 2014

Winner	Race	Course (Distance, Month)
Night Of Thunder	2,000 Guineas	Newmarket (1m, May)
Miss France	1,000 Guineas	Newmarket (1m, May)
Olympic Glory	Lockinge	Newbury (1m, May)
Taghrooda	Oaks	Epsom (1m4f, June)
Cirrus Des Aigles	Coronation Cup	Epsom (1m4f, June)
Australia	Derby	Epsom (1m4f, June)
Sole Power	King's Stand	Ascot (5f, June)
Toronado	Queen Anne	Ascot (1m, June)
Kingman	St James's Palace	Ascot (1m, June)
The Fugue	Prince of Wales's	Ascot (1m2f, June)
Leading Light	Gold Cup	Ascot (2m4f, June)
Rizeena	Coronation	Ascot (1m, June)
Slade Power	Diamond Jubilee	Ascot (6f, June)
Mukhadram	Eclipse	Sandown (1m2f, July)
Integral	Falmouth	Newmarket (1m, July)
Slade Power	July Cup	Newmarket (6f, July)
Taghrooda	King George	Ascot (1m4f, July)
Kingman	Sussex	Goodwood (1m, July)
Sultanina	Nassau	Goodwood (1m2f, Aug)
Australia	International	York (1m2f, Aug)
Tapestry	Yorkshire Oaks	York (1m4f, Aug)
Sole Power	Nunthorpe	York (5f, Aug)
G Force	Sprint Cup	Haydock (6f, Sep)
Kingston Hill	St Leger	Doncaster (1m7f, Sep)
Tiggy Wiggy	Cheveley Park	Newmarket (6f, Sep)
Integral	Sun Chariot	Newmarket (1m, Oct)
Belardo	Dewhurst	Newmarket (7f, Oct)
Together Forever	Fillies' Mile	Newmarket (1m, Oct)
Charming Thought	Middle Park	Newmarket (6f, Oct)
Madame Chiang	Fillies & Mares	Ascot (1m4f, Oct)
Noble Mission	Champion Stakes	Ascot (1m2f, Oct)
Charm Spirit	Queen Elizabeth II	Ascot (1m, Oct)

Irish Group I Winners in 2014

Winner	Race	(Course, Distance, Month)
Kingman	Irish 2,000 Guineas	Curragh (1m, May)
Noble Mission	Tattersalls Gold Cup	Curragh (1m3f, May)
Marvellous	Irish 1,000 Guineas	Curragh (1m, May)
Australia	Irish Derby	Curragh (1m4f, June)
Thistle Bird	Pretty Polly	Curragh (1m2f, June)
Bracelet	Irish Oaks	Curragh (1m4f, July)
Dick Whittington	Phoenix	Curragh (6f, Aug)
Fiesolana	Matron	Leopardstown (1m, Sep)
The Grey Gatsby	Irish Champion	Leopardstown (1m2f, Sep)
Brown Panther	Irish St Leger	Curragh (1m6f, Sep)
Cursory Glance	Moyglare	Curragh (7f, Sep)
Gleneagles	National	Curragh (7f, Sep)

French Group I Winners in 2014

Winner	Race	Course (Distance, Month)
Cirrus Des Aigles	Prix Ganay	Longchamp (1m3f, Apr)
Karakontie	Poule d'Essai des Poulains	Longchamp (1m, May)
Avenir Certain	Poule d'Essai des Pouliches	Longchamp (1m, May)
Cirrus Des Aigles	Prix d'Ispahan	Longchamp (1m1f, May)
Vazira	Prix Saint-Alary	Longchamp (1m2f, May)
The Grey Gatsby	Prix du Jockey Club	Chantilly (1m3f, June)
Avenir Certain	Prix de Diane	Chantilly (1m3f, June)
Noble Mission	Grand Prix de Saint-Cloud	Saint-Cloud (1m4f, June)
Gallante	Grand Prix de Paris	Longchamp (1m4f, July)
Charm Spirit	Prix Jean Prat	Chantilly (1m, July)
Esoterique	Prix Rothschild	Deauville (1m, Aug)
Garswood	Prix Maurice de Gheest	Deauville (7f, Aug)
Kingman	Prix Jacques Le Marois	Deauville (1m, Aug)
Ribbons	Prix Jean Romanet	Deauville (1m2f, Aug)
The Wow Signal	Prix Morny	Deauville (6f, Aug)
Baltic Baroness	Prix Vermeille	Longchamp (1m4f, Sep)
Charm Spirit	Prix du Moulin	Longchamp (1m, Sep)
Full Mast	Prix Jean-Luc Lagardere	Longchamp (7f, Oct)
Olympic Glory	Prix de la Foret	Longchamp (7f, Oct)
Treve	Prix de l'Arc de Triomphe	Longchamp (1m4f, Oct)
Move In Time	Prix de l'Abbaye	Longchamp (5f, Oct)
High Jinx	Prix du Cadran	Longchamp (2m4f, Oct)
We Are	Prix de l'Opera	Longchamp (1m2f, Oct)
Found	Prix Marcel Boussac	Longchamp (1m, Oct)

German Group I Winners in 2014

Winner	Race	Course (Distance, Month)
Sea The Moon	Deutsches Derby	Hamburg (1m4f, July)
Lucky Lion	Grosser Dallmayr Preis	Munich (1m2f, July)
Feodora	Deutsches Stuten-Derby	Dusseldorf (1m3f, Aug)
Sirius	Grosser Preis Von Berlin	Hoppegarten (1m4f, Aug)
Ivanhowe	Grosser Preis Von Baden	Baden-Baden (1m4f, Sep)
Empoli	Preis Von Europa	Cologne (1m4f, Sep)

UAE Group I Winners in 2014

Winner	Race	Course (Distance, Month)
Prince Bishop	Al Maktoum Challenge R3	Meydan (1m2f, Mar)
Vercingetorix	Jebel Hatta	Meydan (1m1f, Mar)
African Story	Dubai World Cup	Meydan (1m2f, Mar)
Gentildonna	Sheema Classic	Meydan (1m4f, Mar)
Sterling City	Golden Shaheen	Meydan (6f, Mar)
Amber Sky	Al Quoz Sprint	Meydan (5f, Mar)
Just A Way	Dubai Duty Free	Meydan (1m1f, Mar)